PARENTAL LOSS
AND ACHIEVEMENT

PARENTAL LOSS
AND ACHIEVEMENT

Marvin Eisenstadt
André Haynal
Pierre Rentchnick
Pierre De Senarclens

INTERNATIONAL UNIVERSITIES PRESS, INC.

Madison   Connecticut

Library of Congress Cataloging-in-Publication Data

Parental loss and achievement / Marvin Eisenstadt . . .
[et al].
    p. cm.
    Bibliography: p.
    Includes index.
    ISBN 0-8236-4111-2
    1. Parental deprivation. 2. Achievement motivation in chil-
dren. 3. Orphans—Psychology. 4. Celebrities—Psychology.
5. Leadership. 6. Parents—Death—Psychological aspects.
I. Eisenstadt, Marvin.
BF723.P255P37 1989
155.2'34—dc19   88-13640
                                                           CIP

CONTENTS

ACKNOWLEDGMENTS

"Orphans and the Will for Power" by Pierre Rentchnick, "Is the Psychoanalytic Biography of Political Leaders Feasible?" by Pierre de Senarclens, and "Psychoanalytic Discourse on Orphans and Deprivation" by André Haynal are translated from the French work *Les Orphelins Mènent-ils le Monde?* published by Stock in Paris in 1978. The translation is by Jacqueline A. Deniz.

"Parental Loss and Genius" by Marvin Eisenstadt is reprinted from *American Psychologist*, 1978, 33:211–223.

THE AUTHORS

Marvin Eisenstadt is Chief Psychologist, Central Nassau Guidance and Counseling Services; Diplomate in Clinical Psychology (American Board of Professional Psychology); clinical supervisor at various times for Adelphi University, Yeshiva University, and Hofstra University; private practice, Clinical Psychology; President of Nassau County Psychological Association.

André Haynal is Professor of Psychiatry, Faculty of Medicine, University of Geneva, and former president of the Swiss Psychoanalytic Society. His work "Le Sens du Désespoir" (*Revue Française de Psychanalyse*, no. spécial, 1977) was awarded the Dubois Prize. (In English: *Depression and Creativity*, International Universities Press.)

Pierre Rentchnick is a Specialist F.M.H. in internal medicine; visiting professor, faculty of Medicine, Geneva University; honorary member of the New York Academy of Science; Chief Editor of *Médecine et Hygiène*. His work "Ces Malades Qui Nous Gouvernent" (1976) was awarded the Littré Prize.

Pierre de Senarclens is Professor of International Relations at the University of Lausanne. He is the author of numerous publications including a critical essay, "Le Mouvement Esprit. 1932–1941."

FOREWORD TO THE ORIGINAL FRENCH EDITION

While studying the illnesses of chiefs of state, Pierre Rentchnick noticed that the number of orphans among them was astonishingly high, and he also observed the same phenomenon among people eminent in the arts and sciences: philosophers, scientists, writers, painters, sculptors, and musicians. In the first part of the book, Pierre Rentchnick examines the issues in the light of psychological knowledge from a psychoanalytic viewpoint for the most part.

What is the role of personality in history? What is the historical significance of the intrapsychic life of a political leader? Is the psychoanalytic biography possible? Pierre de Senarclens discusses the perspectives and limits of the psychobiographical approach.

What is the echo of the missing dimension in the unconscious of orphans, for example? How does psychoanalytic knowledge assist in understanding it, in grasping the forces operating at that level, in apprehending the influence of fantasies, and, more precisely, the fantasies of loss? What do they suggest to us and what can we deduce from psychoanalysis to explain certain troubling facts gathered by Pierre Rentchnick? André Haynal attempts to answer these questions.

Starting from the viewpoint of two different disciplines, history and psychoanalysis, the three authors ask whether or not orphans have a dominant place in human destiny. Their points of view are not necessarily in agreement, but their parallel thinking establishes the foundations for new questions on the controversial problems which simultaneously embrace both human history and the intrapsychic aspects of the individual.

André Haynal
Pierre Rentchnick
Pierre de Senarclens
October 1977

FOREWORD

Parental Loss and Achievement is a work combining psychiatrist and psychologist, psychoanalyst and historian. From the rigid methodology dictated by the requirements of experimental design and statistical analysis to the careful introspection of the intrapsychic self, and as well the interplay between the individual and society, this is a collaborative effort. Each author individually has looked deeply into the historical past, the recent events of the present, and, indeed, has sought to see beyond to a utopian future. Each author, utilizing the tools of his respective profession, has sought to comprehend the worst of man's psychopathology and understand the relationship it might have to the glorious best of humanity.

What can account for the emergence throughout history of the truly eminent—the worthies, the great ones—since time immemorial? What literature exists and what does it say to us? Biographies, in the past laudatory, more recently revealing their subjects, "warts and all," are, of course, available. An overview of occupational groups such as presidents, scientists, artists, and the like can be found offering marginal usefulness to those who seek explanations as to how it is that the select few became the historically great. The question we want to answer is: What transpired psychologically to yield such an achievement? Genius has been feared and rightly so. When a Newton or an Einstein comes along no one and no thing is the same thereafter! When Franklin Roosevelt or Adolf Hitler enters the global stage, he leaves a profoundly altered world behind him.

Negative impact studies abound on the damaging effects psychiatrically of disrupted family life. Death of parents or loss of family by whatever means can have negative results, but the positive overcoming of trauma, the "improved" individual capable of outstanding success and achievement, has been addressed but rarely in the literature. In this work we confront the abundantly clear fact, though many will continue to dispute it, that orphanhood and its sequelae can in its motivational capacity produce a "will for power." The orphan by necessity compensates for nothing with a special something—

a result all the better for mankind in some cases while tragic in its panoramic sweep of historical process and destructive warfare in other cases.

The key is to separate behavior derived from cultural influences from that which is the expression of affective conflict in the historical individual. Psychological explanations do not exclude those which are based on analyzing social conditions. The opposite is also true. Extremes of psychoanalytic reductionistic thinking may not be offered as evidence by those who would eliminate all psychological viewpoints. What is needed is common sense, experimentation, and insightful and carefully reasoned analysis of eminent individuals by psychologically sophisticated scholars who are mindful of the traditional needs for validation demanded by historical research. Rigor as opposed to the enthusiasms of the naive (whether neophyte or experienced professional) is the issue. This collaboration is meant to nourish the skepticism of the reader whenever oversimplification of complex phenomena occurs.

Loss and mourning are not the only existentialist situations which stimulate creativity, but it is compelling how often they are found in the origins of creation and achievement. Is the orphan experience the important factor, the prototype, necessary for either creativity and/or leadership? Can we ask with all seriousness—do orphans rule the world?

Disagreements between the authors can be found, of course, as well as missing facts and incomplete theory. Nevertheless, with restraint and respect for the enormous task at hand, progress in answering our questions is being made.

Marvin Eisenstadt
July 1987

PART I

Parental Loss and Genius

Marvin Eisenstadt

Introduction

A scientific theory is proposed to account for the historically eminent individual or genius by relating his or her development to loss of parents. A parental-loss profile is described that rigorously defines orphanhood, and a study of 699 eminent persons that makes use of this profile is reported. Early orphanhood was found to be characteristic of this eminent group. Comparisons with previous work were attempted despite obvious methodological problems. Theoretical considerations indicating the effects of bereavement and orphanhood are offered to explain the relationship between achievement and parental loss as well as that between the genius and the disturbed psychotic.

There has been renewed interest in the study of genius (Besdine, 1968a,b; Albert, 1969, 1971, 1975, 1983; Sorell, 1970; see also Parts II, III, and IV). Simonton (1984) lists thirty-three references to works published between 1974 and 1984 in his valuable book *Genius, Creativity, and Leadership*. His interest is to apply computer quantitative techniques to data derived from historical populations and develop meaningful abstract statements. He has shown persistence and ingenuity in his use of biographical facts and previous research in eminence. However, to date the sum of its parts is still lacking coherence and it lacks a theory to make the whole project meaningful. His efforts have yet to be integrated.

This chapter was first published in *American Psychologist*, 33/3:211–223, 1978. Reprinted with permission.

Many have tried to explain the development of those who mold civilization. There are leads and there are worthy thoughts on the subject, but few actual facts. Genius was described initially as an act of creativity on the part of the Supreme Creator and until very recently in history was the subject of religious speculation. Beginning in the 1870s, however, scientists attempted to analyze the operational components of genius. Galton (1869) believed that the faculty of genius was transmitted through hereditary principles. Lombroso (1891) believed in a theory of genius that he based on his work as a psychiatrist. He had observed at close range the many forms of mental deterioration, extreme behavioral manifestations, and emotional disturbances of patients in large institutions for the mentally ill. He believed all forms of genius were the result of psychoses and moral degeneracy, and he offered a great number of cases to prove his point. There have been many examples of actual insanity among the famous, yet Ellis (1904) reported that mental illness is not found among the famous in anywhere near the proportions which Lombroso stated it would be. A great step forward in the study of the genesis of genius was made by Wilhelm Lange-Eichbaum (1928, 1932). He explained that psychosis does occur in the lives of many geniuses and that even when psychosis is not found, markedly psychopathic traits can be found in a great majority of the eminent. So, we have (1) Galton and his theory of heredity; (2) Lombroso's degenerative-psychosis hypothesis with its modification by Lange-Eichbaum; (3) the sociological school that cataloged the characteristics of genius (Cattell, 1903; Ellis, 1904; Cox, 1926; Bowerman, 1947; Kenmare, 1960; Goertzel and Goertzel, 1962; Illingworth and Illingworth, 1966; Goertzel, Goertzel, and Goertzel, 1978; and (4) the current historiometric generalizations produced by Simonton which explore biographical, Zeitgeist, creative, and leadership determinants, all four of which are acknowledged to be grossly inadequate theories. There is no theoretical position that can explain the phenomenon of eminence or creative genius, and there are no facts to support any generalized theory. In other words, there is as yet no scientific theory to account for the development of a historically eminent individual.

The present study and the complementary elaboration found in the other chapters of this book attempt a new viewpoint in discussing genius and its origins by relating creative thinking, historical eminence, administrative prowess, and scientific acumen to the variable of loss of parents by death. The study was an outgrowth of previous work in the area of creativity (Eisenstadt, 1966). Interestingly, while this research was being published in America, simultaneously Haynal, Rentchnick, and de Senarclens were publishing in France *Les Orphelins Mènent-ils le Monde?* (Do Orphans Lead the World?) and their contributions appear elsewhere in the present volume.

Genius is defined here as the development of an individual to a high degree of competency and superiority in an occupational field. This is postulated to be due to several factors, including (1) a certain degree of innate, biologically determined characteristics, principally, intelligence, physical abilities, and the like; (2) individual development of those capacities by a unique and specific psychological mechanism of interaction within the family unit; (3) training and educational advancement, leading to (4) accomplishment. The unique and specific psychological mechanism focused upon in this study is the bereavement experience and its resolution or, more generally, the problem of orphanhood.

The essential element in orphanhood that uniquely describes it is that no possibility exists for a return to a former family situation. Once a parent dies, whether father or mother, the family unit is permanently altered. A curious fact of the English language is that the word *orphan* is an inexact term. According to the dictionary definition, an orphan is someone who has lost either one parent or both parents. In this study, orphanhood is defined in three aspects: paternal orphanhood—the loss by death of the father; maternal orphanhood—the loss by death of the mother; and full, total, or double orphanhood—the loss by death of both mother and father. I developed the concept of the parental-loss profile to rigorously define the orphanhood situation of any individual. Thus, Sigmund Freud's profile reads F40, M74, meaning that Freud was forty years old when his father died and seventy-four years old when his mother died. Charlotte Brontë's profile is F after, M5, S38, which states that her father was still alive when she died at age thirty-eight and that her mother died when she was five years old.

In the present study, parental loss by death was the main consideration. Eliminated for the sake of research strategy were sibling loss, the loss of children and its effects on parents, and other loss events including separations, divorces, hospitalizations, mental illness of parents, and so on. It seemed expedient from a research point of view to study the most basic form of parental loss—actual loss by death of the parent, or orphanhood. First, when a parental death is studied, it is easier to determine the actual point in time of the loss. Second, the effects should be more prominent and more easily noticed than those of other forms of loss. Third, the information to be obtained is more readily available.

What is the specific relationship between the loss of parents by death and the desire for fame, eminence, and occupational excellence? Certainly one of the important considerations is the nature of the family unit prior to the disruption caused by the death of the parent. The individual whose parents provided defective care and a disturbed family background would be affected quite differently by the death of a parent than the individual with a healthy family background whose parents showed genuine concern. It has already been remarked in the developing parental-loss literature that various facets comprise the crisis of bereavement. Such factors as the age at which the death takes place, the composition of the household at the time of death, the previous psychological and economic relationships that have existed before the loss, and the capacity of the family members to absorb the crisis have been mentioned as contributory factors to the traumatic nature of orphanhood. Thus, parental loss is conceived in two ways: (1) Parental loss by death has a *direct* result, and depending on the age of the child, this result can be specified, and (2) parental loss by death has an *indirect* result depending on the family dynamics existing before the death occurred.

Researching Genius: The Study Group and
Parental-Loss Profile Results

The study of eminence and the criteria used to define the
eminent has a well-developed history and can be dated for
our purposes as beginning with Sir Francis Galton (1869).
The selection of eminent individuals was personally decided
upon by him, although he was guided in his choice of judges,
statesmen, scientists, poets, and artists by standard reference
works available at the time. Galton later selected Fellows of
the Royal Society who had won medals for scientific work,
had been president of a learned society, had attained member-
ship on the counsel of the society, or were professors at important universities. Havelock Ellis (1904) used the sixty-six
volumes of the *Dictionary of National Biography*. He selected
individuals to whom three or more pages were devoted, but
he also included those whom he believed to have shown a
high order of intellectual ability despite the fewer than three
pages of print. He excluded the notorious and members of
the nobility regardless of their eminence. Cattell (1903) selected
his group of eminent men from six biographical dictionaries
or encyclopedias: two French, one German, and three English,
including Lippincott's *Biographical Dictionary,* the *Encyclopaedia
Britannica,* and Rose's *Biographical Dictionary*. The chosen group
was defined by inclusion in at least three of the sources, with
the greatest average space allotted determining the magnitude
of eminence.

The subjects in the present study were derived from listing
all individuals who appeared in the 1963 edition of the *Encyclopaedia Britannica* with 1 column of space ($^1/_2$ page) or more
and from listing all individuals who were given 1 column of
space ($^1/_2$ page) or more in the 1964 edition of the *Encyclopedia
Americana*. A person with at least 1 column in each encyclopedia
was included; this resulted in a group of 699 individuals, twenty
women and 679 men. The famous spanned the ages from
Homer to John Kennedy, from the Greek and Roman periods
of 500 B.C. through the current eminent of twentieth-century
history. Those studied were found to have an average of $1^1/_2$
pages in the *Encyclopaedia Britannica* (M = 3.31 columns, SD =
3.19) and an average of 1 page in the *Encyclopedia Americana*

(M = 2.51 columns, SD = 2.39). Thus, the average famous individual in this study was found to have a combined space allocation of slightly less than 3 pages (M = 5.85 columns, SD = 5.18).

The death dates of the fathers and mothers and the birth and death dates of the eminent individuals themselves were obtained. Subjects were eliminated from statistical computa-

TABLE 1

Number and Percentages of Individuals by Nationality

Nation	%	n
1. Britain	27.8	194
2. America	17.0	119
3. France	12.6	88
4. Italy	8.2	57
5. Germany	6.9	48
6. Greece	4.1	29
7. Rome	4.0	28
8. Russia	2.1	15
9. Biblical	2.0	14
10. Scotland	1.8	13
11. Spain	1.7	12
12. Ireland	1.4	10
13. Austria	1.3	9
14. Combined Others	9.1	63

Note. N = 699.

tions whenever biographical information was unavailable on the lifespan of the individual or on his or her parents. Of the original 699, it was necessary to eliminate 126 (18%) for whom biographical data on parent death dates were unavailable. This left 573 subjects, which constituted the major statistical group. The greatest number of these, 215 (38%), were from the nineteenth century, while 146 (25%) were from the twentieth century. The eighteenth century contributed 75 (13%); the seventeenth century, 55 (10%); the sixteenth century, 39 (7%); and all others from ancient antiquity through 1499 comprised 43 (7%).

In Cattell's (1903) listing of 1,000 eminent men, the rank order by nationality was (1) France; (2) Britain; (3) Germany; (4) Italy; (5) Rome; (6) Greece; and (7) America. If only the top 500 of Cattell's listing are used, the rank order becomes (1) Britain; (2) France; (3) Greece; (4) Germany; (5) Italy; (6) Rome; and (7) America. The 699 subjects of the present study produced the rank order shown in Table 1. There were 163 subjects (23%) in this study who "moved up" in individual rank order from Cattell's listing, while 203 subjects (29%) "moved down" in rank order. Almost half, or 333 (48%), of the famous individuals in contemporary history included in the present study were not listed at all in Cattell's study. In the total Cattell group of 1,000, 634 eminent individuals (or 63% of his listing), were not included in the present study. Surprisingly, of those not included in the present study from Cattell's group, 10 individuals appeared in his top 100, 23 in the second 100, 47 in the third 100, 56 in the fourth 100, and at least 70 or more individuals were excluded in each of the subsequent 100s up to 1,000. Thus, we can see the cultural influences and/or prejudices that appear in preparing lists of the eminent.

Each subject in the present study was eminent because of his or her occupational abilities. Some individuals were notable because of exceptional accomplishments in more than one vocation, while some made their mark in one area only. In the total sample of 699 subjects, the largest occupational group was writers, followed by statesmen. Philosophers, poets, and scientists-scholars were given essentially equal prominence. Royalty, soldiers, and a special occupational group, founders, were similarly represented by numbers of individuals. Founders were those who achieved fame through establishing religious societies or some new organizational structure. Another special occupational group, reformers, was separately listed. Table 2 gives the numbers and percentages of the various occupational categories found in this study. If individuals were noted for more than one occupation, they were listed in each category of fame. This designation was usually found in the first sentence of the entry in the encyclopedia article. In very few cases was there any question as to the vocational designation to be given each subject.

The subject's age at the time of the death of each parent was considered in relationship to the famous subject's own lifespan. This led to the development of the parental-loss profile notation used in this study. F and an age indicates the mean age of the eminent individuals when their fathers died. M and an age refers to the mean age of the eminent individuals when their mothers died. E and an age refers to the mean

TABLE 2

Number and Percentages of Individuals by Occupational Activity

Occupational activity	%	n
1. Writers	35.9	251
Poets	13.7	96
Dramatists	6.0	42
Novelists	3.0	21
2. Statesmen	25.3	177
Presidents of the United States	4.7	33
Jurists	2.4	17
Diplomats	1.6	11
Prime Ministers	1.3	9
3. Philosophers	15.4	108
4. Scientists, Scholars	13.6	95
5. Royalty	9.9	69
6. Founders	9.3	65
7. Soldiers	9.2	64
8. Artists	8.2	57
9. Reformers	5.4	38
10. Composers	3.3	23
11. Explorers	2.7	19

Note. Some individuals were listed in more than one category if they were noted for more than one occupation. $N = 699$.

age of the subjects when the earliest or first parent died, and L and an age refers to the mean age of the subjects when the last or second parent died. S and an age indicates the mean lifespan of the subjects.

For the total group, the first parent (whether father or mother) died at E21.10 years. The death of the second parent (whether father or mother) occurred at L38.75 years. The subjects lost their fathers at F26.50 years and their mothers at M32.86 years (see Table 3).

It was determined that fourteen fathers (2%) and forty-two mothers (7%) outlived their famous children. In six cases (1%) both parents outlived their child, while in fifty cases (9%)

TABLE 3

Parental-Loss Profile Results for the Total Group of Famous Individuals in This Study

Parental-Loss Profile	M (years)	SD	n
Earliest or First Parent to Die (E)	21.10	14.31	488
Father Death (F)	26.50	15.39	546
Mother Death (M)	32.86	17.63	466
Last or Second Parent to Die (L)	38.75	14.40	446
Age at Own Death (S)	65.38	14.41	564

one parent outlived the child. By age ten, 25.0 percent of the subjects had one parent dead, and by age fifteen, 34.5 percent had one parent dead. By age ten, 3.1 percent of the subjects had lost both parents, and by age fifteen, 5.9 percent had lost both parents. Father death by age ten was experienced by 17.6 percent, while mother death by age ten was experienced by 12.6 percent of the subjects. By age fifteen, 24.8 percent of the subjects had lost their fathers, while 18.5 percent of the subjects had lost their mothers. By age twenty-five, 52.2 percent had lost one parent, 46.1 percent had lost their fathers, 28.6 percent had lost their mothers, and 15.9 percent had lost both parents. See Table 4 for the complete results.

There were 497 subjects for whom complete parental-loss information was available. There were 270 subjects (54.3%) whose fathers died before their mothers. They lost their fathers

TABLE 4

Five-Year Interval Cumulative Percentages by Age at Which Father, Mother, Earliest Parent, and Last Parent Death Occurred in the Lifespan of the Famous Individuals in This Study

Age (years)	Earliest or First Parent to Die (E)	Father Death (F)	Mother Death (M)	Last or Second Parent to Die (L)
Before or at birth	4.2	3.1	1.2	0
0–5	13.4	10.8	4.5	.9
6–10	25.0	17.6	12.6	3.1
11–15	34.5	24.8	18.5	5.9
16–20	45.0	36.0	23.2	9.6
21–25	52.2	46.1	28.6	15.9
26–30	61.4	57.1	31.4	20.8
31–35	68.9	65.3	41.9	29.3
36–40	75.4	74.7	50.1	38.2
41–45	80.6	83.8	59.5	50.8
46–50	83.2	89.2	66.7	60.4
51–55	85.0	92.7	74.5	69.1
56–60	85.3	94.8	78.7	74.9
61–65		95.3	80.6	77.3
66–70			80.6	77.3
71–75			81.2	77.3
76–80			81.3	77.7
After	1.0	2.4	7.3	8.7
Unknown	13.6	2.3	11.3	13.6

Note. N = 573.

at F21.32 years and their mothers at M41.32 years, or twenty years later. Of these cases, 28 percent had lost their fathers by age ten, while 37 percent had lost their fathers by age fifteen. There were 163 subjects (33.0%) whose mothers died first. In these cases, the loss of the mother occurred at M19.22

years, with the father dying at F33.45 years, or sixteen years later. Of these subjects, 34 percent had lost their mothers by age ten, and 50 percent had lost their mothers by age fifteen. There were thirty-six subjects (7.2%) whose mothers died after they did. These subjects lived to the age of S47.72 years, with their fathers dying at F24.56 years. There were only eight subjects (1.6%) whose fathers died after they did. These subjects lived to the age of S42.50 years, with the mothers dying at M21.12 years. There were six cases (1.2%) in which both the father and the mother died after the subject. These subjects died at the early age of S35.17 years.

The One Hundred Most Famous Individuals by Rank Order is found in Appendix E, while the complete list of The Famous Individuals in the Study by Alphabetical Order is found in Appendix F.

The question to be asked is whether these results are unique for the special individuals in the encyclopedia, living in previous centuries when death rates were different, or whether these numbers are average ages at which any group of children and adults lose their parents. The problems in answering such a question are manifold. There are no comparisons to be made between the subjects of 2,500 years of recorded history and any control group. Moreover, insurance-company statistics start in rudimentary fashion only in the nineteenth century. How then to proceed to gain some measure of understanding of the nature of the obtained findings? There are several alternatives. An obvious first step is to compare equal halves of the total group to determine the reliability of the obtained results. Another step is to compare a historical group of individuals not listed in the encyclopedia with the eminent group of this study. Finally, despite numerous methodological problems, base rates of parental loss by death may be ascertained from the literature and used for comparison.

The Alphabet Test

A simple but powerful approach to determining the reliability of the numbers obtained for the total sample is to divide the group into two equal halves. Individuals 1 through 286 (corresponding to last names beginning with the letters A through Kh) were compared with Individuals 287 through 573 (corresponding to last names beginning with the letters Ki through Z) in an alphabetized listing of subjects. No statistically significant differences were determined for any of the ages of death in subject lifespans. These differences ranged from 1.27 years to 2.20 years. The death of the first parent, whether father or mother, occurred at E20.50 years ($SD = 14.29$, $N = 243$) in the A to Kh group and at E21.77 years ($SD = 14.24$, $N = 246$) in the Ki to Z group. The death of the second parent occurred at L37.96 years ($SD = 15.13$, $N = 220$) in the A to Kh group and at L39.56 years in the Ki to Z group. The death of the fathers in the A to Kh and the Ki to Z groups occurred at F25.72 years ($SD = 15.75$, $N = 271$) and F27.27 years ($SD = 15.01$, $N = 275$), respectively. The death of the mothers occurred at M31.76 years ($SD = 17.65$, $N = 233$) in the A to Kh group and at M33.96 years ($SD = 17.58$, $N = 233$) in the Ki to Z group. Thus, the results of the alphabet test enable us to have confidence in the numbers found for the group as a whole. They are stable and reliable facts about the eminent individuals of history selected by inclusion in the encyclopedia.

Comparisons with Fathers Given or Not Given Space in the *Encyclopaedia Britannica*

A special group of fifty-one fathers was found who were famous themselves as well as having eminent children. These fathers had space devoted to them in separate articles in *Encyclopaedia Britannica* (1968 edition), but not necessarily the amount of space to warrant inclusion in the main eminent group. A major characteristic of these fathers was their short lifespan of S53.92 years. They lost their own fathers at F19.79 years and their own mothers at M30.32 years. They lost their first parent at E13.91 years and their second parent at L34.91 years. This parental-loss profile is due primarily to the fact that their first parent to die lived only for an average of 43.95 years. Their fathers lived for an average of 56.18 years and their mothers for an average of 59.71 years. The second parent to die had an average lifespan of 65.86 years.

A separate group of 184 fathers of subjects in this study, who were *not* given space in the *Encyclopaedia Britannica* (1968 edition), was available as a control group. They were found to have lived to S65.21 years. Their parental-loss profile was essentially the same as that found before for the study group. They lost their fathers at F26.93 years, their mothers at M34.28 years, their first parent at E19.60 years, and their second parent at L42.07 years. All these findings were not significantly different statistically from those for the total group.

It became possible to compare the group of eminent individuals so designated by inclusion in an encyclopedia with another group from the same periods of history who were not considered eminent. The first step was to see if they were indeed contemporaries. The eminent came from the following centuries: 53 percent (27 fathers) from the 1600s, 16 percent (8 fathers) from the 1700s, 27 percent (14 fathers) from the 1800s, and 4 percent (2 fathers) from the 1900s. This contrasted with the noneminent fathers as follows: 10 percent (18 fathers) from the 1600s, 24 percent (45 fathers) from the 1700s, 56 percent (106 fathers) from the 1800s, and 10 percent (18 fathers) from the 1900s. Thus, more of the eminent fathers came from the 1600s, while more of the noneminent fathers came from the 1800s. Any differences between the two groups have to be understood in light of this fact. The very limited numbers of cases are another drawback to these results, but nevertheless some real findings do emerge for interpretation.

The parental-loss profile of an average father who was eminent in his own right was found to be statistically significant earlier than that of the noneminent fathers. The earliest parent to die was lost at E13.91 years in the eminent group, compared to E19.60 years in the noneminent group, a difference of 5.69 years (Z score = 2.27). The father died at F19.79 years in the

TABLE 5

Parental-Loss Data in a Special Group of Eminent Fathers of the Individuals in This Study Who Were Themselves Given Space in the Encyclopaedia Britannica *Compared to a Group of Fathers Not Given Space*

Parental-Loss Profile	M (years)	SD	n
Fathers Given Space (Eminent group)			
Father Death (F)	19.79	12.02	48
Mother Death (M)	30.32	17.08	34
Earliest or First Parent to Die (E)	13.91	10.70	33
Last or Second Parent to Die (L)	34.91	13.17	32
Age at Own Death (S)	53.92	15.36	51
Fathers Not Given Space (Noneminent group)			
Father Death (F)	26.93	16.22	169
Mother Death (M)	34.28	19.27	85
Earliest or First Parent to Die (E)	19.60	14.80	77
Last or Second Parent to Die (L)	42.07	14.66	73
Age at Own Death (S)	65.21	16.16	184

eminent group, compared to F26.93 years in the noneminent group, a difference of 7.14 years (Z score = 3.40). In the eminent group, the second parent to die was lost at L34.91 years, compared to L42.07 years in the noneminent group, a difference of 7.16 years (Z = 2.53). The mother's death occurred earlier as well, but the difference did not reach statistical significance (M30.32 years versus M34.28 years, Z = 1.09). These numbers can be examined in Table 5, which also includes the mean lifespans of each father group, their mothers and fathers, and the parental-loss data. A conclusion may be made in regard to the parental-loss profile of the eminent fathers group: Earlier parental loss is found in an eminent group as compared to a noneminent group. On the basis of these results, genius or eminence appears to be related to orphanhood factors, as originally proposed. Certainly, some gain in support for the connection between parental loss and genius was found. The next step is to compare the obtained results with the literature on parental loss.

Comparisons with the Parental-Loss Literature

Table 6 presents a summary of data from the parental-loss literature. The 1921 census data from England and Wales, made useful by Brown (1961), make a good starting point for a comparison between the results of this study and the results reported in the literature. This census stated that in the zero- to four-year category, death of one parent was found in 7.86 percent, death of the father occurred in 6.0 percent, and death of the mother occurred in 2.16 percent. In the present study's zero- to five-year category, death of one parent occurred in 13.4 percent, death of the father occurred in 10.8 percent, and death of the mother in 4.5 percent. In the zero- to nine-year category, the census data of 1921 showed the death of one parent to have occurred among 12.4 percent, the death of the father among 9.4 percent, and the death of the mother among 3.71 percent. This contrasts with the zero- to ten-year category of the present study in which 25.0 percent had lost one parent, 17.6 percent had lost the father, and 12.6 percent had lost the mother. Thus it can be seen that parental loss by age ten is markedly greater among the eminent subjects of the present study than among the more general population of the census data. In the zero- to fourteen-year category, the census data show death of one parent occurring in 16.6 percent, death of the father in 11.9 percent, death of the mother in 5.75 percent, and the death of both parents in 1.2 percent. This contrasts with the findings of this study

TABLE 6

Orphanhood Rates Among General Population, Juvenile Delinquents, and Psychiatric Patient Groups

Group	Father Dead (%)	Mother Dead (%)	Both Dead (%)	One or Both Dead (%)
General population				
Brown (1961): 1921 Census				
To age 4	6.00	2.16		7.86
To age 9	9.4	3.71		12.40
To age 14	11.9	5.75	1.2	16.60
Petursson (1961): 1921–1930				
To age 15				28.5
Metropolitan Life Insurance Co. (1959, 1966): 1900–1902 (estimates; birth depending on age of father or mother)				
To age 17	12.1–32.1	9.7–21.7		
Juvenile delinquents				
Breckinridge and Abbott (1912): 1903–1904	19.9	12.0	4.3	34.0
Rhoades (1907): 1905				
To age 17				35.0
Russell Sage Foundation (1914): 1909				
To age 16	22.7	8.6	5.2	36.5
Shideler (1918)	17.9	12.8	5.7	36.4
Healy and Bronner (1926): 1909–1914				
Chicago	18.0	12.0	3.0	33.0
Boston	15.0	6.5	2.5	24.0
Sullenger (1930): 1922–1927				
To age 17	22.3	16.7	5.5	44.5
Armstrong (1932): 1926–1929	17.7	17.5	3.8	39.0
Brown (1961, 1966, 1968)				
To age 19	31.5	12.25		40.5
Glueck and Glueck (1950): 1911–1922				35.9
Psychiatric patients				
Barry and Lindemann (1960): 1944–1953				
Males to age 27	17.0	13.66		
Females to age 27	18.01	17.80		
Hill and Price (1967):				
To age 30	36.8			
Beck, Sethi, and Tuthill (1963):				
To age 30				30.3
To age 60				54.8
Brown (1961):				
To age 39	60.8	42.9		

in the zero- to fifteen-year category in which 34.5 percent of the eminent had one parent dead, the father's death had occurred in 24.8 percent, the death of the mother had occurred in 18.5 percent, and both parents had died in 5.9 percent. For one parent dead and for father dead, the percentages in the present study are more than twice those from the census data. For both parents dead and for mother dead, the percentages are more than three times greater in this study than in the census data. Naturally, the 2,500 years of recorded history in which the subjects of this study lived had different death rates than found in the England and Wales of 1921. The census population is not meant in any way to be a control group with which the present data can be scientifically compared. Nevertheless, I attempted to make use of the numbers available, and it is readily apparent that orphanhood was essentially more common among the group in the present study.

The Metropolitan Life Insurance Company (1959, 1966) estimates are another source with which a comparison of some significance can be made. In the zero- to seventeen-year category for the period 1900 to 1902, death of the father was estimated to occur for 32.1 percent of the children born to fifty-year-old fathers. If the father was twenty-five years old at the birth of that child, the chances of losing that father by death were reduced to 12.1 percent. In the present study, the finding for zero to twenty years in the death-of-father category was 36.0 percent, and in the zero- to fifteen-year group, it was 24.8 percent. These numbers begin to approach, although they do not equal, the estimates made for 1900 to 1902 by the Metropolitan Life statisticians for children of elderly fathers, but they are greater than the estimates for children of young fathers. Likewise, the death-of-mother estimate at the birth of the child was 21.7 percent if born to a forty-five-year-old mother, whereas it was reduced to 9.7 percent if the child was born to a mother twenty years old during 1900 to 1902. The corresponding findings in the present study were 23.2 percent in the zero- to twenty-year category and 18.5 percent in the zero- to fifteen-year category. Once again, these numbers are comparable if elderly mothers only are considered.

In the comparisons for the zero- to seventeen-year-olds for 1956 and 1964, the estimates for father death were found by Metropolitan Life statisticians to be 32.3 percent and 33.1 percent, or essentially the same as that for 1900 to 1902 for a child born to an elderly fifty-year-old father. However, the percentages for loss of mother by death decreased in 1956 and 1964 to 11.5 percent and 12.4 percent, respectively, for an elderly mother aged forty-five years. Therefore, there was a definite increase in longevity for the mother compared to 1900 to 1902 estimates.

The study by Petursson (1961) for Icelandic Life Insurance policy holders gives a comparison number which is of limited value but useful nevertheless. In the period 1921 to 1930 in the zero- to fifteen-year category, 28.5 percent experienced the death of one parent, which compares to a figure of 34.5 percent in the zero- to fifteen-year group of the present study.

The orphanhood rates for father death, mother death, one parent dead, and both parents dead obtained among the eminent subjects of this study were found to be higher than the general-population results found in the literature. It is clear that the orphanhood rate in the present study is on the high side compared to the rates found in the census data and the Metropolitan Life estimates.

Orphanhood data have also been obtained for specialty groups. Although a specialty group is even less directly comparable to the eminent group in this study, some benefit may be derived by an attempt to compare them. A substantial body of orphanhood data has been amassed in the delinquency field. Of the delinquents processed in the Chicago Juvenile Court who were between eight and seventeen years old (average age of 13), 35 percent had one parent who was dead (Rhoades, 1907). In 1926, Healy and Bronner studied Chicago and Boston juvenile offenders. They found that in the period 1917 to 1923, 23 percent of these offenders in Chicago and 29 percent in Boston had lost one parent. Armstrong (1932) studied the New York City Children's Court during the period 1926 to 1929 and found that in a group of 660 runaway boys, 39 percent had lost one parent. Armstrong also described a study of delinquent boys in four penal institutions; 35.6 percent were found to have lost one parent. The cumulative percentage in the zero- to fifteen-year category of the eminent study was 34.5 percent for the loss of one parent by death. The figure for the loss of both parents obtained in this study was 5.9 percent in the zero- to fifteen-year category, a figure generally reported in the early studies of delinquency as well. For example, in the study by Sullenger (1930) based on the District Court of Omaha, Nebraska, for 1922 to 1927, it was found that 5.5 percent of the boys and 5.5 percent of the girls (combined rate of 5.6 percent) had lost both parents. Thus, the delinquents of the early twentieth century who found their way into a court or an institution were orphaned at rates comparable to those found in the present study of the eminent.

As to father death, a Russell Sage Foundation (1914) study found a 22.7 percent rate in a fourteen- to sixteen-year group. Sullenger (1930) reported a figure for father-death among eleven- to seventeen-year-old boys of 22.3 percent. Similarly, Breckinridge and Abbott (1912) reported that the father-death rate was found to be 19.9 percent in a special group from 1903 to 1904. Shideler (1918) reported father death of 22.7 percent in one New York City study. For death of the mother, the Russell Sage Foundation (1914) reported a figure of 8.6 percent among fourteen- to sixteen-year-olds. Sullenger (1930) reported a corresponding figure of 16.7 percent for eleven- to seventeen-year-old boys, while Breckinridge and Abbott (1912) found 9.8 percent for boys and 20.4 percent for girls, or a 12 percent overall rate. Brown (1961, 1966, 1968) and his associates provide some data for comparison with these numbers for ages up to nineteen: Among women prisoners, death of the father had occurred for 31.5 percent, while death of the mother had occurred for 12.25 percent. In another study it was found that 40.5 percent of the female prisoners nineteen years old or younger had lost one parent. In the studies of delinquency by the Gluecks (Glueck, 1936, 1959; Glueck and Glueck, 1930, 1934a,b, 1950, 1962), the orphanhood rate for the period 1911 to 1922 among male reformatory prisoners was found to be 35.9 percent. These results may be compared to the eminent-study findings of 34.5 percent by age fifteen and 45.0 percent by age twenty for one parent dead. Father death by age fifteen occurred among 24.8 percent; this figure increased to 36.0 percent by age twenty. Mother death by age fifteen occurred among 18.5 percent, and this increased to 23.2 percent by age twenty. Delinquency studies show early twentieth-century juvenile delinquent populations to have roughly similar orphanhood rates, although they are lower than the rates for the eminent group. Prisoners were also found to have roughly comparable orphanhood experiences. Many studies, however, yielded orphanhood-incidence results much lower than those found among the eminent. Overall, my conclusion is that despite methodological pitfalls inherent in the problems of comparison, it once again appears that the rate of orphanhood among the eminent is even greater than that among delinquents given over to courts and state institutions for care. The reader will have to be the final judge.

While a control group for studying childhood orphanhood rates has been extremely difficult (and perhaps impossible) to construct, constructing one to study adulthood orphanhood rates seems even more impossible. Nevertheless, there are some findings in the literature of orphanhood incidence that were collected in connection with studies of bereavement. In the Barry and Lindemann (1960) study of private patients, 17.0 percent of the males and 18.01 percent of the females had lost their fathers by the age of twenty-six. In the same study, 13.66 percent of the males and 17.8 percent of the females had lost their mothers by the age of twenty-six. Hill and Price (1967) found that 33.5 percent of the nondepressed patients and 36.8 percent of the depressed patients admitted to hospitals in 1958 to 1963 had lost their fathers by the age of thirty. The Beck, Sethi, and Tuthill (1963) study of psychiatric outpatients found cumulative orphanhood rates of 30.3 percent by age thirty and 54.8 percent by age sixty. Brown (1961) found that of depressed female patients, 60.8 percent had lost their fathers and 42.9 percent had lost their mothers by age thirty-nine. In the present study of eminence, the findings through age twenty-five were 46.1 percent for death of father, 28.6 percent for death of mother, and 52.2 percent for death of one parent. Through age thirty, the corresponding figures were 57.1 percent for father death, 31.4 percent for mother death, and 61.4 percent for death of one parent, while through age forty the percentages increased to 74.7 percent for father death, 50.1 percent for mother death, and 75.4 percent for death of one parent. By the age of sixty, 85.3 percent of the eminent subjects had lost one parent by death. There is obviously little scientific connection between any of the foregoing to imply whether the orphanhood rates obtained in this study of eminence are systematically greater (which was found) or are an artifact based on the meager and scattered findings for adulthood in a different century with a group of individuals other than the eminent. However, the rates are provided to arouse the curiosity and interest of the reader.

Review of studies of hospitalized patients indicates that the reliability of these studies is much poorer than the reliability of the studies discussed previously. However, with some exceptions it seems that among a psychotic hospitalized population, as many as 28 percent may have lost one parent by age twenty, compared with 45 percent among the eminent. With numerous exceptions, slightly less than 20 percent of hospitalized patients have lost their fathers and somewhat less than 15 percent have lost their mothers. These impressions compare to the figures of 36 percent and 23 percent for death of father and death of mother, respectively, obtained among the eminent. The faulty methodology of the literature of hospitalized psychotics has been fairly and extensively scrutinized in the literature, and further comment is not necessary at this point. (See Barry, 1949; Gregory, 1959; Brown, 1961; Hilgard and Newman, 1961, 1963a,b; Beck, et al., 1963; Forrest, Fraser, and Priest, 1965; Oltman and Friedman, 1965; Dennehy, 1966; Paffenbarger and Asnes, 1966; Gay and Tonge, 1967; Hill and Price, 1967.)

When I examined studies with more specific samples such as depressed or suicidal patients, the percentages reported ranged up to 35 percent for death of one parent by age fifteen, which matches the 35 percent found in the present study. Similarly, father death, with great variations, was found to range from 13 to 28 percent for adolescents, which again roughly corresponds to the 25 percent for death of the father by age fifteen found in the study of the eminent. With great variations, anywhere from less than 10 to 20 percent of a severely depressed teenage population had lost their mothers, which can be roughly compared to the 18 percent of the eminent subjects in this study who had lost their mothers by age fifteen. Thus, once more we see that in a special group of subjects, in this case the severely depressed, just as was true for seriously delinquent populations, there is a reported incidence of orphanhood which approaches the incidence of orphanhood found among the eminent of the present study. Among the more generalized populations studied, the incidence of orphanhood seemed to be much less than among the eminent. Naturally, the lack of true control groups must be repeatedly emphasized. The present speculations and impressions may or may not be helpful in ascertaining the nature of an orphanhood rate in an average population and how it might compare to the results obtained in this study of eminence. I hope that the difficulties in scientifically studying orphanhood throughout the entire lifespan may be overcome and progress in this field will be made in future work. For further information on the topic of orphanhood, see Oltman, McGarry, and Friedman (1952), Oltman and Friedman (1953), Gregory (1958, 1965a,b,c, 1966a,b), Neubauer (1960), Brown, Epps, and McGlashan (1961), Hilgard and Newman (1963a,b), Brown (1966), Greer (1966), Moriarty (1967), Barry (1969), Miller (1972), Marris (1974), and Bendiksen and Fulton (1975).

Is Parental Loss a Primary Pathway to Creativity and Eminence?

Parkes (1972) introduced his study of bereavement by reference to Freud's case of Anna O. Her mental illness, including hysterical symptoms of headaches, paralysis, and anesthesia in her limbs, occurred during the course of her father's terminal illness and became worse upon his death. She was treated during this time (in 1881) by Breuer. Breuer believed Anna O. was helped by talking about these disturbing events of her life—thus the discovery of the link of trauma and symptom. Freud published with Breuer in 1895 (Breuer and Freud, 1895) a description of the case and of the treatment. Anna O. became the first social worker in Germany, founded a periodical, and started several institutes. In the report, trauma and symptom were linked, but trauma and creative productivity and occupational achievement were not linked. One purpose of the present study is to attempt the theory building that would support these overlooked relationships.

The death of a parent in childhood is recognized as a major traumatic event affecting subsequent personality. Not only does the trauma include the separation and loss of the deceased parent but it also alters the relationships with the surviving parent and with other family members. In 1969, Wolfenstein offered a developmental model that helped to explain the relationship between achievement and loss. It is important to know the type of parent surrogate that is identified with following mourning. At times, a child will become his own parent surrogate. If this occurs, an ego ideal may be developed that leads to outstanding accomplishment. Why the child might become his own parent depends on various factors occurring before, during, and after the death. The phase of development at the time of loss, the gruesomeness of the death process if witnessed by the child, and who is available to assume a constructive parent-surrogate role all have to be taken into account. The reaction of rage at being abandoned may assume the proportions of a comprehensive grievance elaborated into an indictment of social injustice. This system of thought can then be transformed into either outstanding accomplishment or outstanding antisocial behavior. If there is a need to "wrest from fate a different outcome" and if a repair of faulty reality testing can take place, then positive achievement may be the result. Even if the need to coerce fate has a pathological aspect to it, it still may be reformulated into an ultimately positive statement. Wolfenstein provides a rationale for the beginning of an understanding of how revolutionaries, founders of new societies, and startlingly innovative social critics, who both attack society and hold out a hope for reconciliation through progressive reformation, appear on the scene. The bereavement reaction can be an impetus for creative effort, a force for good, or it can have the effect of stunting personality growth and producing the concomitant antisocial acts, destruction of social relationships, and even the taking of one's own life.

In the creative mourning process there is a sequence of events whereby the loss triggers off a crisis requiring mastery on the part of the bereaved individual. If this crisis is worked through, that is, if the destructive elements and the depressive features of the experience of bereavement are neutralized, then a creative product or a creatively integrated personality can result. It can ultimately mean an elevation in job, a higher social position, or heightened individual social awareness (Kanzer, 1953; Rochlin, 1961, 1965).

A theory of bereavement leading to creative output can now begin to be developed. Positive results of the bereavement trauma include the fact that many children are able to assume increased responsibility in the family and adopt a new role based on the new circumstances. Some children are able to begin a differentiation toward a unique personality formation. Attempts at restitution for the parent death require the finding of a suitable replacement. Since fears of worthiness might prevent the establishment of a new relationship, steps are taken to become a more worthwhile person. The idealization of the dead parent leaves many openings for such positive growth. The problem of mastering a changed and changeable environment can be translated into strivings for achievement, accomplishment, and power. This desire to control one's own destiny is frequently seen in children who experience multiple separations either due to long-term illness in the parent or to the inadequacy of surrogate parents. Bereavement may temporarily interfere with intellectual development, but as in other areas, once mastery has occurred, there may be a great motivational desire to excel in intellectual pursuits. If feelings of insecurity, inadequacy, emptiness, and, especially, guilt can inhibit functioning by overwhelming the personality, then the mastery of these feelings may be a springboard of immense compensatory energy.

In the mastery of these personal problems and in the previously felt need to master the environment, creative expression may find its deepest roots. The creative effort is thus seen as a restorative act. An attempt is made to produce creative products that will, on the one hand, alleviate those feelings of guilt and apartness and, on the other hand, prove to all the world the individual's essential goodness. The long-term nature of the coping process in bereavement reactions develops a sense of time and persistence that is a fundamental trait necessary in creative effort. The ability to fantasize and the ability to regressively join with a dead parent may lead to a corresponding ruthlessness in dealing with other people. The compensating need for ambition and power of the personally weak but magnetic world leader is obvious.

The question of morality and conscience, a hallmark of creativity, enters with the sense of injustice that the child felt and continues to feel in adulthood. The individual, orphaned child was selected by fate or destiny for the bereavement experience while his peers were not. The capacity to endure a self-punishing regimen might enable a creatively gifted individual to pursue creative studies that others might long before have given up. In all of this we are dealing with preexisting patterns upon which the death of a parent is superimposed and from which subsequent relationships will shape a final conclusion.

There are obvious differences between an outstandingly successful, creative individual, that is, a genius, and a disturbed, psychotic individual. However, there are similarities between them that might lead to a restructuring of theory on the nature of psychosis and genius. Among the similarities often found are, first of all, a certain vulnerability and poor ego defenses. Both the creative genius and the psychotic individual can be easily stimulated as a result of their vulnerability, and each can be considered sensitive despite the fact that at times both appear to turn a deaf ear to those trying to gain their attention. Second, both groups have a great energy investment in themselves and in what the self produces (i.e., narcissism). The accomplished genius is rewarded with societal applause. The psychotic, however, is often condemned on the basis of his or her production. Third, both often have disturbed personal relationships with their parents, siblings, and other relatives. Disturbance is also found in their relationships with their spouses or other love partners. A fourth similarity is their apparent ease of regression to more childlike behavior. The creative person seems to have the ability to control this regression, whereas the psychotic individual seems to have no control over it.

Both groups have a capacity for suffering and exhibit dissatisfaction and unhappiness with their current circumstances. Corresponding to this dissatisfaction is a desire within both groups to master the environment and to strive for an independent stance. Obviously, one group appears more successful at mastery than the other. However, all those who have seen the inner workings of a large institution for psychotic patients can recognize in these patients a form of mastery over that particular environment. The psychotic individual within narrowly defined environmental limits cannot be coerced or medicated or shocked into doing other than that which he or she chooses to do. This characteristic is also found in outstandingly successful individuals who cannot be coerced by society or their associates into being other than what they choose to be. Both groups are capable of original productions that are statistically infrequent and unique in either thought, behavior, or tangible end results. Sometimes the idiosyncratic product can be useful to society, whereas at other times it can be intolerable to society. There is also the possibility that both positive and negative reactions to the thought or work will be elicited from society at the same time or alternating within a narrow time frame. Both the creative genius and the psychotic individual apparently live in exceedingly complex worlds, with their various personality traits reflective of the complexity of those worlds.

In my opinion, the findings of the present study lead to the conclusion that parental loss by death neatly explains these similarities between the genius and the psychotic. However, the parental-loss profile as a research strategy can certainly provide ample opportunity for disproof. Facts can once and for all advance the science of genius and the psychology of the eminent. Its rescue from mysticism and prejudice will not come without struggle. However, I firmly believe that a significant and important beginning has now been made.

References

Albert, R. S. (1969), Genius: Present-day status of the concept and its implications for the study of creativity and giftedness. *Amer. Psychol.*, 24:743–753.

―――― (1971), Cognitive development and parental loss among the gifted, the exceptionally gifted and the creative. *Psychol. Reports*, 29:19–26.

―――― (1975), Toward a behavioral definition of genius. *Amer. Psychol.*, 30:140–151.

―――― (1983), *Genius and Eminence: The Social Psychology of Creativity and Exceptional Achievement*. New York: Pergamon Press.

Armstrong, C. P. (1932), *600 Runaway Boys: Why Boys Desert Their Homes*. Boston: Gorham.

Barry, H., Jr. (1949), Significance of maternal bereavement before age of eight in psychiatric patients. *Arch. Neurol. & Psychiat.*, 62:630–637.

―――― (1969), Parental deaths: An investigative challenge. *Contemp. Psychol.*, 14:102–104.

―――― Lindemann, E. (1960), Critical ages for maternal bereavement in psychoneurosis. *Psychosom. Med.*, 22:166–181.

Beck, A., Sethi, B., & Tuthill, R. (1963), Childhood bereavement and adult depression. *Arch. Gen. Psychiat.*, 9:295–302.

Bendiksen, R., & Fulton, R. (1975), Childhood bereavement and later behavior disorders: A replication. *Omega*, 6:45–59.

Besdine, M. (1968a), The Jocasta complex, mothering and genius, part I. *Psychoanal. Rev.*, 55:259–277.

―――― (1968b), The Jocasta complex, mothering and genius, part II. *Psychoanal. Rev.*, 55:574–600.

Bowerman, W. G. (1947), *Studies in Genius*. New York: Philosophical Library.

Breckinridge, S. P., & Abbott, E. (1912), *The Delinquent Child and the Home*. New York: Russell Sage Foundation.

Breuer, J., & Freud, S. (1895), Studies in Hysteria. *Standard Edition*, 2:1–306. London. Hogarth Press, 1955.

Brown, F. (1961), Depression and childhood bereavement. *J. Ment. Sci.*, 107:754–777.

—— (1966), Childhood bereavement and subsequent psychiatric disorder. *Brit. J. Psychiat.*, 112:1035–1041.

—— (1968), Bereavement and lack of a parent in childhood. In: *Foundations of Child Psychiatry*, ed. E. Miller. Oxford: Pergamon Press.

—— Epps, P. (1966), Childhood bereavement and subsequent crime. *Brit. J. Psychiat.*, 112:1043–1048.

—— —— McGlashan, A. (1961), The remote and immediate effects of orphanhood. In: *Proceedings of the Third World Congress of Psychiatry*, Vol. 2. Montreal: McGill University Press.

Cattell, J. McK. (1903), A statistical study of eminent men. *Pop. Sci. Monthly.* 62:359–377.

Census of England and Wales 1921 (1925), London: General Register Office, His Majesty's Stationery Office.

Cox, C. (1926), *Genetic Studies of Genius: II. The Early Mental Traits of 300 Geniuses.* Stanford, CA: Stanford University Press, 1959.

Dennehy, C. M. (1966), Childhood bereavement and psychiatric illness. *Brit. J. Psychiat.*, 112:1049–1069.

Eisenstadt, J. M. (1966), Problem-solving ability of creative and non-creative college students. *J. Consult. Psychol.*, 30:81–83.

Ellis, H. (1904), *A Study of British Genius*, rev., enlarged ed. New York: Houghton Mifflin, 1926.

Forrest, A. D., Fraser, R. H., & Priest, R. G. (1965), Environmental factors in depressive illness. *Brit. J. Psychiat.*, 111:243–253.

Galton, F. (1869), *Hereditary Genius: An Inquiry into Its Laws and Consequences.* New York: World, 1962.

Gay, M. J., & Tonge, W. L. (1967), The late effects of loss of parents in childhood. *Brit. J. Psychiat.*, 113:753–759.

Glueck, S. (1936), *Crime and Justice.* Boston: Little, Brown.

—— ed. (1959), *The Problem of Delinquency.* Boston: Houghton Mifflin.

—— Glueck, E. T. (1930), *500 Delinquent Careers.* New York: Alfred A. Knopf.

————————— (1934a), *500 Delinquent Women*. New York: Alfred
A. Knopf.
————————— (1934b), *1000 Juvenile Delinquents*, 2nd ed. Cambridge, MA: Harvard University Press.
————————— (1950), *Unraveling Juvenile Delinquency*. Cambridge,
MA: Harvard University Press.
————————— (1962), *Family Environment and Delinquency*. Boston: Houghton Mifflin.
Goertzel, M. G., Goertzel, V., & Goertzel, T. G. (1978), *Three Hundred Eminent Personalities*. San Francisco: Jossey-Bass.
Goertzel, V., & Goertzel, M. G. (1962), *Cradles of Eminence*.
Boston: Little, Brown.
Greer, S. (1966), Letter on parental loss and attempted suicide.
Brit. J. Psychiat., 112:743.
Gregory, I (1958), Studies of parental deprivation in psychiatric patients. *Amer. J. Psychiat.*, 115:432–442.
——— (1959), An analysis of family data on 1000 patients admitted to a Canadian mental hospital. *Acta Genet. et Stat. Med.*, 9:54–96.
——— (1965a), Anterospective data following childhood loss of a parent: I. Delinquency and high school dropout. *Arch. Gen. Psychiat.*, 13:99–109.
——— (1965b), Anterospective data following childhood loss of a parent: II. Pathology, performance, and potential among college students. *Arch. Gen. Psychiat.*, 13:110–120.
——— (1965c), Retrospective estimates of orphanhood from generation life tables. *Milbank Memorial Fund Quart.*, 43:323–348.
——— (1966a), Retrospective data concerning childhood loss of a parent: I. Actuarial estimates vs. recorded frequencies of orphanhood. *Arch. Gen. Psychiat.*, 15:354–361.
——— (1966b), Retrospective data concerning childhood loss of a parent: II. Category of parental loss by decade of birth, diagnosis, and MMPI. *Arch. Gen. Psychiat.*, 15:362–368.
Healy, W., & Bronner, A. F. (1926), *Delinquents and Criminals: Their Making and Unmaking: Studies in Two American Cities*.
New York: Macmillan.
Hilgard, J. R., & Newman, M. F. (1961), Evidence for functional genesis in mental illness: Schizophrenia, depressive

psychosis and psychoneurosis. *J. Nerv. & Ment. Dis.*, 132:3–16.

————————— (1963a), Early parental deprivation as a functional factor in the etiology of schizophrenia and alcoholism. *Amer. J. Orthopsychiat.*, 33:409–420.

————————— (1963b), Parental loss by death in childhood as an etiological factor among schizophrenic and alcoholic patients compared with a non-patient community sample. *J. Nerv. & Ment. Dis.*, 137:14–28.

Hill, O. W., & Price, J. S. (1967), Childhood bereavement and adult depression. *Brit. J. Psychiat.*, 113:743–751.

Illingworth, R. S., & Illingworth, C. M. (1966), *Lessons from Childhood: Some Aspects of the Early Life of Unusual Men and Women*. Baltimore, MD: Williams & Wilkins.

Kanzer, M. (1953), Writers and the early loss of parents. *J. Hillside Hosp.*, 2:148–151.

Kenmare, D. (1960), *The Nature of Genius*. London: Peter Owen.

Lange-Eichbaum, W. (1928), *Genie, Irrsinn und Ruhm* (Genius, Insanity and Fame), ed. W. Kurth. Munich, Germany: Ernst Reinhardt, 1956.

——— (1932), *The Problem of Genius*. New York: Macmillan.

Lombroso, C. (1891), *The Man of Genius*. London: Walter Scott.

Marris, P. (1974), *Loss and Change*. New York: Pantheon Books.

Metropolitan Life Insurance Company (1959), *Family Responsibilities Increasing* (Statistical Bulletin). New York: Metropolitan Life, April.

——— (1966), *Orphanhood — A Continuing Problem* (Statistical Bulletin). New York: Metropolitan Life, December.

Miller, J. B. M. (1972), Children's reactions to the death of a parent: A review of the psychoanalytic literature. In: *Annual Progress in Child Psychiatry and Child Development*, ed. S. Chess & A. Thomas. New York: Brunner/Mazel.

Moriarty, D. N., ed. (1967), *The Loss of Loved Ones: The Effects of Death in the Family on Personality Development*. Springfield, IL: Charles C Thomas.

Neubauer, P. B. (1960), The one parent child and his oedipal development. *The Psychoanalytic Study of the Child*, 15:286–309. New York: International Universities Press.

Oltman, J. E., & Friedman, S. (1953), A consideration of parental deprivation and other factors in alcohol addicts. *Quart. J. Studies on Alcohol*, 14:49–57.

———————— (1965), Report of parental deprivation in psychiatric disorders. *Arch. Gen. Psychiat.*, 12:46–56.

———— McGarry, J., & Friedman, S. (1952), Parental deprivation and the "broken home" in dementia praecox and other mental disorders. *Amer. J. Psychiat.*, 108:685–694.

Paffenbarger, R. S., Jr., & Asnes, D. P. (1966), Chronic disease in former college students: III. Precursors of suicide in early and middle life. *Amer. J. Public Health*, 56:1026–1036.

Parkes, C. M. (1972), *Bereavement: Studies of Grief in Adult Life.* New York: International Universities Press.

Petursson, E. (1961), A study of parental deprivation and illness in 291 psychiatric patients. *Internat. J. Soc. Psychiat.*, 7:97–105.

Rhoades, M. C. (1907), A case study of delinquent boys in the Juvenile Court of Chicago. *Amer. J. Sociol.*, 13:56–78.

Rochlin, G. (1961), The dread of abandonment: A contribution to the etiology of the loss complex and to depression. *The Psychoanalytic Study of the Child*, 16:451–470. New York: International Universities Press.

———— (1965), *Griefs and Discontents: The Forces of Change.* Boston: Little, Brown.

Russell Sage Foundation (1914), *Boyhood and Lawlessness.* College Park, MD: McGrath, 1969.

Shideler, E. (1918), Family disintegration and the delinquent boy in the United States. *J. Amer. Inst. Crim. Law & Criminol.*, 8:709–732.

Simonton, D. (1984), *Genius, Creativity, and Leadership: Historiometric Inquiries.* Cambridge, MA: Harvard University Press.

Sorrell, W. (1970), *The Duality of Vision: Genius and Versatility in the Arts.* New York: Bobbs-Merrill.

Sullenger, T. E. (1930), *Social Determinants in Juvenile Delinquency.* Unpublished doctoral dissertation. University of Missouri.

Wolfenstein, M. (1969), Loss, rage, and repetition. *The Psychoanalytic Study of the Child*, 24:432–460. New York: International Universities Press.

PART II

Orphans and the Will for Power

PIERRE RENTCHNICK

*I have left behind me a young
deceased
man who did not have the time
to be my
father and who could today
be my son.*
Jean-Paul Sartre

*Not everyone can be an
orphan.*
Jules Renard

*On the edge of psychosis, we
always
find the death of the father.*
Jacques Lacan

Introduction:
Serendipity and a
Common Denominator

Following the death of President Georges Pompidou in April 1974, I became interested in the possible political implications of illnesses of chiefs of state; for example, the effect of President Roosevelt's cerebral arteriosclerosis on the Yalta meeting; Lenin's cerebral arteriosclerosis which Stalin took advantage of to oust Trotsky; Hitler's Parkinson's and Alvarez disease at the end of the Second World War; Mussolini's neurosyphilis; Nixon's obsessive-compulsive tendencies during Watergate; General Maurice Gamelin's neurosyphilis at the time of the "phony war," 1939 to 1940, and so on. While thus studying about fifty contemporary political and military leaders for a work which appeared in 1976 (Accoce and Rentchnick, 1976), I had necessarily to analyze a great deal of biographical material with the object of establishing pathographical portraits of these leaders.

A fundamental element became apparent to me, one which appeared to have escaped historians seeking to understand what motivates an individual to become a political or religious leader. The common denominator in a very large majority of great leaders throughout history, both political and religious, is, I believe, that most or many of them were orphans, born out of wedlock, abandoned children, or those who were otherwise rejected as children by their parents.

Hitler, for example, described in *Mein Kampf* his distress and despair at the age of thirteen when he suddenly lost his father, but he did not know how to analyze it; the same is true of Gamal Abdel Nasser. By contrast, Jean-Paul Sartre, orphaned at an even younger age, described and analyzed his existential anguish in a remarkable way in his book *The Words* (1964).

A Genevese, Protestant writer (Tournier, 1977) tells how he reacted to my first study on orphans. "Without knowing it, I am possessed by a will to power . . . greater than I had ever thought" (p. 139).

A successful writer in the United States, Tournier, a great proponent of personal medicine, himself orphaned by the loss of his father at the age of three months, then orphaned by the death of his mother at the age of six, says:

> I have often spoken of the considerable part played in my life, as I believe, by the death of my mother, of the feeling of black solitude into which I was plunged at that time, of my shy, aloof and unsociable character. Then how I slowly emerged from it, helped by my studies, and by a teacher who took an interest in me and who, by talking with me, made me aware of my personal existence, and helped me by means of my intellectual activity to take my place in society. But the importance of my father's death had largely escaped me until now, and the realization of it I owe to Dr Rentchnick. . . . It is not surprising that I chose in medicine a vocation of power. Nor is it surprising that it presented itself to me in a mild and inoffensive light . . . the desire to help others, which seems the complete opposite of the will for power, but which may act as a cover for it. It seems to me that that has been a merciful opportunity granted to me—to work it off to some extent in a career as a doctor, and then as a writer. For after all, this dangerous will to power, which we have to master, is also what saves us! This is true of all statesmen mentioned by Dr Rentchnick. They too were convinced—in their conscious minds—that they were dedicating themselves to their country, that their careers had no other motive than that of service, but in reality they were saving themselves from the feeling of nonexistence into which the frustration of their childhood had plunged them. . . . I have already recognized in myself several of the motivations of my choice of a medical career, and Dr Rentchnick showed me one more, which is valid also for my religious vocation. If medicine is

a vocation to power, the ministry, whether clerical or lay, is much more so! Think of it: to be the bearer of a divine mission, charged not only with contributing to men's health, but also to their salvation, to be the trustee of a religious message! [pp. 140–142].

The one characteristic of the childhood of leaders throughout history seems to me to be an agonizing sensation of "nothing," of "nothingness" against which the orphan or the abandoned child has to struggle. As Sartre and other authors have clearly demonstrated, the orphan does not consciously insert himself into a historical context which then shapes him as an individual and channels his impulses. The social process or the social mold which will shape the individual in such a way as to tame his impulses is not experienced as such by the orphan, who perceives only that a stitch in the biological and historical chain has been dropped. Depending on the age at which the child is orphaned, an identity crisis emerges which seems to be the common denominator of all the great leaders of history. One can see, from the substance of their characters and their intellectual abilities, that they do not become neurotic or psychotic. Rather they become aggressive and domineering vis-à-vis a society or a destiny which does not recognize the necessity for the internalization of the father-son relationship in order for psychological maturation to take place. This takes place along with concomitant crystallization of the conscience (superego), the acquisition of a solid identity, and the simultaneous reaffirmation of an innate confidence, submissive and timid, yet seeking at any price a compensatory social function.

Existentialist justification necessitates that these children, traumatized by death, the absence, or the flight of the father, emerge from this existential nothingness to finally become political, religious, or revolutionary leaders according to the social, national, and geographical context. As a matter of fact, the search for a personal identity can be confused with a search for a national identity in individuals such as Simón Bolívar, who come from colonized countries, who belong to a lower social class (Gandhi), or a combination of the two (Mao Zedong and Bernardo O'Higgins).

Politics and religion appear to these deeply frustrated individuals as the most complete way to modify, create, re-create, or even revolutionize an order which will conform to a conception of the world, conscious or not, in which the individual seeks to avenge himself for what he perceives as a bad destiny. It is probably from this point of view that one must analyze an Evita Perón, a Juan Perón, a Willy Brandt, a Sukarno, a Thiers, a Thorez, a Castro, an O'Higgins, a Ramsay MacDonald, all of whom were born out of wedlock. Furthermore, theology constitutes a systematic attempt to dominate the human existential nothingness by opposing it with the rigors of an absolute metaphysic (e.g., Moses, Jesus Christ, Buddha, Mohammed, Luther, or Confucius, all of whom were either orphans, or abandoned or rejected by their fathers).

Professional historians will criticize or confirm this hypothesis. It remains no less striking to run through lists of orphans and abandoned children and to find there many of the greatest names in history.

Political Leaders and Parental Loss

In general, the biographers of important historical leaders pay more attention to their subject's private and official roles than they do to aspects of character. They almost totally neglect the illnesses that might have affected decision-making ability, and almost never address themselves to what motivated a particular person to become the leader of a particular group, and ultimately of a government or country. Perhaps ambition is the reason, but why precisely does it take the form of an ambition to rule over other people?

We have been struck by the fact that with few exceptions, all the political leaders listed suffered one of the greatest frustrations that a child can endure; that is, the loss of the father by death, because he abandoned the family, or by divorce; or they experienced the death of the mother.

In Appendix B will be found lists of politicians, military leaders, and others throughout history whose childhood was marked by this experience. Ten of the twelve Caesars discussed by Suetonius, lost their fathers during childhood or adolescence. Another example is that of Simón Bolívar, the great liberator of northern Latin America at the beginning of the nineteenth century: He was orphaned by the loss of his father at the age of two, then by the loss of his mother at eight, and widowed by the loss of his young wife at the age of nineteen.

When, in 1827, Simón Bolívar, age forty-four, both parents dead, liberated Caracas and entered it in triumph, he recognized in the crowd the black woman Hipolitá, who had been his nurse during his childhood. He alighted from his horse and threw himself in Hipolitá's arms while she wept with joy. Two years before, he had written his sister: "I am adding a letter for my mother Hipolitá, in order that you give her everything she needs and so that you treat her as though she were my mother; her milk nourished my life and I do not know of another *father* outside of her" (Erikson, 1975, p. 289).

The patriarchal structure of our society follows the law of constraint which the father exerts upon his children. The son, identifying with the father, finds himself with regard to his mother in the conflict that Freud described as the Oedipus complex. He feels that the mother has betrayed him sexually because of her relationship with the father. A man may react by imagining an idealized, pure mother, who has never had sexual relations. He may then seek to impose forcibly on all women a similar purity, at the same time considering women to be impure by nature. Desiring women to be virgins, such men can suspect women of being witches (as occurred in the Middle Ages and on into the seventeenth century). The same conflict can be found when women are divided into two categories: The "good" ones, who feel no sexual desire, and the "bad" ones who do (as occurred in the Victorian and post-Victorian eras).

A son's identification with the father cannot occur without the child first admitting the father's superiority, thus sublimating the sexual issue, internalizing the eventual model of the father, and thereby renouncing his impulses. The son will liberate himself when sexual maturity occurs, but certain persons are so marked that they will continue to observe the taboo by becoming saints or recluses. The apparent suppression of impulses finds its most perfect realization in the life of the Buddha whose mother died soon after he was born.

Thanks to the inhibiting action of reason that training by the father and schoolteachers gradually creates, the self places itself between the energy sources at its disposal and their utilization by the primary drives. In the father's absence, the orphan has at his disposal, like a slow fuse, undisciplined energy sources, and thus the primary impulses, insufficiently inhibited by an almost untouched superego, will become liberated sooner or later.

That is why it seems to us that the child who has lost his father appears so often as a future leader of a group, a political party, a government, or a country. This demonstrates the importance of the impelling forces and the manner in which they seek to attain their goal, and represents a power, not submitted to history, for modifying the history of a given society or of a given era. The absence of the father demonstrates the necessity for social restraint in order for life within a group to be possible. What counts is social restraint and what is under discussion is less the expansion or limitation of social restraints than the degree of comprehension in regard to them and the development of this understanding in spite of the restraints.

Freud said that the center of anguish is the self. And the self must be very strong in order to face the sources of anguish which represent all aspects of life for a young person, especially when he loses his father. Ferocious, diabolical Hitler wrote *Mein Kampf* in prison at age thirty-four. He remembered his father who died. "In my thirteenth year I suddenly lost my father. A stroke of apoplexy felled the old gentleman who was otherwise so hale, thus painlessly ending his earthly pilgrimage, plunging us all into the depths of grief" (Hitler, 1925, p. 17).

In the absence of the father, unconsciously, the orphan learns to realize his own guiding image according to an ideal model, or from the reality of history or daily life, be it political, or from sports, or the movies, or something suggested by his own mother. The son, escaping from the father's narcissistic tendencies, finds a too easy pseudo-maturation, without the frustrations imposed by the father, in his own self ideal, resulting in a structuring of his character for which his absent father no longer serves as a model. The orphan finds himself in the same situation as the spoiled child whom the father allows to do whatever he wants. But the similarity is only apparent, because the orphan in addition suffers from a serious frustration for which he must sooner or later compensate. A father who is present constitutes, notwithstanding his very physical presence, a model of behavior detached from any professional, didactic role, and this makes for the success of the relationship of father and son in our society.

Thus, psychoanalysis has pointed out the primordial role played by the complete family in the socialization of the individual and its importance in the organization of society in its entirety. If we understand better how people adapt to one another and why they do it in one way rather than another, according to their relationships to each other, we shall have captured in a fundamental theoretical scheme the possibilities offered to a civilization in matters of affective contacts and the reduction of conflicts among individuals.

The different modes of behavior that a man can have in diverse life situations, which for him are closely related, are, from our perspective, part of his character. These modes have a direct link with the destiny which the development of impulse restraint has known in the social context, and with the maturation of the self which intervened in these conditions.

The father plays an essential role which is sometimes beneficial and sometimes detrimental. "One can admire one's father, one can feel sheltered and protected by him, or one can fear him; and finally one can despise him. At different times one can do all these things" (Mitscherlich, 1969, pp. 139–140). To these variable affective relationships can be added the following: A person can learn something from his father, who can familiarize the child with the ways of the world, or one can painfully feel his absence during this apprentice period of one's life. In our society, it is evident that the father must, at certain times and in certain aspects of this apprenticeship, delegate his powers to a teacher. The teachers thus embody aspects of the absent father insofar as they understand their task and not often, as now, when they try to become buddies to their students.

The orphan can either deride or surpass the model-guide of his master, and adopt as his ideal the all-powerful father-god, invisible but omnipresent, or even in the concept of the nation or "motherland." But he is missing security, as a direct result of which anguish and aggression automatically occur as a means of combating the very agony which is created by the father's absence.

Film makers raised on psychoanalytic literature have cast adolescents in this role and the audience easily identifies with them. One often sees on the screen a completely antisocial adolescent gang leader who is finally brought down like a wild beast. Certain political leaders or tyrants of ancient or contemporary history may be included in this category, and typically they are driven by, and at the mercy of, their compulsive desires. There is in such a person, outside of his impulses, no definite guidelines by which he could understand himself and direct his life. He lives by exploiting others through violence. We might say, in a more precise fashion, that he has no "self" susceptible of putting itself in the service of culture. This self can only "obey" its impulses. He has either never received any social education, or has received barely enough. Insofar as he perceives his environment and asserts himself, all is placed, without the least scruple, in the service of his impulses. The "civilized self" is the result of a psychic development which, departing from "primitive" introjections, results in the conscious perception of others. It is only with the experience of being really understood and loved that the possibility of taking others into account appears. The first introjections are the archetypes of impulses experienced before the development of the self can influence them by integrating them. The self and the environment are still not precisely distinct forms one from the other. The psychic development has not evolved to socializing identifications due to the absence of the father. Such identifications are founded on an experience of whole and reliable persons. The prepubertal or pubertal adolescent has to seek the experience of a human community in another environment than his own, having been "amputated" from his father. The model, without which man cannot develop, will be found in strong and fearless legendary "heroes." This is a heroic model, fruit of the imagination or of readings by the mother who idealizes her deceased or absent husband (as one of my patients expressed it):

> [It] differs in one essential respect from models who have been really experienced; it never prohibits, never calls for moderation or self-control. Instead, without any protest being made either from without or from within, it combines with hallucinatory trends of the primary instinctual wishes, the primary psychical processes. All the aptitudes which this young person might have developed in more favourable conditions are thus yoked to the services of these fantasy formations. They are reflected in a self-awareness that imagines itself to be omnipotent and indestructible. This failure of social development is discernible in every detail in Hitler. The nucleus of his following was provided by like-minded individuals, his impact and the fascination that he exercised were due to regressive association with these fantasies of indestructibility, and the means of communication was the preverbal cry of excitement [Mitscherlich, 1969, p. 143].

Impulsive desires tempered, hampered, and civilized by the father lead to renunciations and/or long delays in bringing about their satisfactions. Although on the one hand the child without a father does not know the small frustrations and involuntary privations of family functioning in an intact household nor can he even imagine them, on the other hand, he knows how much he suffers from the supreme frustration, the one of being fatherless. One can then understand the compensation he unconsciously seeks in the group in which he lives, or that in comparison with other children who have a father, he feels really frustrated. In our world, the destiny of each individual is not only the product of his own work. It is accomplished in the heart of the group, and under pressure from the conflicts which dominate it. The group in which we come into the world is already an unchosen factor. But these groups can permit their members to develop their aspirations according to a dialectic reasoning which is rich to a greater or lesser extent. Consider, for example, the declaration by the celebrated French revolutionary, Georges Jacques Danton, whose father died when the son was two, and who projected his destiny onto that of society. He believed that the child belongs to his country before he belongs to his father, his self-interest alone requiring that he has an upbringing in common with others. It is not enough that a child be well brought up, he must be well brought up for all. I don't believe that, had Danton not been an orphan, he would have projected the image of the absent father into the notion of the supreme nation replacing all fathers. Did not Hitler say the same thing as Danton when he affirmed: "The underlying idea is to do away with egoism and to lead the people into the sacred collective egoism which is the 'nation!'" (*New York Times* interview, July 10, 1933).

One therefore sees the emergence of a relatively simple mechanism in the child, especially in the boy without a father: he idealizes the notion of the father whom he does not know, or does not know anymore, projects it onto the makeup of the group to which he belongs, and identifies himself with this paternal notion which the concept of the nation represents. Since he has not had a father, he will be the father of the group, the guide, the chief, from which is derived this certainly unconscious will for political power. An example is former President Juscelino Kubitschek of Brazil, a medical doctor who touched upon the explanation that he wanted to compensate for being orphaned at a very young age by studying medicine. The president of the Swiss Confederation, Giuseppe Motta, a lawyer, also ascribed his choice of vocation to the death of his father.

Like the child, society as a whole cannot subsist without constraint, and accordingly, the astute political leader will set up groups which are authoritarian in nature and precisely attuned to sociocultural conditions and political traditions. At the end of this road to political power, such groups will lead to the formation of a one-party system and of a secret police, omniscient and persecuting (persecuting because the leader believes himself to be or is in fact persecuted). One sees, therefore, the appearance under different labels of such individuals as Hitler or Stalin or Franco, or Idi Amin Dada; the process is the same, with tactical applications depending on local environmental conditions.

Finally, after what we have learned of the activities of the C.I.A., one can see that this organization carries within it the seeds of a Gestapo or a K.G.B. The confessions extorted during the Stalin era became a part of the ceremony, as was the case during the Spanish Inquisition or the era of Franco as late as 1975. In a milder version, employing less brutal techniques, Nixon, in the Alger Hiss affair, which preceded the terrible McCarthy era, succeeded in creating the same intellectual doubts with the aid of an all-powerful certainty of salvation which he attributed to himself.

It is also clear how much the experiences of childhood unavoidably define the future possibilities of development. The apparently "soft" pressure behind which there is the pitiless threat of withholding love can lead to the same identification as the tough teaching method of the stick. Both provoke sclerosis of curiosity, the inclination to seek, and both methods predispose the individual to rigidly maintaining the model of behavior and the prejudices he has adopted. It follows that in these circumstances the individual cannot understand himself clearly. To the rare traits of autonomous development of the self, there corresponds an ideal of the self which is remote from reality. It is built upon fantasies of grandeur whose function is to compensate for either powerlessness vis-à-vis the father, or the absence of limits due to the father's absence. The idealized "leader" inserts himself without difficulty into this misreading of reality. When one studies the biographies of contemporary political leaders from the angle we have defined, that is, the physical or moral absence of the father, one sees how these leaders have sought and found in history models with whom they wished to identify in order to surpass the superego of a hated or absent father, or to fix in place the superego they did not see, feel, or predict. Think, for example, that for a while Hitler took as a model not a depraved or crazed Roman Emperor but a figure like Oliver Cromwell.

In entering into competition with his father, the child is led to internalize in his moral conscience the latter's value system. The real experiences that the child shares with his father already determine the manner in which he will be able to test the social field. An emotional disposition toward a particular professional milieu and participation in society will find itself already structured in some way.

Certainly, no one can replace the parents (unless they are quite unable to exercise their parental function) and nothing can replace the relationship with the father. If the father is conscious of his role and knows how to indicate it to his child, the latter will imitate the father and so begin to foresee his future for himself and learn how one deals with failure. It is necessary for the father to frustrate the child, but he can do so in such a way that reconciliation is always possible.

If we maintain the experience, on the one hand, of a father connected to the world outside the family, and, on the other, the relationship with the mother and siblings, it will accompany us throughout life as an introjected object, even if ultimately we escape its immediate influence. The child who has lost his father must replace the image by another, definitive or temporary, idealized or realistic, which does not bear within it the frustrating elements of a paternal education.

Having become in turn a guide, the "father" of a country, the leader of the masses, promising, or terrorizing by his threats, the orphan does not, and indeed cannot really replace the father whose role he acts out before us. He conjures up the image of an all-powerful god who behaves as though he were above the demands of conscience, and invites us to adopt a regressive attitude of submission and of absolute obedience, of mendacity, which can be traced to the child's behavior in the preoedipal phase.

Following the show trial of Basque anarchists which culminated in the death by firing squad of five men on September 27, 1975, most of the Western democracies shunned Spain in one form or another, most typically by the recall of ambassadors, and there were also street demonstrations. Whether it was French President Giscard d'Estaing or Swiss President Graber, Western leaders said approximately what the people thought; that is, on the one hand, we had to apply pressure in order to force the Spanish government to abandon these human rights violations, and on the other hand to indirectly aid the opposition movements in Spain. In part, what took place was foreseeable in a paternalistic society like that of Spain in the mid-1970s; the government stiffened its position, and, furthermore, the Spanish people came to Franco's defense. But they did not come to the defense of the senile Franco's dictatorial methods, but rather to the defense of an old, weakened father whom the children cannot abandon in the face of death, no matter what he has done, simply because he is the father.

Thus we see that the relationships between individuals and governments and political leaders are not well understood in spite of recent progress in researching the psychology of the masses. It is recognized that unconscious factors play a fundamental role in those erroneous political analyses that result in mistakes in psychological understanding whatever the intelligence of political leaders in power or their advisers may be.

In orphans who have lost their fathers and who constitute the great majority of revolutionaries and political leaders, whether the father be absent physically or spiritually, one sees, at a given moment in the individual's psychic development, an identification with the mother, who, alone and courageously has raised the family. It is a constant theme in biographies of all such people. Hitler said, for example, that his wife was the German "motherland." At the death of De Gaulle, Georges Pompidou spoke of France as widowed (as opposed to being orphaned). Others have said the opposite, but what is true is that there is often the idea of a sublimated sexual relationship between the leader and the nation he leads. Some researchers have even wanted to read into it the symbolic expression of latent homosexual tendencies.

Thus, in the absence of the father, the child is automatically drawn toward identification with the mother, and he can later, according to circumstances, project this identification into the mother country that he must liberate and honor, which forms the romantic counterpart of the legend of King Oedipus (e.g., Adolf Hitler, Kemal Atatürk, Simón Bolívar, Napoleon, Joseph Stalin, Mao Zedong, Bernardo O'Higgins, Fidel Castro, Robespierre, Eamon De Valera, Ho Chi Minh, Sukarno, Idi Amin Dada, and so on). If he is linked to a tender and loving mother by a positive fixation, the child identifies himself with her, never to lose her, and will belong to the feminine or passive type. A castrating mother, however, who engenders fear, does not encourage closeness, and the child may develop a hatred for her and, in certain cases, homosexual tendencies.

According to Bonardi (1935), Napoleon was a child condemned from his tenth year to live like an orphan very far from his native land, his family, his young friends, and who saw this hardship coming and accepted it with pride and dignity.

For Marthe Robert (1972), Napoleon exploited the recent regicide which represented a collective patricide for the French, for, as the emperor raised to the throne by his own efforts, he became automatically the father of a guilty people, which first of all permitted him to eliminate from his civil record the cause of his rage and shame; that is, the name of his biological father.

The legend of his illegitimate birth is supported by historians who have no other explanation for his surprising admittance to a military school reserved for the aristocracy. Thus, the legend corresponds to the popular view of the positive aspect of Napoleon's incredible success (we know that, in the myth, the hero cannot be born like others or go through the happy days of childhood without incident). So, for better or worse, everyone is fascinated by the familiar romance whereby the conqueror of Europe was able in a short time to make the reality of his power take roots.

At each stage of his career, Napoleon acted to bring about with unprecedented determination and fearlessness the unconscious or semiconscious program of the bastard frozen at the oedipal stage. Napoleon established himself as head of his family, bestowed princely husbands on his sisters, and bestowed on his brothers as many thrones as Europe was forced to cede to him. This was done not in order to cater to a family esprit de corps, but to exalt, literally, as in a fairy tale, the old desire to engender a family of kings who would both avenge and console the rebellious child for his rage at not being "well-born." Due to Napoleon's literal execution of an infantile myth, the genial adventurer who, like Robinson Crusoe departed from one island, returned to die on an island after having set fire to an entire continent.

"At first, I didn't know I had no mother. I didn't even know you had to have one" (Ajar, 1975, p. 3).

It is possible to feel that those who have lost their mothers do not fit into the framework of this study. The problem is certainly complex, but with the aid of a few examples, we shall see that children who have lost their fathers and those who have lost their mothers represent two aspects of the same problem.

Bowlby (1973) said that physical separation from the mother during early childhood up to a point where it implies the absence or the loss of dependence on the maternal image, will have an unfortunate effect on personality development, particularly in regard to the formation and maintenance of satisfactory object relationships. It is evident that age is a significant factor, but it is certain that the separation from the mother following her death will be the more vividly felt when a stable, secure dependent relationship has been established, before the child is old enough to be more autonomous.

One can imagine that in certain cases a maternal substitute will be able to play a positive affective role with the child and compensate to a certain extent for the absence of the biological mother. However, such cases are rare. In the majority of cases, the widowed father remarries, often a younger woman who wishes to have her own family and, whether consciously or not, rejects the children of her husband's first marriage. Relations become bad, and the orphaned child blames the father for the situation, and in particular holds him "responsible" for the death of the mother. Depending on the age of the orphan, it is identification with the father which emerges again, and we recognize a situation of "abandonment" in which, in fact, the child has finally really lost his mother, and also, to all intents and purposes, his father. In the author's experience, this is a common enough situation, often found in patients.

The child needs always to compare reality with his imaginary life. As Ajuriaguerra (1980) remarks, Freud has shown that "when a child perceives that his parents are not as he thought them to be, he thinks that he is adopted. Therefore, at the time of the Oedipal complex, a child can imagine that the parent who is his rival is not really his parent" (p. 578). It is generally at the adolescent stage or even later that the individual begins to research the subject of his natural parents, often idealized, and that he represents them as being of superior origin. For example, only when Maurice Thorez became vice president during De Gaulle's presidency was he able to speak freely of his problem.

> He felt a dire need to flee all past humiliations. In private and in small groups, to a few people, he said that he was the son of a big Flemish farmer, of a squire who abandoned him. Taking pleasure in embroidering on this theme, he literally reconstructed his childhood, and experienced an irresistible need to invent an end as triumphant as it was moral. He told how, as Vice President of the Council, he had been able to find his father again. The meeting took place with a witness present. At that time, he delighted in describing the embarrassment of the other who called him Mr. President, and in enunciating syllable by syllable his own reply, the final word: "You denied me, and see what I became" [Robrieux, 1975, pp. 321–322].

Thorez needed to build a shining personality for himself. He was drunk with pride, feeling himself long scorned; it is as puerile as it is touching. Thus, always in private, he said (in order to place other paternities in doubt): "When I go to my hometown, in the cemetery, you don't know your ancestors, since everyone slept with everybody else" (p. 322).[1]

On every birthday, Thorez returned to his native town, saw his "nursing" sister, and after the midday meal, went to his room, rested, daydreamed, and slept until four or five in the afternoon. During each visit, Thorez never missed going for a moment to two tombs: that of his adoptive father and that of his natural father (Robrieux, 1975).

Almost two centuries ago, the future revolutionary, Saint-Just, became suddenly undisciplined, quarrelsome, uncontrolled, violent, and a thief, and his mother had him committed to an institution at the age of nineteen. Like Danton and Hitler, Saint-Just stated: "The child does not belong to his parents;

[1]James Ramsay MacDonald, first Labour Prime Minister of England (1924) who carefully hid his illegitimate birth, also lied that his father was a former cabinet minister while in reality he was a laborer.

if it is a son, from the age of five, he passes under the immediate jurisdiction of the State." The state represents here the projection of the idea of the father just as to Hitler it represented that of the mother. Saint-Just again says: "I only see happiness in sacrificing myself for my country and I only have before my eyes the path that separates me from my dead father and from the steps of the Pantheon." In his poem, *Organt*, 1787, which may have misled certain historians regarding Saint-Just's unsavory nature, we discovered these few revealing verses which illustrate our thesis on compensatory fantasies.

SONG III

I wish a lovely fantasy to build
It amuses me and fills my leisure.
I am, for a moment, King of the earth;
Tremble, evil one, your happiness will end.
Humble virtues, approach my throne;
With lifted brow, draw near to me,
Feeble orphan, share my crown . . .
But, at this word, my error leaves me;
The orphan weeps: Ah! I am not King!
If I were, all would be transposed:
On the proud rich who oppress the poor
My heavy hand would smash the haughty
Would fling down the insolent guilty
Would raise the timid innocent
And would weigh, in even balance
Darkness, grandeur, poverty, rank.
To announce royal majesty
I would wish neither guards nor banners.
Let Marius announce his presence
By terror and the key of tombs
I would walk without axes, without defense
Followed by hearts, not by executioners.
If my neighbors were to declare war on me
I would tell them: "Listen, good people;
Don't you have wives, children?
Instead of drenching the earth with blood
Go yield to their embraces;
Leave these arms and terrible weapons

And like ourselves, go live peacefully."
My happy people but happy in its own seaports
Without vilifying on distant shores
Their ashes that should join those of its
                                        forefathers
Would enrich itself from its own treasures
And would flourish in the respectable shade
Of the ancient laws of our wise ancestors.

What more to ask than this fantasy of being king of the earth, of sharing the crown with other orphans, and establishing social justice for all.

What Are the Effects of Becoming an Orphan? Psychiatric Studies

We have attempted to find an answer in psychiatric studies to the question of what the effects are of becoming an orphan. We have not found it, because, by and large, specialists in this field are not interested in the problem of artistic, literary, religious, or even political creativity. In the main, they have only tried to understand whether the loss of either parent can lead to severe psychopathological problems such as schizophrenia.

Nevertheless, in analyzing the ideal conditions for the child's development in the bosom of the family, child psychiatrists (Bowlby, 1952; Ajuriaguerra, 1980) have helped us to better understand how anxiety originates. According to Ajuriaguerra (1980):

[S]ome children can display almost continuous states of ex eeecitation characterized by flight of ideas, psychomotor expressions of omnipotence, expression of fantastic ideas, illusions of grandeur, and a denial of all anxiety. . . . These children often have a history of abandonment . . . these poorly structured children give the impression that their personality represents a defense mechanism against a deep depressive anxiety [p. 464].

What are the defense mechanisms at the disposal of the child who experiences the death of the father, and what are the neurological compensatory reactions when the potential hereditary defenses are no longer sufficient? We see conditions emerge, then characteristics, finally an ego system demanding what is inherently needed in relationship to a society which has to be conquered, then tamed, and finally checkmated.

Bowlby (1952) addressed the issue of the absence of a proper family. As is by now well known this crucial and significant work had serious methodological flaws. "The information is reported in very disparate forms. Often, the status of the normal family is not clearly defined and in some cases must be inferred. Reasons for the parents' negligence are not explained" (Ajuriaguerra, 1980, p. 562). Nevertheless, the causes for the failure to care for the child need repeating.

(1) Natural home group never established:
    Illegitimacy
(2) Natural home group intact but not functioning effectively:
    Economic conditions leading to unemployment of breadwinner with consequent poverty.
    Chronic illness or incapacity of parent
    Instability or psychopathy of parent
(3) Natural home group broken up and therefore not functioning:
    Social calamity — war, famine
    Death of a parent
    Illness requiring hospitalization of a parent
    Imprisonment of a parent
    Desertion by one or both parents
    Separation or divorce
    Employment of father elsewhere
    Full-time employment of mother [Bowlby, 1952, p. 73].

He concluded:

(a) The death of one or both parents is no longer of overriding importance, largely due to low death-rates for adults of child-bearing age and schemes of assistance for widows with children. Such cases probably account for less than 25% of all cases. In two of the largest samples, one British and the other American, the percentages were 10 and 6 respectively.

(b) Illegitimacy features prominently in all sets of figures, varying from about 10% to 40%. In homes for infants and children under 6 in Denmark in about 1945 the percentage was 80 (Simonsen, 1947).

(c) The natural home group being existent but not functioning effectively, resulting in "neglect," "destitution," "lack of parental control," or "maladjustment of child," is prominent in all but one set of figures and shows this condition to be the greatest single cause today. Poverty, neglect, and lack of parental control account for 60% of cases in one large British sample while maladjustment of the child is responsible for 26% of cases in a New York sample.

(d) Where the natural home group is broken up, separation and divorce are common factors, varying from about 5% to 25% of all cases.

(e) Another important cause of the break-up of the natural home group is prolonged illness of a parent necessitating hospitalization (or, in the case of mental defectives, institutionalization). Mental illness and defect predominate and probably account for some 5% to 10% of all cases.

(f) A situation has arisen in the United Kingdom in which it is now legally possible for parents who have been evicted for not paying their rent to leave the children in the care of a local authority and to find accommodation for themselves where children are not accepted. In one area this accounts for about 33% of the children in care" [Bowlby, 1952, pp. 74–75].

The child who has lost both his mother and father is, in effect, abandoned if he does not have a parental substitute. The child who still has one of his parents will react to his loss in relation to the attitude of the remaining parent and whether that parent remarries. Moreover, it is clear that the child's reaction differs depending on his sex and that of the dead parent, depending on whether the orphan has siblings and their age, and depending on whether the parents' death was sudden or foreseen [Ajuriaguerra, 1980, p. 566].

The age at which the child becomes an orphan or is abandoned plays a major role in the outcome. M. Porot (1959) and John Bowlby (1960a,b, 1961a,b,c, 1963, 1969, 1973, 1980) have given us important information on the topic including the issue of the differences between the ways in which children and adults mourn. Arthur and Kemme (1964) studied eighty-three emotionally disturbed children and their families and the children's reactions to the death of a parent. Level of development, previous relations with the deceased parent, and how other family members react to the death will color the emotional reactions of each child. His ability to deal with the abstract concepts of death has significance. The child can react in two ways, either by experiencing feelings of abandonment or by experiencing feelings of guilt.

The Phaeton Complex

According to Maryse Choisy (1950) the superego is heir to the Oedipus complex. The author has asked—perhaps for the first time—what happens when there are no parents, and she is interested in illegitimate children. She was astonished by the drive for power manifested by these children, and she noted, in rural areas, the large number of sorcerers who are born out of wedlock.

The fantasy of the child born out of wedlock may be traced in Ovid's telling of the myth of Phaeton, the illegitimate son of Helios and of Clymene. He seeks his father and finds him in the sun that sees all. The sun represents the censure of the exterior world. When there is no other father, the father is this eye in the sky which symbolizes at the same time the universal gaze, the light which penetrates the interior shadows, and the warmth that is lacking for those who are not loved by a real mother or a real father. But it is a strange warmth that burns and kills. Thus, the sun is an ambivalent archetype of the natural father. Phaeton, who suffered from feelings of inferiority linked to his illegitimate birth, wanted to overcompensate by a flamboyant act. However, he chose an act beyond his strength which led him inevitably to catastrophe—a fiery ending.

Thanks to marvelous intuition, which is still alive before being plunged into the depths of the unconscious, the child knows everything, and from birth hates the parents who have not acknowledged him. "To the illegitimate child who has not known love there remains no other possible relationship than that of hate" (Choisy, 1950, p. 723).

What becomes of this quasi-pure aggression? We know that when it is denied, it manifests itself in asocial behavior, or, it is turned against the self. Projected outward in the first instance, it perverts itself in revolt and nonacceptance of the social contract. In more favorable cases, the "bastard" can become a successful revolutionary.

In the absence of the father, in the absence of an Oedipus, is there a superego? Maryse Choisy indicates that there is a superego even in the absence of Oedipus. I think she is mistaken; it is only an imaginary superego, idealized, which can neither inhibit nor castrate: "Therefore, whether he [the child] finds himself the heir of the Oedipus Complex or of the social guardians, the superego is, either indirectly via the family, or directly, the introjection of the collective soul. The superego already possesses a collective content" (p. 731).

Personally, I am inclined to believe that the Phaeton complex is a better illustration of the failure complex, or the treason complex, but is only a partial explanation of the illegitimate child's motivation. Maryse Choisy has an interesting thought on the subject: "At each moment man makes himself and makes the universe, but at each instant also he is what he made himself to be and what others, all others have made him" (p. 731).

American authors have noted that the loss of a parent constitutes above all a psychic trauma able to affect the personality of the survivor, provoking depressive and melancholic tendencies. It is extremely rare, said Gregory (1966), that we find an orphan able to draw from his distress the necessary force to be able to achieve greater adaptability or greater creativity, with any decrease in vulnerability to psychopathology in adulthood. It is interesting to note that American authors have placed the accent more on the economic problems which result from the father's absence than on identification problems, those relating to the structure of the ego as a function of the superego! Generally speaking, the loss of the father does not lead to grave psychopathological troubles or especially to schizophrenia unless the father was already mentally ill before death, which brings forth the hereditary factor (Brill and Liston, 1966). Other authors do not accept such an optimistic point of view (Bowlby, 1952; Oltman and Friedman, 1965; Gregory, 1966; Meerloo, 1968; Anzieu, 1975).

One can easily imagine that the feelings of insecurity, abandonment, or disarray of a more or less immature child, facing a world to which he no longer has a real link through his father will contribute to perpetuating certain phobias. He may be able to integrate them into his experience by means of fantasies, removing their dramatic character, and transforming them into will power: "I'd like to be a cop myself when I'm [a grown-up], because then I won't be afraid of nothing or nobody and I'll know what to do, because when you're a cop, you've got authority. . . . Cops have the biggest clout of anybody. If a kid has a cop for a father, it's like having twice as many fathers as other kids. . . . There's no better security force . . ." (Ajar, 1975, pp. 68–69).

Sartre and the Orphan State

It is clear that, beyond the shock which results from the loss of parents in childhood, heads of state have never analyzed the unconscious forces, born following this serious trauma, which may have led them to wish to dominate a particular group.

However, certain writers and philosophers have become aware of the importance of the event and analyzed it. Thus, Sartre, in his autobiographical work *The Words*, has been able to describe his orphan state in such a way that we can understand what other orphans have felt who have been unable or did not want to analyze their psychological situation. (Golda Meir [1975], the former Israeli Prime Minister, who left her parents suddenly at the age of thirteen, to lead her own life, was quite unable to analyze her feelings on that subject.)

Sartre (1964) has defined the situation of being without a father in a remarkable way:

A father would have weighted me with a certain stable obstinacy. Making his moods my principles, his ignorance my knowledge, his disappointments my pride, his quirks my law, he would have inhabited me. That respectable tenant would have given me self-respect, and on that respect I would have based my right to live. My begetter would have determined my future. As a born graduate of the École Polytechnique, I would have felt reassured forever. But if Jean-Baptiste Sartre had ever known my destination, he had taken the secret with him. My mother remembered only his saying: "My son won't go into the Navy." For want of more precise information, nobody, beginning with me, knew why the hell I had been born. Had he left me property, my childhood would have been changed; I would not be writing, since I would be someone else. House and field reflect back to the young heir a stable image of himself. He touches on his gravel, on the diamond-shaped panes of his veranda, and makes of their inertia the deathless substance of his soul. A few days ago, in a restaurant, the owner's son, a little seven-year old, cried out to the cashier: "When my father's not here, I'm the boss!" There's a man for you! At his age, I was nobody's master and nothing belonged to me. In my rare moments of lavishness, my mother would whisper to me: "Be careful! We're not in our own home!" We were never in our own home, neither on the rue le Goff nor later, when my mother remarried. This caused me no suffering since everything was loaned to me, but I remained abstract. Worldly possessions reflect to their owner what he is; they taught me what I was not. *I was not* substantial or permanent, *I was not* the future continuer of my father's work, *I was not* necessary to the production of steel: In short, I had no soul [pp. 87–88].

The death of Jean-Baptiste was the big event of my life: it sent my mother back to her chains and gave me freedom [p. 18].

As a child, Sartre is haunted by the feeling that he exists without the right to do so and that, by this fact, his existence is totally illegitimate. It feels as if he is superfluous, an indelible transparency: a flagrant lack of belonging and identity. Around ten years of age, the hero of the novel by Ajar (1975) poses these questions: "I asked her how she knew my name was Mohammed and I was a good Moslem, when I had no father or mother, or document to prove it" (p. 22). This is the "nothing," the "zero" existential state analyzed by Sartre. Had he lived, his father would have served as a model which would have made of him, following a normal resolution of the Oedipus drama, "continuer of father's work." "Command, obey, it's all one. The bossiest of men commands in the name of another—his father—and transmits the abstract acts of violence which he puts up with" (Sartre, 1964, p. 21). "If my father were alive, I would know my rights and my duties. He is dead, and I am unaware of them" (p. 32).

In this work in which such destitution is sublimated, we see Sartre go through two important stages, fantasy and ambition. He makes himself indispensable and creates obstacles in order to give himself the satisfaction of overcoming them. He dreams of having a destiny, of accomplishing a unique and capital mission.

> In the course of my fantasy trips, it was reality that I wished to achieve. When my mother used to ask me, "Sweetheart, What are you doing?", I would sometimes break my vow of silence and answer her, "I am creating a movie." As a matter of fact, I was trying to tear the images out of my head and to bring them to reality outside of myself, among real furniture and real walls, brilliant and visible such as the ones that glowed from silver screens. In vain; I could no longer ignore my double imposture: I made believe I was an actor making believe he was a hero. My pride and forlornness were such at the time that I wished I were dead or that I were needed by the whole world [p. 166].

Sartre begins to write, to plagiarize, because, lacking a father, he found in what he copied the guide, the model, the guidepost that he had always lacked, to oppose himself to a hostile society. It is the anguish of the child whose father is dead facing a society of "controllers" more or less hostile.

> I saw death. When I was five, it lay in wait for me. In the evening, it would prowl on the balcony, press its nose against the window. I saw it, but I dared not say anything. Once

we met it on the Quai Voltaire. It was an old lady, tall and mad, dressed in black. She muttered as I passed: "I'll put that child in my pocket." . . . In that period, I had an appointment with it every night in bed. This was a rite. I had to lie on my left side, with my face to the wall. I would wait, all atremble, and it would appear, a very run-of-the-mill skeleton with a scythe. I was then allowed to turn on my right side. It would go away. I could sleep in peace. During the day, I recognized it beneath the most varied disguises. . . .

When I was seven years old, I met real Death, the Grim Reaper, everywhere, but it was never there. What was it? A person and a threat. The person was mad. As for the threat, it was this: shadowy mouths could open anywhere, in broad daylight, in the brightest sun, and snap me up. Things had a horrible underside. When one lost one's reason, one saw it. To die was to carry madness to an extreme and to sink into it. I lived in a state of terror; it was a genuine neurosis. If I seek the reason for it, I find the following: as a spoiled child, a gift of providence, my profound uselessness was all the more manifest to me in that the family rite constantly seemed to me a trumped-up necessity. I felt superfluous; therefore, I had to disappear. I was an insipid blossoming constantly on the point of being nipped in the bud. In other words, I was condemned; the sentence could be applied at any moment. Nevertheless, I rejected it with all my might. Not that my existence was dear to me; on the contrary, because I wasn't keen on it: the more absurd the life, the less bearable the death [Sartre, 1964, pp. 94–97].

The end of *The Words* is pathetic and shows the drama of the abandoned orphan, at death's door, leaving an account. He must flee:

My sole concern has been to save myself—nothing in my hands, nothing up my sleeve—by work and faith. As a result, my pure choice did not raise me above anyone. Without equipment, without tools, I set all of me to work in order to save all of me. If I relegate impossible salvation to the proproom, what remains? A whole man, composed of all men and as good as all of them and no better than any [p. 255].

Outside of the love that one can have for one's child there exists for all parents a certain ideal of a child which often corresponds either to a predetermined social model, or a happy personal model, or an ideal self which one would like to see in one's child, failing to have realized it in oneself. If it is human to desire a happy future for one's child, it is always to be feared that the static model of the ideal child may prevent the specific blossoming of the actual child.

Sartre evokes the problem of the substitute father. His mother had never assumed the role of mother, she was prevented from doing so by his grandfather, who, by the way he treated her, made her the "elder sister" of her son. The identification with the mother is remarkably expressed. Catching a man looking at his mother, Sartre says: "But I noticed the maniacal look on his face, Anne Marie [his mother] and I were suddenly a single, frightened girl who stepped away" (p. 219).

We were shy and afraid together. One day, on the quays, I came upon twelve numbers of *Buffalo Bill* that I did not yet have. She was about to pay for them when a man approached. He was stout and pale, with anthracite eyes, a waxed moustache, a straw hat, and that slick look which the gay blades of the period liked to affect. He stared at my mother, but it was to me that he spoke: "They're spoiling you, kid, they're spoiling you!" he repeated breathlessly. At first I merely took offense; I resented such familiarity. But I noticed the maniacal look on his face, and Anne Marie and I were suddenly a single, frightened girl who stepped away. Taken aback, the gentleman went off. I have forgotten thousands of faces, but I still remember that blubbery mug. I knew nothing about things of the flesh, and I couldn't imagine what the man wanted of us, but the manifestation of desire is such that I seemed to understand, and, in a way, everything became clear to me. I had felt that desire through Anne Marie; through her I learned to scent the male, to fear him, to hate him. The incident tightened the bonds between us. I would trot along with a stern look, my hand in hers, and I felt sure I was protecting her. Is it the memory of those years? Even now, I have the feeling of pleasure whenever I see a serious child talking gravely and tenderly to his child-mother. I like those sweet friendships that come into being far away from men and against them. I stare at those childish couples, and then I remember that I am a man and I look away [pp. 219–220].

British Prime Ministers

From Wellington to Chamberlain, Britain had twenty-four Prime Ministers, of whom fifteen, or 62.5 percent, were orphans. It is estimated that in general in the British population the proportion of orphans is 1 to 2 percent maximum.

Conclusion

*I would send the sons of
whores and their mothers to
the luxurious palaces in Nice
where they would be sheltered
from life and could later
become the chiefs of state
visiting Paris.*
Ajar, 1975

It is rare that biographies of chiefs of state discuss parental-loss problems though there is sometimes a passing reference to it. Nasser (Stephens, 1973) when only eight years old learned of the death of his mother: "It was a terrible blow which marked my spirit in an indelible manner," and which separated him from his family while he was going through the anguish brought on by the death. Two years later, young Nasser's father remarried and had a new child. Nasser could not get along with his stepmother and was separated from his father and his new family. He was placed with his maternal grandparents where he was not happy; at the age of eleven, he was placed in a boarding school. Thus, as is often the case, the loss of the mother is accompanied sooner or later by the loss of the father at the point at which he starts a new family. (Marshal Pétain's childhood followed just such a pattern.)

Less frequently, the widowed father feels a very special parental responsibility and consciously or not tends to replace the deceased mother by giving more affection, by being less severe, in fact by becoming a substitute for the mother. The child no longer recognizes the father; he is certainly happy about the new relationship, but at a certain moment he can no longer identify with the father that he is in the process of losing. We discussed this with a famous writer who, following the institutionalization of his wife in a psychiatric hospital, mothered his son. It was the intervention of doctor friends that drew the man's attention to the risks inherent in his behavior: after having lost his mother (absent or ill), the child was gradually losing the virile image of the father with which he could no longer identify.

Sometimes, in accordance with the constitution of the family, one sees the older sister play the role of substitute mother; reassured by this, the father draws away to find another companion. We believe then that in the great majority of cases, the child whose mother has died finds himself in a worse situation than the child who has lost his father, because in fact he is abandoned by both parents.

The abandonment syndrome which constitutes for the child either the death of the father, his absence, or his rejection of the child, can liberate impulses which are not restrained by the superego. The anxiety and anguish that are born from this state of maximum frustration initiate aggressive reactions. There is as a result a need for security and this can lead to the type of mental organization imposed by heredity, the environment, education, and a desire to tame society, which in the child's mind is perhaps made responsible for the death of the father. The extraordinary frequency of orphans among political leaders, and more particularly among revolutionaries and creators of religious movements which have shaped human history, allows us to believe that there exists a sequence consisting of the following: death of the father—frustration—absence of model (superego), and identification with the father—search for a grand compensatory model—aggression—search for a sense of security—search for political power in order to tame a group of men. In the case of illegitimacy, revenge can be a sufficient motivation (e.g., Evita Perón). In this respect great religious and philosophical leaders, great writers, and artists have had the same destiny as great political leaders.

It is freely recognized that political geniuses are not formed by the influence of colleges, universities, or technical schools and that they escape psychometric tests and the selection criteria of famous schools. The quality of aggression in the struggle for life is ultimately manifested in concrete fashion. You need not be crazy to be a genius, you need not be an orphan to lead the world. However, given equal potential genes (one should examine the problem of the Y-Y gene), with equal social conditions, and education, children deprived of their fathers appear to have been bequeathed a will for revenge against life, against society, and against men. The function of this will for revenge is to enable them to realize their youthful fantasies, which must compensate and even overcompensate for the emptiness, the abandonment, the humiliation, the nonidentification with the father, which they have suffered unconsciously and sometimes consciously.

To paraphrase what has been said by Sartre, there is a feeling that facing the father's empty place, the orphan or the abandoned child must fill the void, struggle against the anguish by sublimating his aggression in creativity, and a need for political power which alone can liberate him. The example of Thorez, vice premier of France is an illustration.

Finally, I would like to end with a rather bold presentation: we know that the father cuts the umbilical cord of his son twice, the first time at birth, by an intermediary person (the doctor or midwife) to liberate him from his mother's womb, a second time at puberty, when he detaches the child from the tenderness of his mother so that he identifies himself with the role of the father, of the male in the world. In the case of the orphan boy, or the boy who has been abandoned by his father, the second severance of the cord does not take place: there is an identification with the symbiotic greatness of the mother who creates life in the world. Isn't there in the future politician or creator of a religion, in the philosopher, the writer, and the artist a desire to bear a child, to create, to mold, to shape a world, a society, in the image of his mother?

Another type of reaction can be found in the person who is not aggressive and who is aware of his own timidity (e.g., former West German Chancellor Konrad Adenauer): then the need is to transform oneself, step inside the skin of an official, public person in order to publicly honor his sublimated mother in the mother country.

Thus, we have men who sincerely believe in helping others and rendering service, an attitude which appears to be the opposite of the desire for power, but which serves as a camouflage for it (Tournier, 1977; see Appendix A for a discussion with a former chief of state).

Let us end with a whim: it is often said that the man is the father of the child, and perhaps as well the child is the father of the man. One could complete this by saying that the orphaned or abandoned child wishes to be the father or the mother of men in order to tame an agonized and traumatized world.

On the political level, when a group seeks a leader or has a leader imposed upon them, it would be worthwhile to study his biography in accordance with this new concept, not so much to encourage or impede him in his rise toward political power, but in order to propose to him another therapy than political power. On the biological level, one understands that in the face of the overwhelming personality of such a leader, ambitious and dictatorial, democracy, by its control mechanisms, represents the best possible means to limit the force of the impulses; without such restraints there is a risk of dictatorship or political adventurism.

We wonder if writers and philosophers (see Synoptic Tables, Appendix C) have not experienced the same motivations and drives to search for power by means of the word or the idea (e.g., *The Words*, Sartre's autobiography). However, it is worth noting that we could just as easily make a list of literary and philosophical figures who were equally celebrated and influential and who were not orphans.

We could likewise study the great composers and artists from this angle, and the relationship between art and homosexuality due to the absence of the father and identification with the mother. But again, we could as easily make a list of artists and musicians of comparable stature who did not lose their fathers. It is certain that this problem deserves to be studied with the collaboration of literary and art critics. It would also be interesting to verify in what measure Nobel Prize winners are recruited from among orphans or abandoned children.

References

Accoce, P., & Rentchnick, P. (1976), *Ces Malades qui Nous Gouvernent* (The Sick Who Govern Us). Paris: Stock.

Ajar, E. (1975), *Momo*. Garden City, NY: Doubleday, 1978.

Ajuriaguerra, J. de (1980), *Handbook of Child Psychiatry and Psychology*. New York: Masson.

Anzieu, D. (1975), *Freud's Self-Analysis*. Madison, CT: International Universities Press, 1986.

Arthur, B., & Kemme, M. L. (1964), Bereavement in childhood. *J. Child Psychol. & Psychiat.*, 5:37–49.

Bonardi, P. (1935), *Napoléon Bonaparte, enfant d'Ajaccio*. (Napoléon Bonaparte: Child of Ajaccio). Paris: Les Editions de France.

Bowlby, J. (1952), *Maternal Care and Mental Health; Deprivation of Maternal Care: A Reassessment of Its Effects*. New York: Schocken, 1966.

———— (1960a), Separation anxiety. *Internat. J. Psycho-Anal.*, 41:89–113.

———— (1960b), Grief and mourning in infancy and early childhood. *The Psychoanalytic Study of the Child*, 15:9–52. New York: International Universities Press.

———— (196la), Separation anxiety: A critical review of the literature. *J. Child Psychol. & Psychiat.*, 1:251–269.

———— (1961b), Process of mourning. *Internat. J. Psycho-Anal.*, 42:317–340.

———— (196lc), Childhood mourning and its implications for psychiatry. *Amer. J. Psychiat.*, 118:481–498.

———— (1963), Pathological mourning and childhood mourning. *J. Amer. Psychoanal. Assn.*, 11:500–541.

———— (1969), *Attachment*. New York: Basic Books.

———— (1973), *Separation*. New York: Basic Books.

———— (1980), *Loss*. New York: Basic Books.

Brill, N. Q., & Liston, E. H. (1966), Parental loss in adults with emotional disorders. *Arch. Gen. Psychiat.*, 14:307–314.

Choisy, M. (1950), Le complexe de Phaéton (The Phaeton Complex). *Psyché*, 5:715–731.

Erikson, E. H. (1975), *Life History and the Historical Moment.* New York: W. W. Norton.

Gregory, I. (1966), Retrospective data concerning childhood loss of a parent. *Arch. Gen. Psychiat.,* 15:354–368.

Hitler, A. (1925), *Mein Kampf.* Boston: Houghton Mifflin, 1943.

Meerloo, J. A. M. (1968), The father cuts the cord. *Child & Family,* Spring.

Meir, G. (1975), *My Life.* New York: Putnam.

Mitscherlich, A. (1969), *Society Without the Father.* New York: Jason Aronson, 1973.

Oltman, J. E., & Friedman, S. (1965), Report on parental deprivation in psychiatric disorders. *Arch. Gen. Psychiat.,* 12:46–56.

Porot, M. (1959), *L'Enfant et les Relations Familiales* (The Child and Family Relationships). Paris: Presses Universitaires de France.

Robert, M. (1972), *Origins of the Novel.* Bloomington: Indiana University Press, 1980.

Robrieux, P. (1975), *Maurice Thorez.* Paris: Fayard.

Sartre, J. P. (1964), *The Words.* New York: George Braziller.

Simonsen, K. M. (1947), *Examination* of *Children from Children's Homes and Day Nurseries.* Copenhagen: Nyt Nordisk Forlag.

Stephens, R. (1973), *Nasser: A Political Biography.* London: Penguin Books.

Tournier, P. (1977), *The Violence Within.* New York: Harper & Row, 1982.

PART III

Is the Psychoanalytic Biography of Political Leaders Feasible?

Pierre de Senarclens

Do Orphans Lead
the World?

Do orphans lead the world? The question may appear ridiculous, but that is no reason to set it aside without further examination. If the psychoanalyst, as a result of his clinical experience, believes himself able to establish a link between being an orphan and the holding of political power, the historian owes it to himself to consider whether it is possible to verify this hypothetical relationship in empirical terms.

This task, however, is not simple. This hypothesis cannot be proved by a mere haphazard listing of famous orphans. It is not, in fact, important from a methodological point of view to scan the world of the past in search of orphans who have left an imprint on history. The notion of the orphan has evolved so much in the past, it still differs greatly from culture to culture. The mechanisms of transfer of power are so varied, in time and space, that one must necessarily focus research on a single society which is relatively homogeneous from a cultural point of view. But were we to proceed in this fashion, research would stop short. A cursory scan of the biographies of the presidents of the United States in the twentieth century, for example, reveals that in a society where the institutions have left a relatively important place to individual ambitions, one finds only one chief executive who was orphaned at an early age: Herbert Hoover.[1]

[1]If total orphanhood in childhood is meant, then Herbert Hoover and possibly Andrew Jackson may be cited. Perhaps William Harrison would be considered as well. If one-parent orphanhood is to be listed, then among

This does not necessarily invalidate the hypothesis of a correlation between orphans and political power. It is not impossible, in fact, to isolate a particular type of political leader whose search for power would result rather specifically from a psychic trauma provoked by the loss of a father or a mother. If this very general hypothesis were to be verified, one would find a correlation between a certain type of political creativity and the status of a precocious orphan.

Nonetheless, this interesting hypothesis, though vague, risks crumbling into mere intuition if we do not consider the complex problems that are raised by it, such as the role of personality in history, the scientific value of the psychoanalytic biography, and of political typologies.

Biography and the Marxist Vision in History

The biography has been a controversial matter among historians for a long time. There are some who deny that analysis of a particular life can reveal the complex process of history, one which is made dynamic by material forces and social determinisms of a collective type. Others offer innumerable examples of the important and even decisive role of certain individuals in history, and recall, in particular, the essential weight of certain personalities in societies with a Marxist vision

---

the presidents of the United States who were orphaned by the death of one parent by age nine can be found James Garfield (F1, M after, S49), Rutherford Hayes (F before, M44), Herbert Hoover (F6, M8), Andrew Jackson (F before, M13), Andrew Johnson (F3, M47), Abraham Lincoln (F41, M9), and John Tyler (F22, M7). Added to this list are those presidents who were orphaned by the death of one parent by age nineteen, which include Grover Cleveland (F16, M55), Calvin Coolidge (F53, M12), Benjamin Harrison (F44, M17), William Harrison (F18, M19), Thomas Jefferson (F14, M33), James Monroe (F16, M48), Franklin Roosevelt (F18, M59), Theodore Roosevelt (F19, M25), and George Washington (F11, M57). The more inclusive Synoptic Table of Political and Religious Leaders is found in Appendix B—Eisenstadt.

of history. The argument is not new; it was particularly strong in the nineteenth century. In 1841, the English historian Thomas Carlyle (1897) affirmed, in a celebrated work, that "universal history" is essentially the "story of great men," and assimilated the concept of heroic personages to the soul of human evolution.

Contrary to this idealistic position, Marxists have always minimized the role of personality in history, the conscience of the masses or individuals being determined essentially by general conditions of existence. Without denying the role of chance or of individual particularities, Marxists consider that the action of these factors exercise themselves inevitably under predetermined social conditions the importance of which is always predominant. "The character of the individual," Plekhanov (n.d.) was to affirm, "is not a factor of the social evolution except where social connections permit it, as long as they permit it, and only in the measure where they permit it" (p. 331). If Bonaparte had been killed at the Arcole bridge, history would not have followed a radically different path. Military genius, like artistic talent, was, according to Plekhanov, the product of favorable social conditions. Trotsky (1930a) remarked: "Historians and biographers of the psychological tendency not infrequently seek and find something purely personal and accidental where great historical forces are refracted through a personality" (p. 94). Trotsky (1930b) nevertheless yielded to the autobiographical form, but stated precisely that the "only method of making an autobiography objective [was] making it the most adequate expression of personality, conditions, and epoch" (p. xxx). Personality, from this point of view, did have its own autonomy; it was not the undifferentiated reflection of particular social conditions. Trotsky affirmed that one needed to seek the causes of personality more in the circumstances of the times than in oneself. But he also added:

> Of course, certain personal traits were also necessary for the work, good or bad, that I performed. But under other historical conditions, these personal peculiarities might have remained completely dormant, as is true of so many propensities and passions on which the social environment makes no demands.

Above the subjective there rises the objective, and in the final
reckoning it is the objective that decides [p. xxiii].

Trotsky (1937) also defined Stalin as the "personification
of the [Soviet] bureaucracy" (p. 277) which means that he
considered him more or less interchangeable. As was well demonstrated by Tucker (1973), Stalinism was in part the consequence of the tendency of the Bolsheviks to ignore the role
of personality in history. In the twenties, Stalin succeeded in
minimizing his conflicts with his political enemies by accusing
them of attacking his personal qualities in order to avoid considering the fundamental problems.

The problem still appears to be poorly resolved in contemporary Marxist historiography. Khrushchev, at the Twentieth Congress in 1956, attributed a decisive role to Stalin's
personality, in his explanation of the "negative tendencies" which
had appeared in Soviet society, but this extreme personalization
of the Stalin phenomenon was certainly not in accordance with
orthodox Marxist historiography. Jean Ellenstein (1976), twenty
years later, as a French communist historian, protested against
the insufficiency of the Khrushchev criticism, which did not
address itself to the fundamentals of Stalinism. For Ellenstein,
the profound causes of this phenomenon were related "to the
conditions leading to socialism, to the building of socialism, to
the function of the Soviet State, and of the political system
born from the socialist revolution" (1976, p. 4). In other words,
the Stalin phenomenon could not be considered as the unfortunate result of the dictatorship of one person, but translated
into the evolution of an entire revolutionary process confronted
by the particular conditions of Russian society at the beginning
of the twentieth century. From the Marxist point of view, this
position was certainly more orthodox.

Contemporary non-Marxist historiography appears to want
to override this debate by developing a synthesis which would
admit a constant interaction between the individual and society,
and conceive the study of biography as an analysis of this
particular dialectic. Robert Tucker (1973) expressed this position of synthesis when he evoked Stalin's primary Manicheanism with regard to his entourage:

Character and culture coalesced and reinforced each other in this way of perceiving other people. A gifted and unusually sensitive child suffered bad early experiences, including his father's brutality toward himself and his mother, and emerged as a hardened, vigilant youngster with a self-idealizing tendency, on the one hand, and a vengeful streak and indomitable will to fight and to win on the other. The Georgian social setting and its Russifying overseers offered him a ready-made hostile division of people into friends and enemies, together with such cultural traditions as the blood feud and such dramatizations of the situation as the Koba story. (The Georgian revolutionary hero with whom he identified.) As a youth in the seminary, he immersed himself in the Marxian revolutionary subculture; what particularly appealed to him in that, as we have seen, was the ideological symbolism that split the social universe into two great warring classes of oppressed and oppressors: friends and enemies on the scale of all mankind and all recorded history. Within the subculture, he gravitated unerringly to the militant version of the ideology that Lenin presented. . . . Stalin found in his writings a wealth of material that he wrought into his own image of the enemy [Tucker, 1973, pp. 425–426].

Moreover, Stalin had pushed to the extreme a frequent confusion in revolutionary movements between "personal" and "political" relations. But here again this slanted view was derived in part from his education in Georgian society at the end of the nineteenth century where this distinction between the private and the political sphere was little developed. It is therefore difficult to explain this character trait by strictly separating what stems from the idiosyncrasies of his development, from the imprint of the cultural context in which he evolved. The biography, in its global perspective, tends to reconstruct a life defined by the psychological as well as the sociological, cultural, and historical factors. In accordance with this approach, we would concede that Stalinism cannot be reduced to the personality of Stalin, but is the product, rather, of a period in the history of Bolshevik Russia, a history engendered by complex phenomena of a collective type. But one must admit that the phenomenon in question is incomprehensible without an analysis of Stalin's personality, the latter being conceived as a product of multiple psychological, sociological, cultural, and historical determinants. As Saul Friedlander (1975) says so well: "One cannot study Luther without investigating the social and religious context that produced him—but can one study Protestantism without studying Luther, or Bolshevism without Lenin, or Nazism without Hitler?" (p. 44). Certainly, these individuals exercised a decisive influence in their milieu by creating new social norms and symbols.

Phenomena of Long Duration and Brief Political Processes

It is relevant to make an important distinction between the analysis of phenomena of long duration and that of brief political processes. It is recognized that personality factors play a less important role in the long term than in historical processes of short duration. But the analysis of these brief periods is more complicated than is first apparent. The media promulgates the idea that chiefs of state make their decisions in a relatively autonomous manner: "President Carter has decided . . ."; "Leonid Brezhnev, Secretary General of the Soviet Communist Party, has taken the initiative . . ."; it is as if the actions of these leaders resulted from their personal will. The truth is infinitely more complex, as is demonstrated in an abundant political science literature devoted to the decision-making process.

Modern states are made up of enormous bureaucracies, and the decisions made are less the result of thought processes of leaders acting rationally in the performance of their political objectives than they are the product of vast bureaucratic organizations. Inspired by research undertaken in the United States on the function of administrations, Graham Allison (1971) has shown in his study of the Cuban crisis that an explanation can be found for certain illogical or incomprehensible behavior on the part of the United States or the U.S.S.R. during the 1962 crisis in an analysis of American and Soviet bureaucratic machinery. Modern governments consist of a conglomerate of organizations more or less independent of one another, often competing with each other, and functioning according to protocols which are difficult to modify. Chiefs of state perceive the reality across the labyrinths of these organizations, and the decisions they make are a function of the information they furnish, the solutions that they propose, and also the manner in which they execute the resolutions taken. Chiefs of state therefore have a limited liberty, not only in the selection of political-strategic objectives but also in the choice of possible solutions or in the determination of available means. Their capacity for decision is relatively restrained.

One can also envision other limitations on the ability of leaders to decide freely. Allison has indicated that leaders are forced to submit to a variety of political pressures from a guiding elite which is not always homogenous: that is, a group of persons having interests and systems with divergent values, who themselves are subject to multiple political influences, of which incessant political competition constantly orients the direction of governmental action. But the fact that great political decisions are made by a leading elite can have other consequences. In a recent work, Irving Janis (1972) has analyzed certain American foreign policy decisions made as the result of psychic mechanisms which are found in the actions of smaller groups. In certain cases, the "group illusion" would be another factor limiting the decision autonomy of chiefs of state.

It is also relevant to note that certain decisions perceived in retrospect as "irrational" cannot be attributed to the idiosyncratic particularities of the decision makers which are inherent in the very function of the human spirit (Jervis, 1976). As an example, modes of perceiving change slowly, which explains the permanence of images which the decision maker may have of his close or more remote environment. In the domain of foreign policy, one realizes that actors on the international scene continue to pursue over the long term the objectives that they have set for themselves, neglecting data which would suggest a different attitude. The permanence of images and convictions is a source, among others, of errors of perception, and therefore of inappropriate decisions. There exist numerous cognitive factors enabling a "normal" person to have an incorrect perception of his environment. By neglecting them, one can attribute too much importance to emotional factors when analyzing the decision process.

The biographical account which did not take into consideration these sociocultural and historical determinants, organizational mechanisms, complex political processes, factors of perception, and so on, would present an idealized history. This is unfortunately the case in many biographies, or psychobiographies, which believe they can explain Hitlerism by the personality of Hitler or by the young Hitler's oedipal conflict.

Two Biographical Approaches: The Historical and the Psychobiographical

Today there are two principal biographical methods in use. The first approach derives from the traditional historical point of view, and it poses a problem because its criteria for validation are not high when it attempts to reconstitute the character traits of an individual or the psychic factors which have predetermined his actions. The motives of the subject under study are explained via the bias of an intuitive psychology or by recourse to common sense, the scientific basis of which is questionable. The second approach derives from Freudian inspired theories to explain the personality and life of the subject being studied, to anticipate the behavior of an actor on the political scene. This last biographical approach, more hazardous, but also more innovative, presents several problems which we will now examine.

As we know, Freud and his close disciples were the first to attempt to apply psychoanalysis to the study of writers, artists, and famous political leaders. The study of Leonardo da Vinci by Freud (1910) deserves our particular attention, because it raises important problems of methodology. It created an interesting controversy the study of which focuses on the problems rising from the psychobiography.

Freud's Study of Leonardo da Vinci

Freud founded the greater part of his study on the analysis of a childhood memory of Leonardo, the unreal aspect of which led him immediately to believe it a fantasy. Leonardo inserted this strange memory in his scientific writings: "It seems that I was always destined to be so deeply concerned with vultures; for I recall as one of my very earliest memories that while I was in my cradle a vulture came down to me, and opened my mouth with its tail, and struck me many times with its tail against my lips" (cited in Freud, 1910, p. 82). For Freud, the memory that Leonardo expressed was a passive homosexual fantasy, the tail of the animal, the phallic image, symbolizing the maternal breast of childhood. Basing himself on the few biographical notes he had on Leonardo da Vinci, and mainly on his clinical experience, Freud believed that thanks to the interpretation of this fantasy, he could, in part, reconstruct the psychology of this genius of the Renaissance. He believed he could elucidate certain character traits and also explain Leonardo's scientific interests, as well as the inhibitions about painting which he manifested for several years. Freud's interpretation permitted him also to reconstruct certain events in Leonardo's life which had hitherto been of uncertain origins.

In order to explain the image of the vulture, Freud analyzed the significance of this bird within Leonardo's cultural framework. He recalled notably that the Egyptians of antiquity worshipped a maternal deity with the head of a vulture and that the fathers of the Catholic Church had borrowed from mythology the bisexual nature of the vulture fertilized by the wind in order to confound skeptics regarding the Immaculate Conception. It appears probable that Leonardo knew this fable, and this fantasy referred to his situation as an illegitimate child alone with his mother. This fantasy reinforced the plausibility of a story that Leonardo had not known his father before the age of three, perhaps even five, at which time his father legitimized him and took him in. "The fact which the vulture phantasy confirms, namely that Leonardo spent the first years of his life alone with his mother will have been of decisive influence in the formation of his inner life" (Freud,

1910, p. 92). The absence of his father, Freud believed, had brought Leonardo to "brood . . . with a special intensity" on the enigma of life, and these speculations were sublimated into an intellectual and scientific curiosity above the normal.

The fascinating smile of the Mona Lisa would have been reminiscent of the happy bonds which united him to his mother. Freud also believed that the painting of Saint Anne with her daughter and her grandchild is a subject that Italian painting had rarely depicted. "The picture contains the synthesis of the history of his childhood" (1910, p. 112). He in fact compared the theme of this creation to biographical facts which allow us to believe that Leonardo had two mothers: Caterina, his biological mother, from whom he was separated around the age of three, and Donna Albiera, his father's wife, who took care of him from that time on. The painting of Saint Anne suggested the presence at his father's house of a mother and a grandmother that the painter had represented.

As we see it, Freud's methods considerably enlarged the "historian's territory," since a bizarre recollection, apparently insignificant, became for him material of major importance for an understanding of Leonardo's personality, the intelligence which informed his creativity, and even for a reconstruction of the events of his life. According to Freud, Leonardo's recall did not refer directly to an objective event in the sense that a historian bases his work on factual material, but to a fantastic reality filled with desires and interdictions, of symbols, and finally of events that only interpretation could reorient. Thus, interpretation permitted Freud to fill in the blanks in Leonardo's biography.

Freud's thesis was contested from a historical point of view. An English historian (Maclagan, 1923) demonstrated that it was in part founded upon an incorrect translation of the Italian word *nibbio*, which did not mean vulture, as Freud was led to believe on the basis of an incorrect German translation, but kite. This bird did not then have the cultural significance that Freud accorded it. Furthermore, in rereading the notebooks of Leonardo, Schapiro (1956) came to the conclusion that his interest in the kite was above all of a scientific nature, the movements and the form of this bird serving as a model for flying machines. Thus, Leonardo's strange recollection did not necessarily have the psychological significance that Freud had implied. Schapiro explained it by referring to ancient classical legends and to a certain literary genre of the Renaissance, rich in analogous fantasies which were supposed to predict an extraordinary destiny. Schapiro was also able to show that the Saint Anne cult was already established, and that neither her representation with her daughter, the Virgin Mary, nor the child was original at the time that Leonardo developed this theme.

Therefore, without questioning the psychoanalytic paradigm, nor indeed the value of Freudian analysis for comprehending Leonardo's personality and work, Schapiro demonstrated the insufficiency of an approach which tended to explain a complex cultural phenomenon in a monocausal way. Freud had not taken sufficiently into account certain cultural and social factors which could have determined the expression of Leonardo's childhood memory. Schapiro also criticized him for having limited his scope of analysis to certain pictorial works while neglecting those that ran counter to his interpretation.

Kurt Eissler (1961), a Freudian psychoanalyst, author of an authoritative psychobiography of Goethe, was to answer different critics to reaffirm the ground of Freud's theme. The error of the vulture did not negate the interpretation of this recollection as a homosexual fantasy. On the other hand, the legendary factors or the scientific interest in the kite for Leonardo constituted merely a fact derived from an idiosyncratic fantasy. Certainly Schapiro was able to show that the kite, and not the vulture, represented a terrible mother for Leonardo, but this suggestion did not interfere with Freud's hypothesis, since it is also compatible with his theory of homosexuality: in the subconscious, we know, opposite images are intermingled, and that the closeness of homosexuals to their mothers coexists with contempt.

From a historical point of view, we must admit this controversy is insoluble, since only the living Leonardo da Vinci, free associating, could give true meaning to this childhood memory. It does introduce us, however, to the heart of the

controversy released when psychoanalysis is transposed out
of its therapeutic framework. It demonstrates the precarious-
ness of historical hypotheses founded on the psychoanalytic
interpretation of fragile and contestable material. It also shows
us the legitimate tendency of historians trained in the traditional disciplines to exhaust all explanations on a cultural or
sociological level before taking the liberty to cite such explanations as the equivocal and complex manifestations of the unconscious described in Freudian hermeneutics.

Although there may be insufficiencies in this first try at
psychobiography, it is recognized today that Freud's discoveries gave a solid base to the deciphering of the products of
the imagination, and the contribution of psychoanalysis to the
critique of art and literature has been considerable. Outside
of the privileged domain of treatment in psychoanalysis, the
historian and the political scientist are also more aware of the
unconscious processes of the individual or the group. Therefore, the biographer who aspires to use the psychoanalytic
approach will attribute a decisive importance to material which
reveals the subconscious nature of the subject that he is studying: his dreams, his fantasies, his failures, his anxieties, his
inhibitions, his repetitive behavior, his life-style, his character,
the unique aspects of his intellectual work or of his political
acts, and so on. Alert to these subconscious processes, the psychobiographer will point out the importance of facts hitherto
neglected by traditional historians. By following the genetic
approach of psychoanalysis, the biographer will grant a determining role to the childhood and youth of his subject, without
omitting, in dynamic perspective, all the elements of his adult
life, present or past, with individuals or groups, which have
influenced his behavior and his work. But, as we shall see,
this fruitful approach is in conflict with particular obstacles
in the study of political men.

The "Pathography" of Woodrow Wilson

Freud did not limit the application of his discoveries to the
analysis of artists and writers. With William Bullitt (Freud
and Bullitt, 1967) the former American Ambassador to France,

he attempted the psychoanalytic study of a famous chief of state, Woodrow Wilson. It is not known exactly what part Freud played in the conception and writing of this work, but one thing is certain: this "pathography" was a failure. Freud and Bullitt's thesis was simplistic: Wilson suffered from passivity with regard to his father, and his political involvement was an attempt to surmount this alienating dependency. The analysis of the political and social environment in which the president supposedly lived did not exist, our two authors having contented themselves with reducing Wilson's discourse and behavior to terms of simple pathology, in spite of Freud's preliminary warnings relative to the dangers of establishing a clear frontier between the normal and the abnormal in psychic life. Both authors were hostile toward Wilson for different reasons, and this negative view contradicted the explanatory functions of the psychobiographical method. From the psychoanalytic point of view, the schema of the work was equally unacceptable. Paul Roazen (1973) was to write on this subject:

> The book rings with such a curiously old-fashioned language that it has the air of a genuine psychoanalytic antique. There is Freud's own literalistic belief in the existence of fixed quantities of libido to be disposed of. The starkness of the argument and the cheap quality of the interpretations offered have disturbed many readers. What are suggested as explanations of human motivation may be in part true, yet the actions they are supposed to explain can often also be traced to something else entirely. Different situations can mobilize very different qualities in a person. Wilson emerges as a robot, divided up into neat little spheres, with his masculinity in one place and his femininity in another. The true psychologist knows that such sharp lines of demarcation are a ridiculous approach to understanding a person; a human being cannot be described as if he were composed of a set of boxes, with each of his complexes securely isolated. In psychology it is the in betweens which are important [p. 173].

This critique deserves to be quoted, for its pertinence goes beyond Freud and Bullitt's work on Wilson. It is equally applicable to numerous contemporary attempts. Although the discovery of unconscious mental processes was to renew the

biographical method considerably, the psychobiography of political men was to remain a difficult medium, and almost always
unsatisfactory, the particular object of this type of study disap-
pearing from sight as a result of psychoanalytically inspired
investigative methods. It is, therefore, not exactly by chance
that the psychobiography of political personalities took an un-
fruitful turn. One only need consult recent psychoanalytic studies of former President Nixon and his Secretary of State Henry
Kissinger in order to realize that this type of approach remains
hazardous.

The Hazards of the Political Psychobiography

Nixon. The work of American psychiatrist David Abrahamson
(1976), *Nixon vs. Nixon: An Emotional Tragedy,* attempts to reconstruct Nixon's development, then analyze his political behavior
by mixing in historical material of the most doubtful kind with
"wild" psychoanalytic interpretations. From a historical point
of view in particular, this type of psychobiography is characterized by the extensive metamorphizing of chance hypotheses
into objective facts. By taking all kinds of liberties with history
and its methods, but also with the scientific demands of the
psychoanalytic approach, one can prove anything, and notably
that Nixon experienced intense frustrations at the oral stage
of his development, that his passage from the anal stage was
problematic, and that an inharmonious familial environment
rendered the oedipal resolution difficult. Abrahamson reveals
also that young Richard had a profound attachment to his mother
and an unconscious hostility with regard to his aggressive
father, who was also competitive and compulsive, a hostility
which the son necessarily had to project ultimately upon symbols of authority. In a general way, Nixon did not feel loved
by his parents, which made him feel disparaged, self-doubting,
anxious, inclined to daydreaming, obsessional, searching unconsciously for his own downfall, and finally paranoid. It remains
to be understood how such a disturbed individual could reach
a position of supreme governmental power in the United States,
but this kind of question does not enter into the preoccupations
of this psychobiographical journalism where the most complex

psychoanalytic concepts are used as moral bludgeons or for the satisfaction of a general public hungry for pseudoscientific explanations with an odor of scandal.

The psychobiographical analysis of living political personalities, such as Kissinger or Nixon, should not be unachievable. After all, these people had a childhood, like everyone else, and since this took place in the contemporary world certain themes which are susceptible to interpretation could be identified. We sometimes also have the testimony of witnesses to their familial and professional lives, who can furnish salient points on certain aspects of their character, or other intimate aspects of their lives.

Unfortunately, this type of analysis very often encounters insurmountable obstacles. First of all, the most elementary biographical facts are lacking when it comes to reconstructing the significant elements of childhood and adolescence. Second, it is difficult to make a distinction between the private person and the public role he assumes. The political man is in effect the prisoner of standards of behavior imposed by his official function and it is not easy to distinguish in his behavior what is actually part of his personality or an assumed role. Moreover, recourse to an analysis of themes, metaphors, and constant associations is not possible, for speeches have a relatively rigid structure, also imposed by social demand. The conventional rhetoric of the politician therefore escapes more easily from a psychoanalytically inspired interpretation.

Mazlisch's (1973) study of Nixon also adopts this type of uncertain psychobiographical approach, primarily because we do not have at our disposal any significant facts regarding Nixon's family life. Despite long years in public life, Nixon inspired few studies before Watergate, and the basis of his personality, his nonofficial life, has remained impenetrable. To undertake his psychobiography, Mazlisch had only fragmentary information, reaped from studies which may be typified as journalistic and partisan. The thematic analysis of his speeches turns out to be equally difficult, since one does not always know the share of responsibility in this type of creation.

It is certain that the losses of his two brothers were important events in his adolescence, but it is not possible to know the way he responded to them. It is therefore risky, due to lack of data, to affirm that these deaths created in him a feeling of survivor guilt. It is also probable that he responded to the periodic departure of his mother with his older brother (due to illness) as an abandonment, but this isolated hypothesis is without interest. It is also difficult to affirm that Nixon sought to avenge his father's professional failure and that his own success provoked in him feelings of guilt, because nothing allows us to verify these assertions at a level that the psychoanalyst might judge appropriate, while the historian would require verification.

Thus, one must be skeptical in considering as a "massive projection" his Red-baiting electoral campaign against Helen Gahagan Douglas, or his participation in the McCarthy era witch-hunts of the 1950s. It is possible that his position resulted from simple demagogy, inspired by his political ambition and by the demands of an electorate which favored this type of Manicheanism (Mazlisch, 1976a). To win, a politician often must utilize the very processes whose use he denounces in others, and this behavior does not need to be interpreted in terms of projection. Likewise, Nixon's raising of the issue of a communist plot does not necessarily arise from a "paranoid fear," but from an ideology broadly circulated in certain circles. Let us note that Nixon did not bear his own aggression well (who can bear it?), and that he showed himself as irresolute in times of crisis. Mazlisch believes he can trace this character trait to the advice of his mother to avoid political conflicts, a piece of advice which was contrary to the "fiercely" competitive tendencies of his father. But the biographical data available on Nixon are so ambiguous that it is very difficult to find in them the emotional basis for a particular character trait. This results in interpretations proposed by Mazlisch that are poorly supported, either because the facts quoted are sparse or insufficient, or because they can have different psychological explanations.

Kissinger. Without sharing the opinion of *Time* (April 1, 1974) which saw Kissinger as "the world's indispensable man" (cited in Mazlisch, 1976a) we can recognize that the former Secretary of State for presidents Nixon and Ford has played a leading

role in the conduct of world affairs. The psychoanalytic interpretation of Kissinger's personality and work is clearly of interest. Unfortunately, such studies have had the same negative
characteristics as the psychobiographies of Nixon.

Thus, in Diana Ward's approach (1975), there is a constant
back and forth between unclear psychoanalytic concepts on
the one hand, and chance biographical facts of little value on
the other hand. Accordingly, Ward attempts to explain the
development of Kissinger's personality by gathering little clues
from what is known about his childhood, and, when the biographical facts are missing, by referring to data on the Jewish
situation in Germany during the mid-1930s. Believing in the
importance of the theme of opposition between order and chaos,
she refers to her own experience as a Jewish child under Hitler.
This preoccupation with chaos, she affirms, by referring to
clinical literature, is a characteristic of the depressed personality. Surely it is necessary to demonstrate that young Henry's
childhood actually followed the schema of the development
of a depressive personality. However, failing the availability
of this information, the interpretation of rare bits and pieces
concerning his childhood and adolescence is supposed to fill
the gap between theory and reality. Using this perspective, *A
World Restored* (1957), Kissinger's book on Metternich, is understood as expressing his deep desire to restore his proper self.
In other words, in order to compensate for his feelings of
inadequacy, he would have taken as identifying models in history or in the present personalities symbolizing assurance, vitality, and power. Thus, Vietnam would become the "test" of his
own capacity to overcome the doubts which he experienced
with regard to himself and in regard to his environment. The
invasion of Cambodia would illustrate his permanent need to
confront chaos, to show force; it would also express his obsessional anguish over the decline of America.

Mazlisch's study of Kissinger is no more solid. He thus
"cannot help suspecting" that young Henry Kissinger experienced feelings of hostility toward his father which were strongly
repressed, a hypothesis not in itself of interest since this type
of hostile sentiment is found in the normal development of
every personality. Mazlisch remains on the level of generality
and speculation when he seeks to reconstruct the emotions

felt by young Kissinger at the time when the Nazi menace rendered departure into exile inevitable:

> Henry's deepest reactions, unconscious of course, must have been mixed and chaotic: great insecurity and fear for himself; a resentment of his father's "authority," which nevertheless could not protect those under it from the Nazi threat; and a desire to redeem his beloved father's failure (coupled with feelings of guilt that, in doing so, he might "show up" his father and surpass him) [p. 35].

Mazlisch then takes up the concept of Kissinger's feelings toward the Germans in 1945, and later toward the communists and other groups to which he was opposed, but still his thesis relies on partially known data, badly documented, and loosely interpreted.

Should one conclude that neither Nixon nor Kissinger has any characteristic traits susceptible to interpretation by a psychoanalytically inspired biographic study? In the absence of rigorous attempts, it is difficult to answer this question. Together and individually they have incontestably made a personal imprint on their times, but this has given rise only to intuitive interpretations in the absence of other sources directly relating to their emotional life, and without any serious biographical indications allowing the reconstitution of the development of their personalities.

Erik Erikson (1950, 1962, 1970) has considerably renewed the psychoanalytic biography, notably by seizing on the importance of numerous historical and sociocultural determinants which condition the stages of personality development, and also by showing how certain historical personages negotiated their conflicts with their social environment in order to transcend them in a political or religious project which anticipated the ideas and the affective demands of their contemporaries. Unfortunately, the works that he dedicated to Luther, Hitler, and Gandhi display such license with the scientific requirements of the historical approach that it is difficult to consider them in any other way than as a type midway between the psychobiographical novel and the philosophical essay.

Bismarck. Inspired by Erikson, certain authors impose abstract schemes of development to fill in the void left by the inexplicable. Thus it is with the "psychosocial moratorium" hypothesis defined by Erikson as a universal period of gestation preceding maturity, which appears to explain the anticipation of very diverse vocations. Otto Pflanze (1972) utilizes this noion to explain an entire period in the life of Bismarck, the one during which the Prussian Junker was not yet involved in the career which was to make him a historical figure (see also Jardim [1970] and Kakar [1970] for this same unsatisfactory type). He also refers to the work of Anna Freud in order to interpret Bismarck's submission to the service of the Prussian state as a projection of his need for power over and renown in this institution. According to this projection mechanism approach, had Bismarck's aspirations been used for personal profit his level of guilt would have been intolerable.

Pflanze then utilizes the notion of the "phallic-narcissistic" character developed by Reich to explain Bismarck's personality. Even if we agree that this type of character singled out by Reich can be placed in a particular category, is it possible to use it to encompass the personality of Bismarck? Is it so evident that his behavior manifested an exaggerated masculinity? The number of duels that he had to his credit, his boasts in the domain of alcohol consumption, his need to surround himself with enormous and vicious dogs, his taste for parades in military uniform, weren't these behaviors suggested by his sociocultural, his Prussian, environment? But if we admit that Bismarck corresponds to the type singled out by Reich, what are the origins of these character traits in Bismarck? To answer this question, we have a summary of biographical data. Certainly, Pflanze brings out an interesting letter in which the future statesman confessed to having a mother who was harsh and cold, his hatred for her, the love mixed with remorse that he felt for his father. Moreover, Bismarck had detestable memories of the boarding school to which his mother sent him at the age of six. Consequently, he felt rejected, and the avowal that he made one day that his mother had "spoiled his character" is heavy with significance. But how can we interpret autobiographical facts that are so deficient? Are they enough to affirm that "in the successive stages of Bismarck's development can be discerned the emergence of an inner conflict whose origin may lie in the oedipal triangle with his parents" (p. 431). This type of conclusion is so general that it has no interest for the historian. It is also difficult to integrate Bismarck's bulimia, his insomnia, or his hypochondriac nature into a coherent clinical framework. Above all, one cannot clearly see the relationship between the psychological factors and Bismarck's political career. Pflanze modestly titles his article "Toward a Psychoanalytic Interpretation of Bismarck." It appears doubtful, however, that one can go beyond the statement of a few interesting though not always convincing hypotheses.

Stalin. One might assume that personalities would be more accessible to the psychobiographic approach when the individual in question exhibited political behavior that was obviously irrational or deviant, as though pathological phenomena lend themselves more readily to the psychoanalytic method. This is not necessarily the case, first, because the line between the normal and the pathological is not clear, these standards being natural offshoots of a given political and cultural environment. Furthermore, the psychobiographical approach does not content itself with examining the pathological behavior, but also attempts to explain its inception, which assumes, as we have seen, the existence of information sufficiently rich and well documented to undertake a reconstruction. Now, though we may know the most insignificant details of the public life of important personalities or charismatic leaders of our era, we lack almost all knowledge of their childhood or adolescence, a decisive stage of development, if we assume the foundation of the psychobiography to be correct. We can generally retrace in broad terms the circumstances of their birth, education, and stages of intellectual development, but, besides these few factual details, the biographer is confronted with large gaps in the individual's life which remain unknown. Therefore, from the historical point of view, it is generally not acceptable to reconstruct by inference significant factors in the childhood and adolescence of these personalities.

This is the principal stumbling block encountered by the psychobiographer. Some adjust to it, and do not hesitate to derive definite conclusions from odds and ends of information. Thus, Gustav Bychowski (1971) summarizes Stalin's entire personality by retracing certain aspects of his childhood (p. 125).

But we possess very little information on Stalin's personal life, and the psychological essay by Robert Tucker (1973), although infinitely richer from historical, political, and cultural points of view, also proceeds from the hypothetical interpretations. How else could it be, when all we have available to understand Stalin are scraps of testimony from his close relatives? We also know the political project which he put into operation and his behavior as a statesman. His hatreds, his mistrusts, always more extreme concerning his immediate circle, his crimes, reveal to us important elements of his personality. On the other hand, we know nothing concerning his intrapsychic life, and the analysis of his speeches, or of his political actions does not permit us to reconstruct coherently the development of his personality. In Tucker's psychological essay on Stalin, an important place is assigned to his relationship with his father and its effect on his character formation. According to the testimony of a childhood friend of Stalin, partially corroborated by his daughter, it does appear that his father was brutal and that his death did not move the young Djugashvili, who was then eleven years old. It is therefore probable that Stalin openly hated his father. But what significance should be given to this apparent hatred? How did he experience his father's violent and premature death?

> Soso [Stalin] must have felt that an ominous shadow had passed out of his life. By now, the boy was showing a vindictiveness and mean streak reminiscent of the father whom he despised. The alien force that his father represented had somehow been internalized within him. The parent with whom he identified positively was his mother. Whether or not we think of him as directly assimilating her traits of mind and character, it is evident that he formed a strong mother-attachment which greatly influenced the development of his personality. . . . Encouraged by her idealization of him, he started idealizing himself. . . . Anxieties and threats to self-esteem that beset him in early life from inside must have spurred him on in the process of self-idealization, making a compensatory fantasy life psychologically indispensable [Tucker, 1973, pp. 75–76].

As pure hypothesis, this type of interpretation is perfectly admissible, especially if you take into account with Tucker the historical and cultural factors which conditioned Stalin's vindictive and rebellious spirit, as well as the "feeling of [being a] conqueror" which he was to express throughout his political career. A historian conscious of rigorous causal determinants will use this type of explanation with caution, however, as it does not refer to any objective character factor anchored in agreement with irrefutable sources.

Hitler. The case of Hitler is equally representative of the difficulties inherent in psychoanalytically inspired biographical studies. No one will deny the pathological characteristics of his frenetic ideas, of his megalomaniac projects, of his anti-Semitism in particular. His delirious hatred of Jews, which was associated with other neurotic problems which were manifested in his problematic relationships with women and his hypochondriacal fears, all these elements constituted an unequivocal clinical chart of a disturbed nature. On the other hand, it is much more difficult to discover with precision the inception of these problems by reconstructing the development of his personality, for, in this case as in others, biographical data are rare and controversial, always insufficient to pinpoint the origin of his pathological behavior and the structure of his psyche. As for the symptoms of his psychic conflicts, they are not always clear. We have, for example, every reason to believe that his sexual relationships were perverted, but the information available on this subject is often contradictory, and naturally equivocal.

In his chapter "Nazi Anti-Semitism" Saul Friedlander (1971) cites several pieces of testimony regarding the conflicts in Hitler's relationship with his father, and suggests that this deep hostility, partly repressed, was one of the possible causes of his pathological anti-Semitism. The death of his father when the young Hitler was only thirteen years of age would have reinforced the consequences of this inhibited hostility. The other side of this oedipean conflict would have been the particularly strong attachment toward his mother, which was reported by two witnesses of his childhood, one being Dr. Bloch, his family doctor, who was of Jewish origin. The Jew would have become for Hitler the symbol of the bad father, and this projection would have been nurtured by the care that Dr. Bloch gave his dying mother, and also on the doubts that he had about the purity of his father's Aryan origins. With some variants, one finds the same kind of explanation in most of the psychobiographies dedicated to Hitler.

It is a question of hypotheses, plausible ones, of course, but ones which cannot be validated with certainty, taking into account the paucity of source material relative to Hitler's childhood. Friedlander (1975) admits this and in citing the different interpretations dedicated to Hitler, he writes in *History and Psychoanalysis*:

> Whatever hypothesis one chooses, one can find a way to integrate it into a total context that will appear coherent, for the possible variations are extremely numerous. For each hypothesis, one can find sufficient proof in the huge mass of Hitler's writings, speeches, and conversations, the texts of which have been preserved. . . . One can define an unconscious structure, both in its typical and its specific characteristics, *but its genesis is sometimes inaccessible to historical study* [p. 48].

To fill in the gap in historic sources, the psychobiographer risks attributing too much importance to known events, forgetting that psychoanalysis teaches us precisely to separate reality and the experience of this reality. We know that the events marking a life from the psychological point of view very often have little historical consistency. It is generally awkward to reconstruct the reality of an affective relationship by its exterior appearances or by the testimony of a third party. And as Freud was to prove, a psychic trauma cannot necessarily be traced back to a precise historical event. But it is here that the historian's methods and those of the psychoanalyst are not always in agreement. The first often tends to seek causative sequences made up of objective facts, while the other explains the formation of the unconscious in the functioning of psychic elements which are rarely objective. In the life of an individual, the notion of the biographical event covers only very partially that of the psychic event. This is the reason why it is difficult to accept Rudolph Binion's thesis that he has discovered the traumatic origins of Hitler's anti-Semitism (1973). For this historian, Hitler's desire to annihilate the Jews would have derived from a trauma which developed in two phases, the first being manifested in 1907, when his mother received medical care for her breast cancer, the second being at the moment when the psychological shock linked to this event was to be revived by the German defeat of 1918.

Hitler was eighteen years of age when his mother died of cancer. The idle life which he had led with her up to that time is testimony, according to Binion, of a clear intellectual and emotional retardation. Consciously, he loved Dr. Bloch like a father, but unconsciously he hated him as being responsible for his mother's degrading illness, for the harmful medication with which he inoculated her, and finally for the expense of this treatment. All this would result in an indelible hatred for the "Jewish cancer," the "Jewish poison," and the "Jewish exploiters." But this delirious hatred would not affirm itself until the time of the German defeat, more precisely after Hitler's hospitalization for gas poisoning in October–November 1918, an event that he would have unconsciously associated with the iodoform treatment to which Dr. Bloch subjected his sick mother. After a brief hallucinatory episode, Hitler would have believed he had been called upon to redress the German situation, and to avenge Germany's defeat, Germany becoming the objective support of the image of his mother poisoned by the Jew. The "Final Solution" would have germinated in this delirium of 1918! The extermination of Jews by gas, and before that his program of euthanasia, also by gas, directed against the mentally retarded, would duplicate Dr. Bloch's injurious treatment which Hitler believed had brought about his mother's physical and mental failure.

By taking upon himself the notion of "living space," Hitler would have unconsciously taken the shock experienced by the German people, defeated in 1918 shortly after the victories in the East, as his own traumatic experience. He would have also expressed the trauma which must have been experienced by his mother as a result of losing three children in infancy. Hitler's relationship with regard to food, like his theory of "living space," would have emanated from his "oral-aggressive

fixation," a consequence of the prolonged symbiotic relationship which he had with his mother!

Despite the enthusiasm that one can feel with regard to
the psychobiographical method, it is evident that Binion's thesis
is not acceptable as such. Historically, first of all, Binion bases
his examples on uncertain facts, because historians are not
in agreement on the reality of the events which could have
influenced Hitler's childhood and adolescence. Even his first
years of militancy remain relatively poorly documented. Thus
it is not certain that Hitler witnessed his mother's agony. It
is not evident either that the origins of Hitler's anti-Semitic
fervor can be traced to the autumn of 1918. We are not sure
of the origin of his adherence to the theory of "living space."

At any rate, his anti-Semitism, like the totality of his options and political demeanor have complex historical origins,
and it is not acceptable to reduce them to the effect of an
intrapsychic traumatizing experience. On the other hand, as
we have suggested, a psychic trauma remains hidden from a
certain type of historical deduction, as there is no simple causal
relationship between an event and its symptoms. Finally, the
psychology of nations remains an uncertain undertaking. We
cannot seriously evoke "traumatic" origins for the German
people's expansionist attitude toward the East, because it is
always hazardous to explain a collective behavior by means
of individual psychology.

Himmler. The case of Himmler also illustrates the difficulty
inherent in reconstructing by psychoanalytic means the links
of causal explanation between the son of the German bourgeoisie and the monster of the Third Reich. Without question,
the leader of the SS has left his imprint on the crimes of the
Third Reich, and his name is intimately associated with the
Hitlerian adventure. Psychobiography should enlighten us as
to the origins of Himmler's motives, and through him, as to
certain psychic bases for the Nazi crimes.

In the case of Himmler, the psychobiographical approach
is facilitated by the existence of important biographical material
which throws an interesting light on the formation of his personality. The intimate journal which he kept from 1910 to
1922 has been discovered. We also have his list of reading

matter during this same period and a few documents allowing us insight into certain aspects of his family life.

Bradley Smith (1971), in an excellent work devoted to Himmler's formative years, has studied the biographical material without using the conceptual framework of psychoanalysis. The results of his research deserve to be examined before taking into consideration Loewenberg's psychobiographical approach to the same subject (1971).

Himmler's intimate journal contains no sensational revelations. It certainly does not provide the key to the genocide. Himmler remains "a meticulous little man, pedantic to the point of caricature, who loved dogs, children and family life" (p. 2), to quote Bradley Smith. There is nothing extraordinary to point out in his childhood and adolescence. His father, tutor to Prince Arnold of Wittelsbach, then teacher in the Gymnasium in Munich, appears to incarnate, with his wife Anna, the aspirations, the faults, and the virtues of the Bavarian bourgeoisie. Young Himmler grew up in a world that was tranquil and conscientious, cultured, obsessed with neatness and cleanliness, rather pedantic, very concerned with conventions, respectful of the social hierarchy, even somewhat snobbish. But these values and this behavior is rather typical of the German bourgeoisie of the era preceding 1914, of a stable, structured, and peaceful world. From the psychological point of view, one finds no unusual event in young Himmler's childhood and adolescence. As we have seen, his family environment was apparently harmonious. He received affection, enjoyed certain cultural preoccupations, loved nature, and enjoyed vacations and trips throughout Germany. In sum, the development of Himmler's personality appears to have followed a completely normal road, and one cannot really explain his progression to the extremist positions which he adopted in the 1920s.

Bradley Smith notes his anxiety concerning sexual problems, but such taboos and obsessions were apparently common to the entire era. Thus, we find him very preoccupied in avoiding all premarital sexual relationships, which signified avoidance of all affective, compromising relationships with young women of his own age. Smith points out Himmler's embarrassment, even indignation, that a little three-year-old girl could show herself naked. He was also troubled with homosexuality, which he associated with the degeneracy and absence of morality after World War I. His character was aggressive: He was a moralist, condescending, and relatively intolerant with regard to those who did not share his system of values. And naturally this aggressiveness depressed him: he experienced doubts about himself, had remorse; he blamed himself for talking too much.

Himmler's papers attest to conservative but not extremist opinions. It was in early 1922 that he appeared to evolve toward a fascist position which would make him a disciple of Hitler. But how are we to explain this evolution? Smith suggests the conjunction of personal problems and outside events. This is certainly probable, but the causal relationship is not easily established with precision. Immediately after the war, he seemed particularly troubled with the fate of Germany. He detested France and feared Bolshevism. During this period also, his anti-Semitism appeared more virulent. The "Jewish question" increasingly became a central preoccupation. It is associated with stereotyped aspirations based on Volkisch German values. Himmler, who had always been fascinated by militarism, now considered that the solution of Germany's problems resided in the resurgence of the military might of the Reich. Moreover, this period of political and social problems was also a period of uncertainty for Himmler in relation to his social identity. But the German Army soon gave him a sense of personal identity, and in turn provided him with a professional future. Progressively, in the course of 1923 to 1924, he became a fanatic.

Is Smith's detailed study of Himmler's formative years then sufficient to explain the Reichfuhrer SS? Apparently not, since traditional historiography cannot reconcile the young Himmler, a banal, even insignificant personality, with the SS of the death camps.

Such is not the opinion of Peter Loewenberg (1971), who, basing himself on identical sources, but examining them in the light of psychoanalysis, offers us a very different interpretation of Himmler's childhood and adolescence. Loewenberg first of all questions the singular emotional platitudes of the intimate journals left by Himmler. The need to transcribe his intimate thoughts already suggests the necessity of expressing a particular affective reality. Nevertheless, for almost ten years, Himmler filled pages full of details, apparently without importance, relative to his daily life. He did so in a totally obsessional way, noting the hours of his least important railroad trips, the minutiae of the hour at which he took a bath, his meals, dressing, and so on. On the other hand, he never expressed a single emotion in his journals, and the name of his mother appeared only twice. Loewenberg interprets this attitude, manifestly contradictory with the need to keep a record in an intimate journal, as the sign of an obsessional personality having repressed most of his affects.

For Loewenberg, indeed, Himmler's interest in hourly records is not a chance fact but expresses his compulsive need to exercise meticulous control over all his activities for fear of succumbing to his own instinctual exigencies. The timetable becomes a protection against the threat of an unbridled spontaneity. This interest is considered by Loewenberg to be evidence of an anal fixation since the experiences of this period are decisive for the control of reality, and for the control of time in particular. Loewenberg also sees Himmler's desire to be physically strong, as being progressively transformed into a need to repress all spontaneous expression of his personality. Himmler indeed expresses constantly in his journal the fear and shame inspired in him by the feeling of losing control of himself. This need for control is also expressed on the sexual level. For Loewenberg, this obsession with self-control was Himmler's defense against immature coping skills.

Loewenberg also discovers a very contrasting view of men and women in Himmler. In his journals, Himmler describes as a pitiless tyrant a father who refused dance lessons to his daughter: "The poor little girl wept tears. I truly pitied her. But she had no idea how pretty she was in her tears" (p. 620). In relating this anecdote, Loewenberg presents the hypothesis that this scene was a reflection of the relationship between his parents. According to him, this episode seems to indicate Himmler's identification with those who are dominated by the father, because this type of chivalrous reaction with regard to women frequently appears in Himmler's inti-

mate journals. Loewenberg interprets it as a reaction formation
to sadism which the tears of the young girl arouse in him.

He believes that Himmler found a means of erotizing
his aggression via German nationalistic fervor. His dream of
Romantic German conquests was apparently a displacement
of his repressed desires. Loewenberg believes he can discern
in Himmler an important conflict between his feminine and
masculine identifications, a conflict which is expressed by a
pseudomasculine attitude and by an image of women associated
with weakness and tears. An episode in which a hypnotist makes
a young girl submit to his will is intolerable to Himmler: "I
could have strangled the dog in cold blood," he wrote (cited
in Loewenberg, 1971, p. 625). The idea of submitting to a
man appeared insupportable to him at that time. Himmler
frequently also associated women with unbridled sexuality, which
could signify a projection of his own instincts toward women.

Loewenberg thinks that the transition from his controlled
anti-Semitism to his virulent and pathological anti-Semitism
is the result of an identification to a new paternal image: Hitler.
This anti-Semitism permitted him to resolve the problem of
his social standing and of his identity which had been problematic
up to that time. The Jew would have become a projection of
all that he did not tolerate in himself, particularly his identification to his mother, and in a more general manner, his homosexual tendencies. His new paternal ideal would have permitted
him to freely express the desires prohibited by his father and
his Christian morality.

The procedure, we see, is coherent. Certainly, the positiv-
ist historian could discuss the value of this analysis by asserting
that it is possible to reconstruct certain aspects of young Himmler's
intrapsychic experience on the basis of an intimate journal
in which emotional platitudes are evident. For Loewenberg,
on the contrary, the apparent indigence of this source already
clearly reveals the bureaucrat of the death camps, and the
interpretation of this material constitutes the only plausible
link of causality between the young Heinrich and Himmler,
the chief of the SS. In other historical circumstances, and Loewenberg does not ignore this point, Himmler would have remained
an insignificant person, and his personality problems would
have been placed at the service of beneficent and socially ap-

proved professional activities. There is no way to reduce the explanation of the concentric universe to the sadism of Heinrich Himmler.

Wilson. The absence of intimate journals or of literary sources, the lack of biographical testimony on the childhood and adolescence of a political figure, does not present definite obstacles to the psychobiographical approach. A repetitive political behavior, a strongly emotional political speech, can shed light on the affective structure of a personality. The work of political scientists Alexandre and Juliette George (1956) dedicated to analyzing the steps which led to Wilson's failure is very suggestive on this point.

President Woodrow Wilson is certainly a fascinating personality in twentieth-century history. Few American presidents have left such a mark on international events; few political leaders have left such a controversial heritage. He was largely responsible for the creation of the League of Nations, but was also the unwilling architect of the failure of this grandiose project in relation to the U.S. Senate, the historical consequences of which are unfathomable. In spite of the many studies of Wilson, he remains an enigmatic figure, and the responsibility for his failure with the Senate in 1919 has not ceased to intrigue historians. All those who were close to him have attested to the complexity of his personality, of his "divided nature," to use the words of a Protestant minister who knew him well. Wilson's strangely rigid behavior at the time of the Versailles Treaty, and then at the time of the fight for the ratification of this document in Washington, certainly constitutes one of the most incomprehensible moments in his political career. There exist also specific traits of his personality, his Messianic stance, for example, which the historian trained in the traditional disciplines finds inexplicable. Freud and Bullitt (1967) analyzed this rigid behavior as the product of a reaction formation to the passivity toward his father, and also to his identification with Christ, resulting from this passivity. But, as we have seen, their thesis was schematic and unacceptable from the historical and political point of view. Without knowing this work (written in the 1930s, but published in 1967), Alexandre and Juliette George attempted to identify President Wilson's psychic structure and the unconscious dynamics of his inauspicious political behavior. By referring to the works of Adler and Lasswell on the relationship between personal feelings of inadequacy and the need for power, and also basing themselves on the psychoanalytic literature relative to the compulsive personality, Alexandre and Juliette George arrive at a psychological portrait of great coherence, and solidly etched from the historical point of view.

It is in Wilson's childhood that the authors searched for the enigma of the future president. Almost nothing is known about young Wilson's relationship with his mother, but we have good reason to believe that it was tender and affectionate. It even appears that the people around him considered him as somewhat of a "Mama's boy." On the other hand, we know that he always totally venerated his father, Reverend Joseph Ruggles Wilson, and that he felt throughout his entire life strong feelings of inferiority with regard to this idealized figure. His father, an austere and caustic theologian, intervened early in his education. Being very demanding, Joseph R. Wilson did not hesitate to humiliate his son when he did not respond to his expectations on the intellectual level. Young Wilson must have experienced aggressive feelings when faced with the demanding authority of his father. It nevertheless appears that he never expressed them openly and consciously, so strong was the paternal hold. The latter therefore always remained his "incomparable father." He did not succeed in freeing himself from a strong feeling of incompleteness with regard to him. According to A. and J. George, who do not cite their source, Wilson once admitted that the most difficult speech of his political career was one he made after having noticed his father in the audience. They also give other testimony as to his continuing devotion and feelings of inferiority toward his father.

A. and J. George ascribe a great part of Wilson's political behavior thereafter to this paternal complex. As president of Princeton, then as governor of New Jersey, and finally as president of the United States, Wilson would never tolerate any challenge to his authority in the field of his responsibility. For the Georges, this attitude to authority is reminiscent of the passive behavior which he adopted as a child in relation to his father. "Throughout his life his relationships with others seemed shaped by an inner command never again to bend his will to another man's" (p. 11). And that is the reason why he considered all those who tried to oppose him as an untenable menace, and why he personalized conflicts of principle in an extreme manner. Political power was a means for him to compensate for the humiliations of his childhood.

The authors note furthermore that his need for power could not express itself fully if he did not encounter the approval and emotional support of his inner or outer circle. Colonel House therefore played a decisive role in Wilson's presidential career. His low-key presence, his refusal of honors, the subtle manner in which he reassured the President himself, convincing him and also flattering him, were decisive elements in the bonds that united the two men. For A. and J. George, it is symptomatic that House and Wilson quarreled in 1919 when Colonel House assumed an official position for the first time and appeared competitive. The Georges show moreover that Wilson never succeeded in fully enjoying his success. His insatiable drive impelled him toward ever more complex political confrontations, and in the process his ideals became more problematic.

His Messiah complex would be the sublimation of a need to dominate, a need which could only be manifested in the service of grandiose projects. His political action then became the expression of a Divine will. Wilson furthermore identified himself with a suffering humanity, certain that God had endowed him with the mission of reorganizing the relationships amongst nations. Later, at the time of the confrontation with the Senate, his aggression toward his opponents was tolerable only at the price of immense physical sacrifices and because he was convinced he was serving an important cause.

Let us note that Wilson nevertheless did not always manifest a rigid and intolerant political attitude—his extraordinary career is proof of that. Under certain circumstances, and notably in his efforts to gain the presidency, he knew how to exercise great flexibility, even what might be regarded as opportunism. A. and J. George have demonstrated that Wilson's political career developed along the lines of a repetitive schema. As president of Princeton, governor of New Jersey, and then president of the United States, he was initially intensely active, and this was crowned with success; he then became involved in a more arid period of controversies and political conflicts, before experiencing a major and avoidable failure. This repetitive behavior is particularly striking if one compares his accession to the presidency of Princeton and his career as chief executive.

The obvious merit of A. and J. George's thesis is that they fulfilled the methodological demands of the classic historic discourse, thus avoiding the facile short-cuts of a psychoanalytic synopsis. Nevertheless, this work raises a number of delicate questions.

First of all, are the biographical facts available sufficient to explain Wilson's behavior and political aspirations? A. and J. George are certainly right to link Wilson's uncompromising attitude, his authoritarianism, his great need to be comforted by his entourage, to a deep feeling of inadequacy. But what is the real origin of this need? Our authors present the hypothesis that Reverend Joseph Wilson's attitude to his son was the essential cause of this complex. Can we accept this hypothesis without really knowing young Wilson's relationship with his mother, his sisters, his immediate circle? Wasn't Reverend Wilson's attitude with regard to his son rather typical of certain religious circles and a particular period? Isn't the need to accomplish also a characteristic of this American Protestant culture of the late nineteenth century? Isn't Wilson's messianic posture a typical product of American culture? In other words, how would one separate in his political behavior that which is derived from a typical cultural influence, or that which is the manifest expression of an affective conflict peculiar to the young Wilson? As a matter of fact, the cultural explanation would be insufficient, because, as A. and J. George have well demonstrated, Wilson did not adopt stereotyped behavior, and in certain circumstances, he manifested political attitudes very far from the ethical norms of his circle. It is therefore regrettable that the authors have based the essential part of their work on studying Wilson's repetitive behavior while neglecting other pertinent areas of study.

Leopold III of Belgium. In general terms, it is always difficult, outside of the therapeutic framework, to explain a political action from a psychoanalytic point of view, and if A. and J. George's approach is convincing, the Rudolf Binion (1969) study dedicated to the conflicting psychic foundations of Leopold III's diplomacy illustrates on the contrary the hazards to be found in this type of approach.

Binion asserts that in pursuing a neutral policy to the point of absurdity, which circumstances rendered problematic, Leopold III of Belgium was unconsciously trying to relive the traumatic experience of the death of Queen Astrid, whom he had killed in an automobile accident. The king never got over this tragedy for which he was responsible. Not being able to mourn his wife, he took in hand the "conduct" of Belgian foreign policy, and led his nation to catastrophe, to gratify his unconscious need to relive his guilt-ridden trauma. While his armies fled without hope toward the sea, Leopold realized the fatal nature of the imminent catastrophe and relived the moment when he lost control of his car which landed in a river. "In the wake of his battered army, Astrid died a second death in his arms" [p. 250].

That certain of Leopold III's political options were determined in part by his psychological conflicts, that the "small anecdote" can sometimes explain the course of great international events, should not surprise us. But its validity remains to be demonstrated in this particular case. The foreign policy adopted by Leopold III and his government found adherents in large segments of the Belgian population. It was also in the mainstream of European appeasement with regard to the Third Reich, a position which apparently owed nothing to the individual idiosyncrasies of the Western leaders. From the historical point of view, the schematism of Binion's psychological approach borders on the grotesque. From the psychoanalytic point of view, as we have already noted, his approach is derived from an erroneous conception of the notion of trauma.

Psychic Distress and Trauma in Childhood

The psychic distress of an unhappy childhood, the loss of a father or mother at a young age, a psychic trauma, a disability, can certainly create the psychological repercussions which favor the blossoming of a political career, or of an artistic vocation. During the 1930s, Harold Lasswell (1951) even formulated the hypothesis that the quest for political power was a means to compensate for a personal lack; that success in this domain would enable the politician to modify the image that he had of himself or to change the environment in which he functioned. If the hypothesis appears too general in nature, it must be recognized that in the childhood of great statesmen one often finds a lack of love, a loss, a humiliation, or a physical or psychic trauma. We know, for example, that Churchill suffered intensely as a result of the lack of love he received from his parents, his mother in particular. It is not impossible that his periodic depressive tendencies—his "black dog," as he called it—were the direct consequence of this abandonment. As Anthony Storr (1973) has suggested, his ambition, his creativity, certain aspects of his political career, were perhaps a result of this childhood wound. We also find in Disraeli's childhood the impenetrable shadow of a conflictful relationship with a rejecting mother. His later relationships with women were conditioned by this initial deprivation. It is not inadmissible to link certain aspects of his political life to the affective privations of his childhood (Blake, 1967).

Of interest is another enigma in the childhood of a political genius: Thomas Jefferson's father died when the son was aged fourteen. We have few facts on the relationship that Jefferson had with his father; we also know nothing about how he reacted to this loss. Fawn Brodie (1974) mentions the great physical strength of his lost father and hypothesizes that Jefferson experienced a great feeling of inferiority with regard to his father's imposing stature. She associates this early death with Jefferson's ambivalence regarding power. It is indeed not impossible that this event engendered in him a certain feeling of incompleteness, notably the feeling of not having the capacity to carry out his responsibilities. On the other hand, it is more difficult to understand the relationship Jefferson had with his mother. We know that he lived by her side until the age of twenty-seven, but strangely he mentions her only twice in his thousands of letters and in his autobiography. Brodie concludes that he experienced very hostile feelings toward her and he felt it an act of slavery to be obliged to live such a long time with her. This conflicting relationship would explain in part certain of the revolutionary positions Jefferson adopted against England.

One could find other analogous examples, as, for instance, Maurras' deafness, a disability which struck him in his adolescence and which revived the psychological wounds caused by the death of his father when he was only five (McCearney, 1977). Let us also examine the political destiny of Robert Brasillach, conditioned surely by the premature death of his father (Senarclens, 1976).

The German socialist leader Kurt Schumacher lost an arm during the first months of the 1914 War, and this mutilation appears to have been a decisive influence on the orientation of his personality. Edinger (1965) even discerns in the accident the origin of Schumacher's political career. The loss of a limb often entails important psychic consequences. Edinger refers to clinical studies regarding this type of mutilation which reveal that amputated subjects frequently consider themselves devalued and impotent, a feeling coupled with profound anguish. It is not impossible that his aggressive and tense character was determined in part by this mutilation. A close relative who knew him well during this period attested to the fact that he did not feel himself a complete man, and did everything from that time on to affirm his virility. He also became a heavy smoker. It is not unthinkable then that he transferred this desire for affirmation of his manhood to the political plane. Edinger is careful, and justly so, not to attribute Schumacher's entire political career to this trauma, neither the positions he adopted nor his influence on the masses. On the other hand, Edinger attributed to his victory over this deficiency, his capacity for exceptional resistance to the Nazi concentration camps.

Forrestal. The case of James Forrestal is particularly troubling. As Secretary of the Navy for presidents Roosevelt and Truman, then Secretary of Defense, this man had considerable power, and played an often decisive role in the development of American policies at the onset of the cold war. Having been an excellent organizer and a frequently perspicacious political observer, Forrestal was one of the principal shapers of "containment" pursued by the U.S. Administration after the Second

World War. It manifested itself by consistent positions favorable to the rearmament of the United States and by a vigilant hostility with regard to Communism and Soviet expansion. At the end of his career, he suffered psychotic episodes and committed suicide a short time after having relinquished his important responsibilities.

This tragic end testifies to an obviously fragile psyche. In retrospect, it allows us to better understand his character, certain aspects of his ideology, and his political behavior. Arnold Rogow (1966) pointed out with finesse the links between Forrestal's psychic fragility and the vigor of his anti-Communism. His personal insecurity, a consequence of the lack of affection from which he had suffered as a child, translated itself into compulsive work habits, obvious interpersonal relationship problems, and impelled him to recommend intransigent positions in the field of United States foreign policy. Nevertheless, the pathological symptoms of an exhausted man do not shed a full light on the entire political career, and Rogow understood this well by refusing to establish a simple correlation between Forrestal's mental illness and his political attitudes. For in the final phase of his career, at a time when the symptoms of his illness were clearly revealed, Forrestal was not a fanatic, and none of his actions while in office bear the clear imprint of his psychic troubles. And in this case, as in all others, the psychological explanation could not exclude the one offered by analyzing existing social conditions. Forrestal was the spokesman of the business world which was generally not much inclined to compromise with regard to the Soviet menace.

In a general manner, it appears as inadmissible from a psychoanalytic as it is from a historical point of view, to reduce the origin of a political project or of any creation whatsoever to a conflictual intrapsychic core. This schematism is all the more so unsatisfactory as the historical facts in which these conflicts originate remain somewhat ambiguous and always uncertain insofar as their psychological consequences are concerned. On the other hand, it appears necessary to recall these childhood wounds, to understand their psychic significance, in order to highlight certain aspects of a political career.

Recapitulating the Causes of Failure

The psychobiography of politicians constitutes, therefore, a hazardous historical format, and most of the present attempts have been unsatisfactory from both the historical and the psychoanalytic point of view. It seems necessary now to recapitulate the causes of their failures.

It is certain that psychoanalysis has considerably expanded the "territory of the historian," by making one aware of all facets of the unconscious processes. This enrichment has nevertheless not excused the historian from the procedures of validation traditionally demanded by historical research. The problem of sources of information is presented with a particular sharpness. The unconscious is so rebellious, unorganized, and surprising, as Eissler (1963) recalls in his psychobiography of Goethe, that one cannot be satisfied with simple probabilities. It is easy to single out the general expression of an oedipal conflict, but it is more difficult, outside of the analytic situation, to uncover in a specific manner the consequences of this conflict in the behavior or the thinking of the historical figures. The chameleon manifestations of the unconscious force to which the biographer has recourse requires very complex procedures of validation. Interpretation continues to play a primary role. But this interpretation always runs the risk of being subjective, unless it is corroborated by a converging accumulation of factual indices, personal testimony, of themes, or of characteristic repetitive behavior. The problem of sources also appears on another level. We have known since the earliest days of psychoanalysis that the testimony of the subject studied or of other people can be tainted by their affects. But we also know that the emotional links between the historian and the object of his study constitute another source of distortion with regard to discovering the truth about the past. The analysis of these links, which can constitute a source of fertile investigation, complicates the historical research even more.

These studies which we have examined are quite representative of the psychobiographical approach. If one does not have any reason for rejecting these approaches a priori one cannot avoid a certain uneasiness about them, especially if one is dedicated to classic historical methodology. At one ex-

treme, one encounters manifestly unorthodox methods characterized by a naive or undisciplined utilization of psychoanalysis
and historical methods. The search for the sensational, the
desire to reduce the destiny of "great men" to a few elements
of their personality considered as pathological, appears to
constitute the primary motivation for this kind of enterprise.
The absence of biographical facts permitting a validation of
the hypotheses, the hasty correlations between certain "objective" events and the interpretation of behavior or ideas, the
summary manipulation of psychoanalytic categories, their schematic application, the neglect of nonpsychological determinants in the formation, then in the political behavior of the
personalities studied, appear as so many negative characteristics of this type of study.

Linked to two disciplines demanding complex formats,
the psychobiography (or psychohistory) is attacked by psychiatrists or psychologists who have no mastery of historical methodology or by historians who utilize in a mechanical and
abstract way complex psychoanalytic concepts with multiple
meanings. A certain enthusiasm on the part of the neophyte
often leads them to utilize psychoanalysis as a surreptitious
weapon of a highly ideological nature or to believe it is the
key to a definitive analysis of the most complex historical
phenomena.

At the other extreme, one can single out very believable
partial explanations, but they sometimes provide an uncertain
basis for the historian anxious for rigorous causal determinants.

The Application of Psychobiography to Artists and Writers

It is practical, however, to distinguish our degree of skepticism
by clearly indicating again the fields in which psychobiography
applies. Although psychoanalysis does not always clarify the
lives of political personalities in a very precise manner, its
value can be considerable in the biography of artists, notably

of writers. In the work of art, and more particularly in the novel, the author gives free rein to his fantasies, and his creation reveals itself as an artifact of the unconscious, like, for example, the dream. Freud and his disciples immediately perceived it by laying the foundation of their scientific discovery with many artistic references, by exploring the vast domain of folklore, myths, and legends, and also, as we have seen, by preparing the fertile foundations for a psychoanalysis of the artist and of his creativity. Today, in its most elaborate form, which is probably the one developed by Charles Mauron and his disciples, the psychoanalytic critique points out, in the course of a long and detailed study, themes, associations, and obsessive metaphors the interpretation of which permits us to enrich our understanding of the work of its author. From the historical point of view, the work becomes an important source for the comprehension of known biographical facts, and, in a general manner, for the interpretation of the destiny of its creator.

"Adolphe" et Constant *by Han Verhoeff*

As a particularly attractive example of this type of study, let us examine the work of Han Verhoeff (1976) *"Adolphe" et Constant.* Verhoeff provides an absolutely coherent and realistic exposition of the themes and structure of the novel, their analysis, and the confrontation of the facts as set out in the novel with those of the biography, notably with the author's autobiographical writings.

What is striking in this type of study, is the fusion with the classic thematic approach. In other words, the psychoanalytic reading highlights recurrent themes, associations of ideas, obsessive metaphors that the traditional critic can recognize even if he refuses to accept the interpretation offered. Verhoeff does not invent the theme of indifference which appears with such force in *Adolphe,* and also in the autobiographical writings of Constant. He does not invent the need for affection expressed by Adolphe or Ellenore, their obsession with abandonment, and death, the contempt for women expressed by Adolphe, the identification of the author with the two heroes, the fixation with the past, the identification of the author with the abandoned woman, the theme of the abandonment of the children, and so on. A psychoanalytic reading seems to impose its own coherence, for one has the impression that a traditional critic would single out the same themes and the same source of associations.

Thus the critic does not seek the author behind the work, but the work itself, for, following the road paved by Charles Mauron, Verhoeff believes that it is the texts that enlighten us on the biography, and not the reverse. And this seems important to me for explaining our skepticism with regard to psychobiographies of political figures. In the type of interpretation proposed by the psychocritic, the known elements of the biography determine nothing a priori. Psychoanalytic concepts, their validation by means of clinical experience, explain nothing either a priori. In other words, the psychocritic will not brandish at the onset notions related to aggression, identification, parental imagoes, to fixation or depression, and so on, but he will introduce them via a rigorous analysis of the text in order to give a meaning which would remain largely unintelligible without the aid of psychoanalytic interpretation. Verhoeff remains prudent:

It goes without saying that the mother fixation is not the magic formula which would permit us to resolve all the problems or to give a definitive explanation of life or even less to the work of Constant. It is a question of a mere hypothesis, and this hypothesis is not directly verifiable due to lack of documentation. Constant never spoke of his mother, and this silence, although significant in a man who has been so long engrossed in his psychological difficulties, does not allow for drawing conclusions.

The hypothesis, however, appears useful to us to seize at a more profound level the psychic mechanism which governs his emotional life.

In fact it permits the unification of certain themes which appear everywhere in his work and which would remain disconnected without it; it also allows for focusing on Constant's central psychic conflicts and for identifying the forces which play on his personal myth and constitute the personalities of his interior drama.

The notion of fixation, fixation to the mother, could cover the themes of abandonment and imprisonment which, as we have seen, both express the lack and the need for affection: emotionally, Constant is tied to his mother who abandoned him. The mother died. The theme of death is omnipresent in Constant's work. It results from the themes of aggression and identification which command Adolphe. It is also found in the story of his liaison and is manifested in the truly obsessive nature of the rupture, which for him is linked to the death of the abandoned woman, and to identification with the victim which makes him imagine his own death. His deceased mother, whom Constant, without knowing it, mourns all his life, also causes his aggression. Therefore, the aggression of the child, provoked by the abandonment, is reactivated by his liaisons, since he sees in each woman the image of the vanished, beloved mother. The hostility which he cannot turn upon the true object of his hatred is turned upon other objects, the women that he has loved, and also against himself [pp. 101–103].[2]

This type of approach, obviously, does not exhaust the field of interpretation; its pretension is not to provide us with an all-encompassing explanation of the writer and of his work. It is enlightening, however, regarding certain emotional bases of a literary creation.

The Political Speech

One has to recognize, however, that a political speech lends itself less to a psychobiographical investigation than a novel or any other artistic creation. Psychocriticism, as we have seen, finds points of agreement between the romantic creation and the dream, that "royal road" to an understanding of the unconscious. The analysis of recurrent themes, of associations and metaphors, reveals in part the unconscious personality of the writer, and biographical elements provide helpful information of relative importance, as in the analytic relationship. But one

[2]Benjamin Constant is the author of *Adolphe* (1816). His parental-loss profile is F44, M0—Eisenstadt.

perceives immediately the difficulty of comparing the political speech to the dream, as the former is focused toward action and is a good deal more dependent on the social environmental factors than is the artistic creation. Undoubtedly, politics derives from desire. Political creation is related to art, therefore to the dream, and, in a general way, there is no absolute separation between the analysis of a political speech and literary criticism. Nevertheless, the political speech conceals more of the unconscious processes than the true literary speech or manifestations of the plastic arts.

In his work *History and Psychoanalysis*, Friedlander (1975) expresses a very interesting analogy between the action of the charismatic leader and the language of the artist: "The fundamental nature of charisma resembles the symbolic language of the artist, applied to the reality of the political or social world. Further than this, we cannot go" [p. 73]. One naturally could wish to go further. One could wish to be capable of interpreting the political gesture with the same confidence as the language of the novel, but this is still unattainable. Napoleon would have said, "I love power. But I love it as an artist, as a musician loves his violin, to derive sounds from it, arrangements, harmonies" (Sieburg, 1957, p. 9). There are numerous chiefs of state who seem to have established with power the relationship of the artist with his instrument. Erikson (1950) rightly compared Hitler to an actor, "because he must always be ready to personify, as if he had chosen them, the changing roles suggested by the whims of fate" [p. 330]. Inge and Stanley Hoffman (1973) have considered De Gaulle as an "artist of politics." If it is possible to relate intuitively to the language of the artist and the charismatic leader, one must also recognize that the political gesture of the latter is still difficult to approach by means of psychoanalysis.

Is the Psychobiography of Political Figures Feasible?

Is the psychobiography of political figures feasible? If one defines this historic type in a restrictive manner as the system-

atic recourse to psychoanalysis in a coherent explanation of
a personality and of his political project, the answer should
be negative, except for exceptional circumstances which would
entail the existence of a personality leaving testimony of a
particular emotional quality; and of a biographer qualified
from the psychoanalytic point of view, knowledgeable in historical methodology, and the related sciences. On the other
hand, if one designates by the term *psychobiography* the partial
and complementary recourse to psychoanalysis in the biographic
study, one will admit the decisive and novel contribution of
this particular approach, as shown in certain works that we
have examined, and as is also proven in the excellent study
by John Mack (1976) on Lawrence of Arabia.

Lawrence of Arabia

Lawrence of Arabia was above all an exceptional being. Endowed with a prodigious intelligence, curious about everything,
capable of adapting to a great variety of situations, to very
different cultural worlds, a man of action, a charismatic personality, Lawrence played an important role in one of the
great heroic adventures of our time: the liberation of the Arab
world from Ottoman domination. But Lawrence was also an
unhappy person. At the end of his glorious adventure, he
appears consumed with remorse, tortured by the need to pun-
ish himself, unable to cope with his own legend, invaded by
a perverse sexuality. The traditional historian is absolutely incapable of explaining such a complex personality, and his interpretation would still leave vast gray, disorganized zones.
But, on the other hand, the psychobiographer could be tempted
to reduce the creativity of Lawrence to the intrapsychic conflicts
of his childhood, while forgetting that these were overcome
in a lasting work, which affirmed a historic destiny.

It is the great merit of John Mack's biography of avoiding
these two impasses. To take a significant example, Mack ex-
poses multiple facets of the life of his hero but without risking
an interpretation. For Mack, Lawrence's exceptional gifts, his
knowledge of the Arab world, his courage, his capacity to
empathize with the cause of a foreign people, and the particu-

lar historical circumstance, of course, and also pure chance, essentially explain his adventure in the desert. Does it mean that Lawrence's psychological conflicts in no way determine his historic destiny? Certainly not, but the relationship is difficult to demonstrate. With caution and modesty, Mack writes: "Up to the time of the war, it is difficult to establish precise connections between Lawrence's sexuality and its related conflicts and the directions of his life, although I believe such connections exist. After the war, however, they are unmistakable" (1976, p. 416).

Nobody will ever know the entire truth of the episode at Deraa, evoked by Lawrence in the *Seven Pillars of Wisdom* (1926). The author gives several versions of it, all apparently incomplete and mysterious. One thing is certain: at Deraa, Lawrence was brutally sodomized, and this traumatizing experience was to be "The Shattering of the Dream," to borrow the title of Mack's chapter on this episode. From that time on, he would be haunted by this trauma which he sought to exorcise by literary creation: from 1919 to 1925, he wrote and reworked the chapter on Deraa nine times, as if he were seeking in writing a form of therapy, obsessed by the shame of invoking this humiliating incident, yet pursued by the need to recall it publicly. His resistance to the publication of the *Seven Pillars of Wisdom* was in part linked to the Deraa chapter. Lawrence admitted himself that this event had "damaged his nerves in a permanent way," and it is very clear that the strange punishment which he imposed upon himself after the war was related to his trauma.

After the war and the Versailles Conference, while he was at the height of his glory, Colonel Lawrence decided to enlist in the Air Corps as an airman, then in the Army as a private soldier, and this strange penance, as he clearly explained, was related to this tragic episode of his desert adventure. Lawrence also felt the need to relive this traumatic experience. He imagined from that time a rather complicated scenario to fulfill his repeated desire to be periodically flagellated, and, apparently, this perversion was linked to Deraa.

How can one explain this psychic disorder? What importance does it have on Lawrence's life? To the first question, Mack gives a rather simple answer: For Lawrence, Deraa was a true trauma, that is to say, a psychic wound with lasting effects, the consequence of an external event, but the effects of which are inscribed in the individual's personality.

The origin of this trauma is situated therefore within the confines of particular accidental events and psychic problems rooted in Lawrence's childhood. The genesis of the psychic problems is complex and equally overdetermined. As Mack pointed out, Lawrence was a child of the Victorian age, a cruel period due to the rigidity of its Puritan constraints. He suffered the more in that his parents imposed the severest standards on their children, thereby compensating for the feeling of guilt arising from the fact that they were not legally married. Lawrence discovered at the time of his adolescence the trench that existed between his parents' religious values and their concubinage. This discovery disturbed him profoundly and appeared to have influenced the development of his personality in a decisive way. "The same mother for whom Oscar Wilde was a dirty word and who disapproved of theatres and dancing was herself living in an adulterous relationship, to which the father had also subscribed" (Mack, 1976, p. 418). This disillusion was all the more difficult to accept in that Lawrence's mother was very demanding emotionally, which made it difficult for Thomas to assert his own autonomy. Lawrence remained fixated on his mother's image, and was unable to free himself from the feeling of being under siege from her affective demands. The Deraa flagellation, a torture which also gave him pleasure, appeared to have revived memories of the spankings that his mother gave him to curb his rebellious will.

Without diminishing the talent and work of John Mack, one must recognize that his hero lent himself particularly well to psychobiographic analysis. Lawrence, in reality, left us with very rich material from an emotional point of view. His literary creation, his numerous letters, his taste for introspection, and abundant testimony both from those close to him as well as those more distant, favored the psychoanalytic approach to his personality and his work. The absence of this kind of material, as we have already noted, makes the psychobiographical endeavor a problem.

Is There a Typology
for the Revolutionary
Personality?

Is it possible to conceive a less ambitious, more utilitarian approach, allowing one to seize the personal dynamics of a political role? For example, in isolating certain psychological characteristics common to all persons in positions of authority, could one hope to better understand their political behavior, and even anticipate their future attitude? Does there exist, for example, a type of revolutionary personality; that is, persons knowing best how to exploit the potentialities of a troubling social situation? Do charismatic leaders have clearly definable psychological characteristics? Within the framework of a given function, for example, the presidency of the United States, can we classify the holder of power in terms of a simple psychological type? We immediately perceive the interest of this sort of investigation for the historian and for the political scientist.

We know the essays on typology by Jung. Freud, in a less systematic way, also outlined the embryo of a typology, notably by describing the anal instinct. In political science, the study of Adorno (1950) and his associates on the authoritarian personality contributed excellent essays on this subject, for the scientific value of these authors' definition of the authoritarian syndrome is certain, even if we can dispute certain aspects of their methodology. This study and certain later research which it has inspired have clearly shown the affective factors which condition certain ideologies, certain political attitudes.

These general typologies can be useful in order to encompass better certain characters, to give a more general coherence to certain aspects of a personality, even to a formulation of certain hypotheses relative to the development of an individual where the known biographic facts are lacking. But can the historian or the political scientist expect more from typologies? Before answering this question, it is necessary to formulate two possible procedures. The first would consist of isolating a well-determined category of political leader (e.g., the revolutionary or the charismatic leader) to find the psychological type or types to which he belongs. The second approach would proceed in a more restrictive manner by isolating the psychological types to which correspond, in a given institutional framework, certain modes of political functioning.

The first approach is not, for the moment, very fertile, for it appears that no political category clearly corresponds to a particular psychological typology. The syndrome of the authoritarian personality is not to be found only among conservatives. We find it in a large array of political attitudes. If we were able to isolate in certain Nazi fanatics some typical psychological traits, nothing could prevent us from asserting that these individuals might well be engaged, in other circumstances, in political movements of a different orientation (see further Dicks [1974]; Barker, [1974]).

Victor Wolfenstein (1967), on the basis of a comparative study of Lenin, Trotsky, and Gandhi, has attempted to show that these three "revolutionaries" had a common oedipal problem. The revolutionary personality would be a possible avatar of the Oedipus complex. It is an enticing hypothesis, but it is nevertheless not valid, and Wolfenstein, when he applies developmental theory in a mechanical way, is far from convincing.

From the start, the hypothesis had little chance of being fruitful, since revolutionary situations are so diverse that the search for a common denominator in the personalities who inspire or animate these political and social upheavals does not appear in the least adventurous. This first failure did not discourage Bruce Mazlisch (1976b). If he refuses Wolfenstein's Oedipus hypothesis as too general and simplistic, he believes that he can isolate in most great revolutionaries of our time particular ascetic qualities which would also explain the puritanical tendencies of all revolutions. Being at the same time inspired by the libidinal theory of Freud and Max Weber's thesis on the Protestant ethic and the spirit of capitalism, Mazlisch sees in Robespierre, Lenin, and Mao Zedong typical representatives of the revolutionary personality, and the spokesmen of a modern ascetic movement which encompasses political rather than economic or religious activities. These people have learned to focus all their emotions on their political project and this intense discipline goes together with the rupture of normal emotional relations in favor of the particular emotional links that they establish with abstract ideals, the only objects of their interests. But if we find in Robespierre, Lenin, or Mao Zedong common character traits, analogous periods of asceticism, an influence on their entourage and the masses the psychological dynamics of which may be similar, it does not appear possible to fuse them into a typical portrait of the revolutionary personality without having recourse to the most doubtful psychobiographical typology.

The Charismatic Personality

If the revolutionary personality remains elusive, what can be said of the charismatic personality?

In his essay on sociological types, Max Weber (1971) tried to single out three types of authority: the rational authority, in which reposes a belief in the legality of accepted norms; the traditional authority founded on a belief in the sanctity of venerable traditions and of the leader who incarnates them; and finally the charismatic type of authority which is essentially magical or religious. This last concept, the most difficult to define, but also the most useful for the comprehension of certain relations of contemporary power, has inspired a rather abundant literature (Tucker, 1968).

Charismatic leaders, according to Max Weber, impose on themselves qualities inaccessible to most mortals. They are "the bearers of specific gifts of body and mind, that [are] considered supernatural (in the sense that not everybody could have access to them)" (p. 112). The charisma is a vocation, a *grace* in the full sense of the word. The latter is validated by the "recognition" of those who accept it and who abandon themselves to the veneration of their heroes. Charismatic domination implies "a strictly personal social relation." It is not linked to a role; it is not institutionalized by a system of beliefs. It is therefore a type of ephemeral domination which rests upon the capacity of the leader to inspire faith in his action (Weber, 1971).

The concept of the charismatic leader, even if it is defined in an imprecise manner by Weber, seems particularly appropriate to the analysis of certain political phenomena of our times. In an era inherited from the century of the Enlightenment, we have seen dictators multiply who established links of a religious nature with the masses, and who based a part of their influence upon this type of magical domination. Today, most of the new nations of the Third World have set aside Western constitutional practices and are dominated by charismatic leaders.

But if one perceives intuitively the importance of such a concept, one is also obliged to admit the difficulty of encircling it with precision. How does one identify charisma? What are the characteristic traits of a charismatic leader? Can one single him out from the dictator who imposes his thinking by virtue of instruments of repression or of propaganda, or should he simply be regarded as a leader who enjoys a great popularity?

Ruth Willner (1968) believes that the charismatic leader engenders an emotional response of a particular and singular character: he does not inspire affection, but devotion; he does not engender apprehension but terror, and so on. It is therefore in examining the feelings inspired by a leader that we have the proof or disproof of his charisma. The charismatic leader is seen by those who follow him as a supernatural being, inspired, omnipresent, and his vision of the world becomes theirs. It is well documented that Hitler, Roosevelt, and De Gaulle exercised this kind of influence. We must, however, remember that this type of testimony is always partial, and we ask ourselves if all persons invested with a certain authority do not provoke, in various degrees, the same type of emotions and convictions. Nevertheless, in spite of these reservations, one knows intuitively that the concept of the charismatic leader defined by Weber and his successors sheds light on the reality of a certain form of authority.

But if, as Weber believed, and as Willner recalls with insistence, the proof of charisma resides in the emotional reaction engendered by the leader, the intrinsic qualities of an individual are insufficient to make him a charismatic personality. Like all forms of authority, charisma would be above all a relational phenomenon. It would therefore not be possible to establish a rigorous psychological typology of the charismatic personality. Charisma is a relationship of authority which would result not only in the individual qualities of the leader but also in the response of the masses who support him. Therefore in the last analysis, the sociocultural center favors the appearance of this type of political phenomenon. The particular qualities demanded from the charismatic leader would vary with the particular culture in question along with the political and social conditions.

Can we, nevertheless, isolate certain characteristic traits common to charismatic leaders? In an inquiry regarding about twenty such charismatic leaders, Ruth Willner has demonstrated that personalities of this type show an exceptional vitality and an uncommon capacity for work. They appear animated with a determination out of the ordinary as if they were inspired by an internal focus which enabled them to overcome apparently insurmountable obstacles. In situations of crisis or danger, they remain absolutely fearless. Most charismatic leaders also singled themselves out by the magnetic influence that they exercise on their immediate entourage, and also by the quality of feminine emotions they inspired. Leaders of this type seem to illustrate a strange political creativity, and, as already noted by Max Weber, they manifest little concern for economy, refusing to behave rationally in this domain. Due to their social origins and their particular psychological development, charismatic leaders often have the capacity for manifesting a number of identifications. They are therefore able to internalize and express the values of a plurality of social groups, which favors their influence on the society to which they can give the greater part of their potentiality. There are various causes for this particular aptitude: the family origin of charismatic leaders has little homogeneity from the social, religious, or ethnic point of view, and they have little geographical and cultural stability either.

As has been noted, the sociological and psychological determinants are narrowly linked in this sketch of the typology of the charismatic personality, and the more so in that the character traits such as capacity for work, courage, influence upon others, and so on, are apparently conditioned in part by a political or social situation favorable for the expansion of these individual qualities.

Analysis of American Presidents

If we cannot classify revolutionary leaders or their charismatic personalities into certain well-defined psychological categories, is it possible, in a given institutional framework, to explain certain modes of political functioning by a psychological typology? At present the best attempt is James Barber's (1972) work in which he analyzed the characters of American presidents. According to this author, American presidents since Theodore Roosevelt have manifested the following four types of character: active-positive, active-negative, passive-positive, and passive-negative. The *active-positive* type were highly active and took pleasure in such activity, manifesting a relatively good opinion of themselves, and were quite successful in adapting to the environment. This is a fundamentally rational person who sometimes experiences difficulty in comprehending the irrational aspects of politics. According to Barber, Franklin D. Roosevelt, Harry Truman, and John F. Kennedy would belong to this psychological category. The *active-negative* type manifests compulsive character traits. He works hard, but receives little emotional satisfaction from his effort. His attitude toward his environment is aggressive. His self-image is uncertain. For him life is a fight to attain and then retain power. He is constantly handicapped by a perfectionistic conscience. Woodrow Wilson, Herbert Hoover, Lyndon Johnson, and Richard Nixon would have this type of character. The *passive-positive* type (Calvin Coolidge, Dwight Eisenhower) is flexible, receptive, and cooperative. With this conciliatory attitude, he seeks affection above all. We can note in him a contradiction between a weak opinion of himself and a superficial optimism. Presidents of this type know how to soften the angles of political life, but their dependence with regard to their entourage, the fragility of their hopes, render their political success unlikely. The *passive-*

negative type (William Taft, Warren Harding) does not experience pleasure in his functions. He accepts it as a necessary duty. He has a poor opinion of himself and feels useless. He has a marked tendency to hold himself apart, to escape from conflicts by affirming some vague principles, and on insisting on agreements of procedure.

Character, which is defined by Barber as the definite way to orient one's life, is not the only element determining the personality of the president. His style and his vision of the world are other aspects of the presidential personality which will have a definite effect on his political behavior and which permit us to classify him in this typology. If character is formed in childhood, then the vision of the world takes shape in adolescence, while the style appears early in adult life. Barber defines the style of the president as his habitual manner of assuming three political roles inherent to the presidential function: rhetoric, his relationship with others, and work. His vision of the world expresses the totality of his political convictions, his conception of human nature, and his ethical position.

Lyndon Baines Johnson

To illustrate Barber's approach, let us examine certain problems posed by the analysis of President Johnson, classified by Barber as *active-negative*. Immediately following the death of President Kennedy, Johnson affirmed to Henry Cabot Lodge, who had just briefed him on the Vietnam situation, "I am not going to lose Vietnam. I am not going to be the President who saw Southeast Asia go the way China went" (Barber, 1972, p. 32). Kennedy, we know, had deferred the decision of direct involvement in Vietnam, and certain witnesses have led us to believe that he wished to avoid it. Johnson, on the contrary, immediately and forcefully asserted the policy of intervention; that is, to prevent South Vietnam from passing into the orbit of Hanoi and of the communist world. This war, Barber stated, was not a product of the American political system, but really the consequence of Johnson's fundamental options, in his obstinate flight into an engagement that already appeared destined for failure. In other words, this war was essentially the product of Johnson's personal system; that is, of his character type *active-negative*. In the manner of Wilson and Hoover, he pursued an unrealistic policy with blind obstinacy, and therefore without hope. How can this blindness be explained? Johnson, like Wilson and Hoover, in analogous circumstances of failure, took the Vietnamese tragedy as an eminently personal matter; both his speeches, and his actions reveal that this war had become his personal war. He spent without counting the cost in this hopeless enterprise, and became overly sensitive to any criticism of his policy. In other words, the failure of Johnson in Vietnam, of Wilson with the Senate, or of Hoover in the Depression crisis, are not solely due to outside circumstances, but also result from personal affects. Therefore, in each of these political tragedies, asserts Barber, we note that the president fights against a form of letting things take their course, as if this abandonment constituted an attempt against which they had to fight with all their might.

The political objective is defined by reference to great idealistic principles. All compromise is experienced as a grave moral mistake. The conflict is expressed in terms of strength and weakness, and the refusal to capitulate appears linked to a fear of losing personal integrity. When the personal implications of the policy appear, the president falls into a depression which expresses itself in even more compulsive work habits, and by more overt feelings of persecution. He demands from then on from his close or more distant followers an unfailing loyalty to his own person, and all those who oppose his policies are discredited as immoral or weak beings.

Barber's analysis gives rise to several delicate problems. We can question the importance he grants to the variable personality in the development of American policy. Taking into account the American leaders' consistent definition of their objectives in Vietnam, the evidence of a psychological variable to explain the attitude of President Johnson seems of rather limited interest. Johnson's itinerary was not a solitary one. Indeed we need only consult the *Pentagon Papers* (1971) to become aware that members of the Kennedy administration concerned with this problem were convinced that it was necessary to follow the objectives formulated since 1950, and therefore take appropriate military measures to attain these political ends.

Johnson's obstinacy in the pursuit of this war was shared for a long time by his immediate entourage. Their error arose as a result of complex and largely overdetermined phenomena. It must also be admitted that the political and strategic consequences of the American disengagement were not simple. Furthermore, Johnson, in spite of his adamant attitude, did not remain insensible to the change of opinion in his immediate entourage after the Tet offensive. He agreed to modify the attitude that he had adopted up to that time, and opposed the new demands from the military. We can analyze Johnson's attitude in essentially political terms. In other words, it is not certain that the personality variable singled out by Barber is as determining as this author indicates.

Barber's study illustrates the difficulties inherent in attempting to classify holders of power according to simple psychological categories. A typology constitutes by definition a classification into abstract psychological categories. He singles out a dominant one, but recognizes that each president is a mixture of the four types. In other words, a typology is always somewhat schematic, incapable of including, with the necessary nuances, the psychological traits of an always complex personality. But, if the character of the president is a composite of the four types, how are we to predict political behavior when facing unforeseen circumstances and in diverse roles? A. George (1974) poses this question in the excellent critical analysis which he devotes to the work of J. Barber. Certain situations, certain roles, couldn't these cause a particular aspect of the presidential personality to appear which had not been previously apparent but is a latent tendency? This question brings out the problem of a diagnosis as formulated by Barber. Johnson failed in the Vietnam affair, and this failure, like his whole behavior during this tragic episode of American foreign policy, appears to confirm Barber's hypothesis which places Johnson in the category of *active-negative* presidents. But is this type of deduction sufficiently probing? Facing analogous circumstances, can we be sure that presidents Truman, Eisenhower, or Kennedy would have reacted in a very different manner? On the other hand, if, on the phenomenological level, Truman, Kennedy, or Roosevelt correspond to the *active-positive* type, what does their apparent behavior conceal? Isn't a proud and determined attitude often a reaction formation to the unconscious fear of passivity?

The explanation of the genesis of the presidential character remains as problematic, because we find ourselves confronted with the insoluble problem of sources permitting the reconstruction of the psychodynamic development of the personality analyzed. Going back to President Johnson, it appears difficult to determine the beginning of his hypothetical *active-negative* character, and Barber's reasoning based on brief and conflicting information appears unconvincing. Johnson knew poverty in his childhood, but what does this material reality signify on the emotional level, when we learn that he was particularly nurtured by a mother who had great ambitions for him? Barber also stands on uncertain ground when he states that Johnson suffered "severe wounds to his pride" during his childhood, or when he has us believing that Johnson's parents were overly domineering. On the other hand, it is possible that the recital of Texan lore, and the example of his father's political career made an impression on his vision of the world and his political style.

Richard M. Nixon

Barber's presentation is imperfect, and his retrospective analysis of presidential characters is not always very convincing. But whatever the imperfections of his typology, Barber affirmed in 1972 that Nixon would probably follow the road to failure of his predecessors Wilson, Hoover, and Johnson, because his *active-negative* character risked leading him into a disaster. Nixon belonged to those types of presidents who are able to follow, through winds and tides, in an absolutely rigid manner, a line of conduct destined to fail. Barber's perceptive analysis of Nixon's political behavior, of his compulsive attitude, of the themes of his speeches, permitted him to anticipate that this president would weave the threads of his own tragedy. When we reread his study of Nixon's character in the light of Watergate, we cannot fail to be impressed by the acuity of his analysis.

New and Seductive Perspectives

In terms of this brief research on the problems posed by the psychoanalytic biography, and the typologies of political leaders, it is clear that there is no easy shortcut to understanding the intelligence of the princes who govern us. Psychoanalysis manifestly opens new and seductive perspectives to the "initiated" biographer by offering to him important means for probing the emotional life of the persons being studied. It does not authorize one to submit to the temptation of simple causal explanations. If the Oedipus complex is universal, there exist infinite ways of living it, and the psychic processes revealed by psychoanalysis vary greatly in the course of epochs, according to cultures. This affirmation should reinforce the preconceived notions of the psychobiographer contrary to the schematic utilization of abstract psychoanalytic concepts and of clinical data socially and culturally conditioned. In particular, it should nourish his skepticism in regard to oversimplification of complex political phenomena, and encourage one to be tentative when attempting to reduce to a few psychological types the infinite diversity of personalities who have held or will hold power.

This prudent position casts doubt on the hypothesis that orphans would be able to play a determining role in the history of humanity, or, at any rate, on the possibility of validating this hypothesis. The psychoanalyst can explain very well the psychic factors which favor an artistic or political creation. He will never delineate coherently the numerous and knotted threads which form the fabric of this creativity. A creative destiny is always the fruit of exceptional circumstances where complex idiosyncratic factors and endless exterior social conflicts are mixed together. In this, the creative person escapes from the outlines of simple explanations.

References

Abrahamson, D. (1976), *Nixon vs. Nixon: An Emotional Tragedy.* New York: Farrar, Straus, & Giroux.

Adorno, T. (1950), *The Authoritarian Personality.* New York: Harper.

Allison, G. (1971), *Essence of Decision: Explaining the Cuban Missile Crisis.* Boston: Little, Brown.

Barber, J. D. (1972), *The Presidential Character: Predicting Performance in the White House.* Englewood Cliffs, NJ: Prentice-Hall.

Barker, E. N. (1974), Authoritarianism of the political right, center and left. In: *Personality and Politics*, ed. G. J. Di Rienzo. Garden City, NY: Anchor Press/Doubleday, pp. 283–300.

Binion, R. (1969), Repeat performance: A psychological study of Leopold III and Belgian neutrality. *History & Theory*, 8:213–259.

——— (1973), Hitler's concept of lebensraum: The psychological basis. *Hist. Childhood Quart: J. Psychohist.*, 1:187–215.

Blake, R. (1967), *Disraeli.* New York: St. Martin's Press.

Brodie, F. (1974), *Thomas Jefferson: An Intimate History.* London: Bantam Books.

Bychowski, G. (1971), Joseph V. Stalin: Paranoia and the dictatorship of the proletariat. In: *The Psychoanalytic Interpretation of History*, ed. B. Wolman. New York: Basic Books.

Carlyle, T. (1897), *On Heroes, Hero-worship and the Heroic in History.* London: Chapman & Hall.

Dicks, H. V. (1974), Personality traits and national socialist ideology. In: *Personality and Politics*, ed. G. J. Di Rienzo. Garden City, NY: Anchor Press/Doubleday, pp. 160–225.

Edinger, L. (1965), *Kurt Schumacher: A Study in Personality and Political Behavior.* Stanford, CA: Stanford University Press.

Eissler, K. (1961), *Leonardo da Vinci: Psychoanalytic Notes on the Enigma.* New York: International Universities Press.

———— (1963), *Goethe: A Psychoanalytic Study, 1775–1786*. Detroit: Wayne State University Press.

Ellenstein, J. (1976), La porté et les limites du rapport Khrouchtchev (The bearing and the limits of Khrushchev's view). *Le Monde*, 30 December.

Erikson, E. H. (1950), *Childhood and Society*, 2nd ed. rev. & enlarged. New York: W. W. Norton, 1963.

———— (1962), *Young Man Luther*. New York: W. W. Norton.

———— (1970), *Gandhi's Truth*. New York: W. W. Norton.

Freud, S. (1910), Leonardo da Vinci and a memory of his childhood. *Standard Edition*, 11:57–137. London: Hogarth Press, 1957.

———— Bullitt, W. C. (1967), *Thomas Woodrow Wilson*. Boston: Houghton Mifflin.

Friedlander, S. (1971), *L'Antisémitisme Nazi* (Nazi Anti-Semitism). Paris: Editions du Seuil.

———— (1975), *History and Psychoanalysis*. New York: Holmes & Meier, 1978.

George, A. (1974), Assessing presidential character. *World Politics*, 26:234–282.

———— George, J. (1956), *Woodrow Wilson and Colonel House: A Personality Study*. New York: John Day.

Hoffmann, I., & Hoffmann, S. (1973), *De Gaulle, Artiste de la Politique* (De Gaulle, Artist of Politics). Paris: Editions du Seuil.

Janis, I. (1972), *Victims of Groupthink*. Boston: Houghton Mifflin.

Jardim, S. (1970), *The First Henry Ford: A Study in Personality and Business Leadership*. Cambridge, MA: M.I.T. Press.

Jervis, R. (1976), *Perception and Misperception in International Politics*. Princeton, NJ: Princeton University Press.

Kakar, S. (1970), *Frederick Taylor: A Study in Personality and Innovation*. Cambridge, MA: M.I.T. Press.

Kissinger, H. (1957), *A World Restored*. Boston: Houghton Mifflin.

Langer, W. (1972), *The Mind of Adolph Hitler*. New York: Basic Books.

Lasswell, H. (1951), Psychopathology and politics. *The Political Writings of Harold Lasswell*. Glencoe, IL: Free Press.

Lawrence, T. E. (1926), *Seven Pillars of Wisdom*. Garden City, NY: Doubleday, Doran, 1935.

Loewenberg, P. (1971), The unsuccessful adolescence of Heinrich Himmler. *Amer. Hist. Rev.*, 76:612–641.

Mack, J. E. (1976), *A Prince of Our Disorder: The Life of T. E. Lawrence*. Boston: Little, Brown.

Maclagan, E. (1923), Leonardo in the consulting room. *Burlington Mag.*, 42:54–57.

Mazlisch, B. (1973), *In Search of Nixon: A Psychohistorical Inquiry*. Baltimore: Penguin Books.

——— (1976a), *Kissinger*. New York: Basic Books.

——— (1976b), *The Revolutionary Ascetic: Evolution of a Political Type*. New York: Basic Books.

McCearney, J. (1977), *Maurras et Son Temps* (Maurras and His Time). Paris: Albin Michel.

The Pentagon Papers as Published by the New York Times. New York: Quadrangle Books, 1971.

Pflanze, O. (1972), Toward a psychoanalytic interpretation of Bismarck. *Amer. Hist. Rev.*, 77:419–444.

Plekhanov, G. (n.d.), Concerning the role of the individual in history. *Selected Philosophical Works*. Moscow: Foreign Languages Publishing House, 1961.

Roazen, P. (1973), *Sigmund Freud*. Englewood Cliffs, NJ: Prentice-Hall.

Rogow, A. (1966), *Victim of Duty: A Study of James Forrestal*. London: Rupert Hart-Davis.

Schapiro, M. (1956), Leonardo and Freud: An art-historical study. *J. Hist. Ideas*, 17:147–178.

Senarclens, P. de (1976), Brasillach, le fascisme et l'Allemagne (Brasillach, Fascism and Germany). In: *Les Relations Franco-Allemandes: 1933–1939* (French-German Relations: 1933–1939). Paris: C.N.R.S.

Sieburg, F. (1957), *Napoléon*. Paris: R. Laffont.

Smith, B. (1971), *Heinrich Himmler: A Nazi in the Making, 1900–1926*. Stanford, CA: Hoover Institution Press.

Storr, A. (1973), The man. In: *Churchill: Four Faces and the Man*. Harmondsworth, UK: Penguin Books, pp. 203–246.

Trotsky, L. (1930a), *History of the Russian Revolution*. Ann Arbor: University of Michigan Press, 1957.

——— (1930b), *My Life*. New York: Pathfinder Press, 1970.

——— (1937), *The Revolution Betrayed*. New York: Pathfinder Press, 1972.

Tucker, R. (1968), The theory of charismatic leadership. *Daedalus*, 97:731–756.

——— (1973), *Stalin as Revolutionary, 1879–1929: A Study in History and Personality*. New York: W. W. Norton.

Verhoeff, H. (1976), *"Adolphe" et Constant: Une Étude Psychocritique* ("Adolphe" and Constant: A Psychocritical Study). Paris: Klincksieck.

Waite, R. G. (1971), Adolf Hitler's guilt feelings: A problem in history and psychology. *J. Interdisciplin. Hist.*, 1:229–249.

Ward, D. (1975), Kissinger: A psychohistory. *Hist. Childhood Quart.: J. Psychohist.*, 2:287–348.

Weber, M. (1971), *Economy and Society*. Berkeley: University of California Press, 1978.

Willner, A. R. (1968), Charismatic political leadership: A theory. *Research Monograph*, 32, May. Princeton, NJ: Center of International Studies, Princeton University.

Wolfenstein, V. E. (1967), *The Revolutionary Personality: Lenin, Trotsky and Gandhi*. Princeton, NJ: Princeton University Press.

PART IV

Psychoanalytic Discourse on Orphans and Deprivation

André Haynal

Orphans

Every man is born to be an
orphan.
S. Bellow, *Herzog*

While children with living parents dream of being independent or of having other parents more powerful and more perfect than their own, orphans, whose destiny is marked by the *fact* of the loss of one or both parents, dream of their own survival and fear being responsible for their parents' death. These images or fantasies (in accordance with psychoanalytic terminology) by which children modify reality with regard to their desires form what we call the "family romance." Otto Rank (1909) has reassembled the fundamental fantasies surrounding the "birth of the hero": the child sees himself as a deprived baby, having survived by his own efforts, and, as he was close to death, was saved by a loving mother whose presence was necessary to his survival. Sometimes, the deceased parent takes demonic form, or else it is the survivor who has killed the parent and bears the entire responsibility for this misfortune.

By the term *precocious trauma*[1] is meant a tragic and highly perplexing event which imposes such pressure on the psyche

[1] *Trauma* from the Greek word for *wound.* "A situation is considered to be traumatic when the events evolve and are precipitated in such a way that the concerned subject is forced to repress a powerful need or a great desire at the very moment when he claims the satisfaction in the intimate certainty that this satisfaction is perfectly legitimate and necessary" (Odier, 1950, pp. 120–121). Or, more simply: That which overwhelms the integrative capacities of the self is traumatic.

137

that it can in itself stimulate the mental faculties, which explains why certain individuals become creative once they are orphans. Without a doubt, Freud's self-analysis was set off by the death of his father, and the personal experience related in *The Interpretation of Dreams* (Freud, 1900) is linked to this event, "the most poignant loss, of a man's life" (p. xxvi).

To qualify the grief, the pain which accompanies creativity, Freud created a word, *Mittelelend,* which could be translated as "average misery." In the *Studies in Hysteria* (Breuer and Freud, 1895), Freud speaks of transforming hysterical misery into a common unhappiness. If we too often forget the link that exists between creative people's *Mittelelend* and neurotic misery, it is probably due to the pathological connotation attached to the word *neurotic.* However, as we have said, suffering appears to have the effect of stimulating some people's creative capacities, and they then succeed in developing work which originates from painful and even tragic experiences. Thus *losses* destroy a state of equilibrium, and the capacity to internalize or interiorize, to take from within what one has lost, appears to be a stabilizing and gratifying factor.

Everyone undergoes losses, and these determine the path of human evolution; for example, at the time of weaning, and especially at the time of the birth of the child's own personality, when, little by little he slowly becomes conscious that he is a different entity from his mother, becomes aware of his limits, both of his body and his self, with regard to his mother. This self-awareness recurs later, during adolescence and upon entering adulthood, when the individual's capacities for sustaining separations and losses are put to the test, and while at the same time he experiences intense emotion as a result of the fruitful moments of life. Freud (1908) noted that "we can never give anything up; we only exchange one thing for another" (p 145); the features of the loving and caring mother will thus become (by introjection) the features of the personality of the individual and contribute to its enrichment. Orphans only live more intensely than others what is a fundamental human experience. Here, as elsewhere, the variations in the seriousness of an experience do not form qualitatively different fields, but rather, they constitute a continuous field. The most painful losses are those relating to ideals, which give a sense of order to one's life, because their loss calls into question the individual's self identity.

If we believe with Freud (1923) that the self is a "precipitate of abandoned object cathexes" (p 29), we can imagine the effect when the lost object is one of the parents. The loss of one or both parents provokes a crisis which imposes new adjustments, in particular with regard to the internal changes which such a rupture demands of a relationship.

"If we don't succeed in mastering our difficulties, they will master us." Children who have undergone the trauma of parental loss can turn the loss into a creation or be submerged, marked for all time by an experience from which they have drawn nothing positive. Certain political leaders, such as Hitler and Stalin, were marked by hatred of their fathers and the need to dethrone them. Yet, though their fathers had died while the sons were still young, there remained an image, an introjection, which determined their future way of seeing and behaving. However, other children who have also retained but a vague memory of the early loss of their father present a totally different psychological constellation: they idealize him.

A little boy who had lost his father at the age of three-and-a-half imagined at the age of five that his mother would meet the father again every night on the other side. Insomnia appeared during psychoanalysis, as an attempt, at the price of suffering, to prevent these meetings. We see in this example all the ambiguity of the Oedipus constellation: in spite of the loss of the father, absent, dead, the fantasy of reunion persists, of particular relationships between father and mother (the primal scene) from which the child is excluded, the oedipal jealousy, and self-punishment by insomnia.

If it is true that all creation re-creates what we have loved and then lost, which has been ruined, destroyed, it focuses also on the restoration of an interior world damaged by this loss. Perhaps this explains the high percentage of orphans among creative people. Let us take the example of the great English Romantic poet, John Keats: he was eight years old when his father was killed; his mother remarried two months later; she left her second husband shortly thereafter to live with a third man, leaving her children. John was placed with a grandmother. The following year, the grandfather died. Why be surprised in finding traces of these events in his works? Later, mirroring his mother's behavior toward his father, the woman he loved would not be faithful to him; he tried to repair the pain by taking care of his tubercular brother, contracted the disease himself, left for Rome to be cured, and died there of hunger and misery. He wrote, "Each man is able, like a spider, to weave within himself a citadel of air." This citadel of air is the reconstruction of his fortress, but the latter is made of an unstable and invisible element upon which one cannot lean.

Beauty is truth, truth beauty — that is all
Ye know on earth, and all ye need to know.

A thing of beauty is a joy for ever.
The search for beauty ends implicitly in death:
Verse, Fame, and Beauty are intense indeed,
But Death Intenser—Death is Life's high meed.

For beauty is fragile, closely related to death. The work of the poet is haunted by this comparison. In his study of John Keats, Hamilton (1969) brings out the relationships that exist between the creative processes and dreams, the latter seeking to compensate for the loss of maternal gratifications. In his poems, Keats seems to have tried to end the process of mourning and to compensate for the numerous losses which had afflicted him in his childhood, by, among other methods, recounting his dreams. Mircea Eliade (1959) shows how the poet re-creates a language which abolishes the prior one, in order to reinvent a personal language, private, new, and secret, bringing him back to the primary paradise where he spontaneously creates, where the past had not yet existed since he was not conscious of the passage of time. Thus, for the poet, the past never exists: he rediscovers the world as if he were living at the moment of the first day of creation. We could add that by means of denial, he erases the traumata of the past: his art is outside of time, of history. But when this type of dream is presented as a scientific discovery or a political conception, the abolition of the past risks placing society in great danger. False prophets sometimes try to lead their country out of reality, the existence of which they deny, toward an era of wild dreams following which the community will pay the price in suffering. For the poet, on the contrary, the attempt to liberate himself from his bad experiences is a work of reconciliation. We expect him to triumph over death, that he break his chains and our own, which Hölderlin (cited in Stierlin, 1976b) expresses as: "Because I am more easily destroyed than other persons, I must try all the harder to obtain an advantage from those things which have a destructive influence on me" (p. 60). Stierlin's subtle analysis shows how Kafka succeeded in reconciling the painful events of his existence in his work.

Is it possible to speak of a personality profile typical of orphans? Although it does not constitute a true psychoanalytic problem, numerous psychoanalysts have considered this question. Certain characteristic traits appear notable. Throughout this work, we have included under the heading of orphans those who have lost one parent, or abandoned children who have suffered partial or total parental deprivation. The deprivation that members of these different categories underwent really seemed to bring them together and consequently served as a basis for our reflection.

It is Freud (1910) who in his *Leonardo da Vinci and a Memory of His Childhood* (see also Part II) set the first marker for the psychoanalytic investigation of the pathology of deprivation. Freud placed Leonardo's homosexuality in relation to the absence of paternal influence during the oedipal phase, and suspected that the enclosed relationship between mother and son had blocked the child's psychosexual evolution. A few years later, Ferenczi (1914) attributed such a blocking to the avoidance of normal conflict between father and son. Others then accentuated the idealization of the missing parent and the child's guilt in regard to this. According to Ajuriaguerra (1980), a feeling of abandonment and guilt characterizes orphans in general:

> The feeling of being abandoned is experienced by the child in an emotional emptiness and feelings of despair, being lost, and alone. Confidence and previous security are replaced by

apprehension, and the child wonders whether he or other members of the family are also going to die. Because he is convinced that he was abandoned, the child often has fantasies about a reunion with the dead parent and the desire to see the parent again may be reflected in his refusal to consider death as a finality [pp. 566–567].

For the unconscious, the disappearance of the parents brings out the son's responsibility, as though it were he, by his guilty desires, who had been the cause of the disappearance. The belief in his guilt reinforces his conviction in the power of his thoughts, from which he deduces the evil effects upon others. How often revengeful ghosts will appear in his dreams, forcing him into the miserable life in which many orphans take refuge in order to escape from punishment and not defy the dead parent who must not be overtaken, who is no longer there, who can no longer be confronted, and whom the child feels as more dangerous now that he is invisible.

Boys who have lost their father have difficulty in assuming the male role, as well as the sexual role of fertilizer, father of a child. To be superior to his father, and surpass him always poses a problem in the son's unconscious; but when the son cannot measure himself in reality with the father, and has never been able to do so, then this defiance is not feasible. We find an analogous attitude in the daughter who has lost her mother.

Anna Freud and Dorothy Burlingham (1944) demonstrated, during World War II, how orphans build an image of the father which does not exist in reality, as if this creative sketch were destined to fill in the gap left by the absence of the parent. Naturally, with an imaginary father created from many pieces, there is no danger of being in conflict: he remains an ideal, perfect father; but also, you cannot revolt against him, and, during adolescence, you cannot get rid of him. Individuals who are creatively gifted will find an outlet, either by giving him life through their art (painting, music, literature, and so on), or, by gathering him within themselves, they act in his stead as politicians or statesmen. For others, however, the deceased or absent father will remain an obstacle heavy with consequences, a shadow with which they will constantly collide.

The mechanisms which bring about the development of guilt are complex. The latter will be all the more archaic because the loss activated the oedipal problem. This problem is often expressed by means of a search for someone "responsible," so much so that the surviving parent becomes the object of reproaches from the orphan. Sometimes, a sharp feeling of injustice finds an outlet in sublimation, for example, the struggle against the injustices of the world, but it can also lead to a turning into oneself. The subject drowns in bitterness, complains of being crushed by his surroundings, never blooms, and always nurtures a grudge against life for not having spared him from pain.

As stated above, boys who grow up without a father experience a particular evolution, from the *absence* of a "third" real person who comes to interrupt the dual relationship with the mother. (This, of course, takes place in circumstances other than a remarriage or the existence of a paternal substitute, uncle, or grandfather, who can assume the role generally assigned to the father in daydreams.) Thus, the father who would have cut the umbilical cord, "symbolizing separation from the magic kingdom of the mother," is absent (Meerloo, 1968, pp. 225–229).

In such circumstances, the mother-child relationship will be all the closer, generating anxiety and difficulty in the expression of aggression. The child, indeed, will not always find the necessary strength to separate from the mother and to assume for himself the father's role of "exploding" the mother-child dyad. We have evoked the name of Jocasta in alluding to the particular intimacy between the little boy and his mother. Besdine (1968) described different aspects: "Overevaluating, overprotective, close, binding, intimate, overindulgent, overstimulating, seductive, exclusive, doting, narcissistic, infantilizing, momistic, symbiotic, etc." (p. 575).

According to the author, "geniuses like Michelangelo seem to have an unresolved oedipal problem, unusual attachment to the mother. . . . This is not only true of Michelangelo and his illustrious contemporaries; Elizabethan England exhibits the same phenomenon" (p. 575). He also adds:

Since Jocasta mothering is a common factor to all the condi-

tions mentioned, it is not uncommon to find geniuses who
are alcoholics, drug addicts, asthmatics, homosexuals, or even
psychotics. The alcoholism of Poe, Dylan Thomas, Robert Burns,
and Brendan Behan; the drug addiction of De Quincy and
Poe; the asthma that dominated Proust's life; the madness
of Van Gogh; Goethe's psychotic break at age 16; and Einstein's leaving high school in his senior year: may all have
their roots in Jocasta mothering [p. 575].

Besdine cites David Levy (1943), who appears to confirm
"the importance not only of overprotection but of Jocasta mothering: Sex maladjustment occurs frequently in the overprotective
mother. . . . In difficult marriages, some women turn to their
children. . . . There is overevaluation and attachment to the
child as love object . . . "(p. 575).

How does the child see himself in this situation? What
is his family history? Let us recall the myth of the little solitary
shepherd, imagining himself to be the son of powerful and
idealized parents. The boy whose father has died will conjure
up an idealized image of him; because of his absence, the
child will often lean on a feminine model, accounting for the
frequency of homosexuality, either acted out or sublimated,
as Freud stressed. It is difficult to measure the relations between this situation and creativity, not only artistic, but also
scientific and political. Nevertheless, we have often placed in
parallel the creativity of men versus that of women—the latter
"procreates" although she is not the unique agent of the pro-
creation; her role is more evident, more "visible," while that
of the man is more distant, mysterious, and a source of anxiety.
It can be said that in certain sociocultural conditions, women's
creativity is biological, while men's is symbolic: woman creates
life and man creates symbols. Here we enter into a psychosoci-
ological domain rather than a psychoanalytic one per se. Indeed, it is only by taking these social factors into consideration
that one can explain the particulars of feminine creativity,
and the fact that, in the past, feminine charismatic political
leaders, such as Joan of Arc, were the exception. On the other
hand, the creator, the artist, the writer, and even the psychoanalyst have often felt that the ideal of virility seems linked
to the stereotypic schemata of the type "introversion-femi-

ninity," "conquest of the world-virility." It is possible that these links may have a biological basis from the outset; however, given the almost unlimited choice of behavior and ways of fulfilling oneself that are open to human beings, the environmental, social, and economic factors probably influence these types of attitudes more than the actual biological aspects, as the observation of animal behavior would suggest.

Outside of this question, it is important, in general, to take into account the numerous elements which modify the orphan's situation and complicate the problem. The age of the child at the time of the loss is a determining factor: thus, the loss of the mother appears particularly traumatic between the age of six months and two years, at a developmental stage when stable emotional relationships are established. On the other hand, the child will be more sensitive to the loss of the father during the oedipal period, between three and six. The quality of the relationship with the mother before the separation, the nature of the maternal care being replaced, the relationship with other adults and with siblings, previous experiences, all this reinforces or mellows the "trauma." Other elements are sometimes incriminated, with regard to the accompanying biological structure (heredity, "constitution"). Thus, each case is different, and each individual is unique in terms of his life events, exterior and interior circumstances, and the moment at which the event or events have taken place.

Researchers from Lyons (Aimard, Guyotat, Laurent, and Confavreux, 1976) examining more than 200 patients stricken between the ages of fifteen and twenty-eight by psychosis, discovered that there was the loss of the father in 25 percent of the cases (7 percent in the control group). Thus, evolution is sometimes directed toward the disorganization of the personality, and creativity could be a means to maintain harmony and equilibrium.

There is an element of deficiency in the evolution of all human beings. In the early days of psychoanalysis the accent was placed on infantile sexuality. Freud systematized the knowledge in this domain, he opened the eyes of his contemporaries to those phenomena which appeared to await only the coming of an observer, they are so self-evident today. The impact of infantile sexuality originates also from conflicts, often unconscious, which it engenders. Thus the "castration complex" becomes a central complex linked to the Oedipus complex, and we find here the dimension of deficiency. The initial deficiency of being becomes deficiency on the level of desire: deficiency with regard to needs, the absence of the person the baby desires, can awaken his capacity to penetrate the mysteries of his surroundings by means of his perception and his budding intelligence. It will encourage his comprehension, in other words, deficiency on the level of desire will profoundly impregnate the structure of his affect.

The problem of evil introduces that of death as the ultimate limitation on human existence. More than other people, the orphan, abandoned, is forced to confront this problem. He will either descend into a pathology of bitterness and irritation (which Odier and Guex have called "abandonism"), or this "trauma" will stimulate the evolution and precocious maturation of the child (Ferenczi, 1933) and will push him to artistic, scientific, or political creativity.

Our knowledge of the birth of culture allows us to believe that it is linked to an awareness of death. According to Géza Róheim (1943): "Civilization is a huge network of more or less successful attempts to protect mankind against the danger of object-loss, the colossal efforts made by a baby who is afraid of being left alone in the dark" (p. 100). Some of the earliest works of art have been inspired by tombs. As already noted, we cannot accept the loss of something without replacing it, at least intrapsychically. Raising a statue in the image of the one who has disappeared, using art to breathe life into the image, trying to understand or avert a bad destiny, death in particular, by science—which was at first only magic—trying to extinguish the feeling of culpability born of the realization of our death wishes, that is the cradle of culture (E. Morin, 1973). Myths respond to questions about the origins of evil and death. Magic, myths, these precursors of science, as well as the representations, the first tentative feelings for art, are all linked to deficiency, to those who have vanished, to the warding off of this destiny.

The image is at the outset a symbolic-communicative entity appearing at the earliest moments of human intelligence, as Piaget noted: the surpassing of the sensorimotor intelligence common to men and animals begins with the birth of the inner image. It occurs at the same time as the "mirror stage" (Lacan), of the awareness of the possibility of doubling by reflection, in the light of the mother's eyes, but also in the dream. At night, the child can symbolize the presence of the mother by a piece of cloth or a toy, the transitional object of Winnicott, birth of illusion, of symbolism filling the void left by *absence*. By how many threads are these linked to our capacities for thinking, imagining, and feeling? Isn't one of the greatest Freudian discoveries the refined elaboration of these fundamental facts, their intertwining with our deepest feelings, with our needs and our desires, their *rapport* with this dimension of deficiency?

Aristotle says amazement is the source of all science; isn't the source also in suffering, the unexpected, the strange, which provokes intellectual questioning, or anguish which obliges man to question, and in turn evokes still more questions?

We have understood that the process of mourning plays a role in the birth of science, art, thought, and imagination in all senses of the term, *form into images*. Mourning, however, does not uniquely have the sense that is generally attributed to it at first glance: namely, to abandon one's attachment for someone, to resign oneself to his absence. It is also an "effort" in which the individual fills himself with memories of the lost person, through which he *will preserve* something of him, and thanks to which, at the same time, he will liberate "structures" in order *to become attached* to someone else. It is in fact the great paradox of mourning[2] that the abandoned one abandons the deceased, internally, in the course of difficult and painful moments, and at the same time, he incorporates him, he consumes him cannibalistically, he fills himself with him, so that he does not abandon him to lose him but *to preserve his memory*; therefore, the earth is covered with memorials to all the vestiges of our ancestors. There is the fascination of splitting off, the paradox of the immortality of those whom we know to be dead. It is in this fashion that our past is linked to our present by

---

[2] We would like to underline the importance of the mechanism of mourning and the restoration of ruins and internal losses in creation: "Lost life is found again (as time [is found again] in Proust), chaos is reorganized by a psychic gesture and a musical magic. A promise of salvation is acquired under the assurance of beauty" (Mauron, 1962, p. 234).

a thousand threads that we cannot tear. We must accomplish a work with this past which returns in our dreams and in our nightmares, like phantoms. We can attempt to chase them away, repress, deny, disavow them, but they remain inscribed in our memory, and man, through rites, magic, art, and scientific questions which he poses, transforms them into an accomplishment.

Creativity

I am more convinced than ever of the cultural value of psychoanalysis and I would hope that someone whose perspectives are large enough would draw legitimate conclusions for philosophy and social life.

Letter from Freud to Jung
The Freud/Jung Letters

A number of psychoanalysts, of whom I am one, are convinced that a relationship exists between the mourning process, loss, need, and creativity. One cannot help but be impressed by the high number of orphans among creative people. While the psychoanalyst, as a result of the slowness of his investigation, can have only a limited number of patients, which in practical terms excludes all statistical proof, on the other hand, testimony gathered in the course of psychoanalysis appears to confirm the above impression.

There is a danger that dissimilar facts may be grouped under the same heading; namely, that psychologically disparate situations will be grouped under the general category of orphans. For example, a boy who has lost his father at the age of one, and is then brought up by his mother alone in a one-to-one relationship, would have fundamentally different problems from a boy who has lost his mother in adolescence, or again of a child with siblings, with uncles, aunts, grandparents, or whose mother remarried, and so on.

The shorter lifespan in past centuries does not satisfactorily explain why the proportion of orphans has been higher among creative people than in the general population; nor why it is among orphans that Pierre Rentchnick has discovered the names of the most creative persons in history; nor why creativity often arises after the death or loss of a loved one (Proust, Freud, and so on). In a previous work (Haynal, 1977), I have noted that some of the greatest French writers were orphans or abandoned children.

> Molière, whose mother died when he was a child, wrote a masterpiece following each of his depressions stemming from marital problems;
> Racine was orphaned at the age of [three] and raised by a grandmother;
> Rousseau's mother died when he was born, and he was left to fend for himself from childhood. . . .
> Stendhal lost his mother and rebelled against his father;
> Baudelaire's father died when he was six; and
> Camus and Sartre both lost their fathers in childhood [Haynal, 1985, p. 145].[3]

Creativity blossomed after some writers, already adults, had lost a loved one—generally, the father: Victor Hugo, Joyce, Pascal, Proust, and Freud; Montaigne, after the death of his friend La Boétie; Max Weber, five years after the death of his father, wrote his greatest work, *The Protestant Ethic and the Spirit of Capitalism.*

Jean-Michel Porret (1977) tried to prove, by using a control group, whether in a relatively recent epoch, the predominance of orphans or of children separated from their parents could be confirmed in a population of creative people. He therefore chose the names of the greatest writers of the nineteenth century and examined their biographies. Of course, the numbers obtained only give an indication of a characteristic trait overrepresented in a given population. It is still astonish-

[3]The inclusive Synoptic Table of Artists, Philosophers, Scientists, and Writers is to be found in Appendix C. The above named French writers have the following parental-loss profiles: Molière (F47, M10), Jean Racine (F3, M1), Jean-Jacques Rousseau (F34, M0), Stendhal (F36, M7), Baudelaire (F6), Albert Camus (F0), and Jean-Paul Sartre (F2)—Eisenstadt.

ing to realize that of thirty-five writers, seventeen suffered the death or separation of one or both parents in childhood, while eighteen others had not experienced anything like it; furthermore, in fifteen out of seventeen children, the loss took place during the first twelve years of life. It would be worth making analogous studies on important political leaders.[4]

One of the pioneers of psychoanalysis, Karl Abraham (1911), had already pointed out the link between loss and creativity in an essay on Giovanni Segantini, an Italian-Swiss painter. At the age of five, Segantini was confronted with the death of his mother, then abandoned by his father who left for America with a son from his first marriage, leaving Giovanni with the father's half-sister; he never heard from his father again. Karl Abraham analyzed the course of Segantini's life. A childhood remembrance of the painter is briefly cited:

The first time that I ever took a pencil into my hand to draw was when I heard a woman tearfully say to her neighbours: "Oh, if I only had her picture; she was so beautiful!" As these words were spoken, I saw the beautiful features of a young despairing mother before me and was deeply moved. One of the women present pointed to me and said, "Let this boy make a picture; he is very clever." The beautiful tear-filled eyes of the young mother turned towards me. She said nothing, but went to her room, and I followed her. In a cradle lay the body of a tiny girl, who could not have been much more than a year old. The mother handed me paper and pencil, and I began. I worked for several hours, as the mother wished me to draw the child as if she were still alive. I do not know whether my picture was an artistic success, but I remember that for a moment the poor woman looked so happy that she seemed to forget her grief. The pencil, however, remained at that poor mother's house, and it was not till many years later that I took up drawing again. This incident may have been the seed from which the thought developed that I might use this medium to express my feelings.

[4]See Part I and various appendices for further information on orphanhood data among creative individuals and political leaders—Eisenstadt.

Separated From 2 Parents Between 0 and 7 yrs.	Death or Separation From 1 Parent Between 0 and 7 yrs.		Death or Separation From 1 Parent Between 7 and 12 yrs.	Death or Separation From 1 Parent Between 12 and 20 yrs.	Parents Present From 0 to 20 yrs.
	Father	Mother	Father	Father	
Balzac (brought up by nurse) Nerval (M. deceased when he was 2 F. in military & absent)	Hugo (sep. from F. up to 9–10) Renan (at 5, loss of F.) Rimbaud (at 6, separated from F.) Sainte-Beuve (death of F. before his birth) Sand (at 4, death of F.) Zola (at 6, death of F.) Baudelaire (at 6, death of F.) Dumas père (at 3, death of F.) Dumas fils (separated from F. until 7)	Constant (at 3 wks., death of M.) Stendhal (at 7, death of M.)	Huysmans (at 8, death of F.) Maupassant (at 10, separated from F.)	Loti (at 20, death of F.) Vigny (at 19, death of F.)	Barthélemy Comte Daudet Flaubert France Gautier La Rochefoucauld Lamartine Maeterlinck Maine de Biran Michelet Mistral Musset Rostand Mme. de Staël Verlaine

After J. M. Porret (1977), *Orphelinage et Créativité* (Orphanhood and Creativity). Genève: Thèse, p. 3.

And Karl Abraham added: "For the sake of a mother he becomes an artist," and "Segantini states that the reason for staying for hours beside the corpse was to represent the dead child as living, in accordance with the wishes of the grief-stricken mother. So there was an art by which one could, as it were, summon the dead back to life! (pp. 219–220).

We will not dwell further on this biography in which Abraham also tried to show in what forms and by what transformations the themes of Segantini's childhood arose in his work. Segantini suffered from what he himself called his "melancholia": "Thus was my spirit imbued with a deep sadness which reverberated in my soul with infinite sweetness" (p. 231). "The weary melancholy ceased to be the dominant mood; it gave way to an exuberant joy in creative activity" (p. 232).

A year later, Karl Abraham (1912) wrote "Amenhotep IV: Psycho-Analytical Contributions Towards the Understanding of His Personality and of the Monotheistic Cult of Aton," on a political leader of the fourteenth century B.C. (18th dynasty), who introduced the first monotheistic cult in history. He had lost his father, and Abraham attempts, in the light of historic works of his era (Breasted, Weigall, Niebuhr, Sethe, Petrie) to do the first psychohistorical study, and from an angle which interests us.

In 1953, Marc Kanzer (1953) studied the influence of the early loss of parents on creativity. He cited numerous authors who became orphans in childhood: Baudelaire, the Brontë sisters, Dante, Dumas, Rousseau, Poe, Sand, Tolstoy, and Voltaire. Let us further name in Anglo-Saxon literature: Byron, Keats, Wordsworth, Coleridge, Swift, and Gibbon, who were orphans before the age of fifteen, as well as the famous case of Dostoyevski, whose father was murdered.[5]

---

[5]Parental-loss profiles on the above named are as follows: Baudelaire (F6), Anne Brontë (F after, M1, S29), Charlotte Brontë (F after, M5, S38), Emily Brontë (F after, M3, S30), Dante (F17, M6), Alexandre Dumas père (F3, M36), Jean-Jacques Rousseau (F34, M0), Edgar Allan Poe (F1, M2), George Sand (F4, M33), Leo Tolstoy (F8, M1), Voltaire (F27, M6). Lord Byron (F3, M23), John Keats (F8, M14), William Wordsworth (F13, M7), Samuel Coleridge (F8, M37), Jonathan Swift (F before, M42), Edward Gibbon (F33, M10), Fedor Dostoyevski (F17, M15)—Eisenstadt.

In their book *Cradles of Eminence*, Victor and Mildred G. Goertzel (1962) analyze the characteristics of the childhood of these people. They list in the chapter "Early Agonies," a good number of orphans, semi-orphans, neglected, rejected, or illegitimate children.

In 1975, George Pollock (1975) published a study in which he examined the effects of losses undergone in childhood in leaders, political theoreticians, writers, painters, sculptors, composers, and scientists. He counted 1,200 writers (whom he does not list) as "having undergone such a trauma." The act of creation would consist in closing up a breach, of "repairing the object," or of repairing oneself. In other words, the subject, feeling deprived of something which he once possessed, seeks to replace the lost object (often a person) by a creation. And since the creation does not fill all his needs, narcissistic desires, and omnipotent expectations, the artist is always dissatisfied in not having succeeded in creating the object that he had unconsciously desired. He must then begin again; new failures, accompanied by feelings of incompleteness, will follow new attempts at restitution and re-creation. The failures cannot be canceled except by the product of a new creation, and it is thus that work always continues, without respite, in that quest for immortality which creation promises, whether it be artistic or scientific. The replacement objects never appear as beautiful as the ones lost and idealized; that is why there is always a gap between the dream which incites to creation and its accomplishment. The "restoration of the object" can only be imperfect.

L. Trilling (1945) cites Edmund Wilson who compares the artist to Philoctetes, the Greek warrior forced to live in isolation because of the repulsive odor of a festering wound, but whose compatriots nevertheless sought him out because of his magic arrows which never missed their target. In like manner, artists, scientists, and leaders gifted with creativity are separated from others, suffering from a lack which they try to fill by means of creation, and because of which they are different, marked, as by a "wound," by the loss suffered which engenders the "creative malady" (Ellenberger, 1964). Likewise, others need them, for what they possess, for this power which allows them to give to the community.

Edgar Allan Poe lost his father before the age of two and lost his mother before he was three. According to Niederland (1976), the child spent the night with the body of his mother until the neighbors came in the morning to separate them. We are right to see a link between this event and the sublimation of this pain which caused him to attain the apex of English poetry. Let us cite in particular "Never more" in his immortal poem *The Raven* (1846).[6] Poe takes us through a world of visions of dark and mysterious lakes, of abysses, of river banks lined with lilies growing between lava flows, and of glaciers where fallen angels whisper above separated, tragic, or dead lovers. It is the end of the world, and the names that he chose suggest the distant and abandoned (*Ulalume, The Haunted Palace, Dreamland, Silence, Eldorado*, and so on). The dead lover is always present and this mystic union is so gentle that we don't know whether the dead one is still alive or if it is the living that is dead (*Annabel Lee, For Annie*, and so on). All these themes appear reminiscent of that terrible night when his mother died, and his poems, like his life, often begin on the corpse of the dead woman. We have the right to believe, as psychoanalysts, that the night which made him an orphan deeply marked Poe's sources of inspiration and indeed his entire life (he was a gambler, alcoholic, and depressive). He was suspended from the university because of gambling debts and he died as a result of falling asleep in the road while drunk. We can therefore say that his pathology is related to the night with his mother's corpse, which was the hinge of his life, as well as of his poetic inspiration and his short stories where the caves of the Inquisition, the wine cellar where a demented Italian walls up his victim keep reappearing. Perhaps Poe himself is the victim in every case. Likewise, the confusion between living and dead, living-dead and dead-living, lovers dead and living, would only be the presentation of his idealized mother who survived in the depth of

[6]In *The Philosophy of Composition* (1846) Poe insisted on the importance of sources of rational and conscious inspiration by taking the famous poem *The Raven* as an example. We can ask ourselves if there is a question of an explanation following the creation, of a rationalization in "good faith," or whether he had other personal motives for doing so. Whatever it may be, numerous critics doubt the credibility of his reasons.

his solitude. *Alone* (all-one—as in German *allein, all-ein*) appears to make allusion to a unity found once more in solitude, the former dual unity with the mother.

Therefore, the individual rich in inner resources seeks to "re-establish the lost object" by an artistic or scientific creation. A loss is often to be found at the source of what will result in a "creative malady" (Ellenberger, 1964; Pickering, 1974), whether loss of a beloved person, loss of health, or other matters. The mystery of creativity was invoked a number of times by Freud. He referred to it as "the riddle of the miraculous gift that makes an artist" (Freud, 1930, p. 211); or he stated "before the problem of the creative artist analysis must, alas, lay down its arms" (Freud, 1928, p. 177) with regard to Dostoyevski; a view he repeated in his foreword to Marie Bonaparte's work on Edgar Allan Poe (1933).

Can psychoanalysis itself contribute to an elucidation of the creative process, particularly in relation to orphans? The British psychoanalyst D. W. Winnicott believed that the source of creativity resides in the transmission of a maternal feminine element, the investment of "the very process which gives value to life" (Green, 1977). This could apply to the orphan who lost his father, whose identification to the maternal element is particularly strong.

Earlier we mentioned other authors in whom we find the idea of a great closeness between mother and son in the absence of the father and of all other persons capable of modifying their relationship. Besdine (1968) alludes to Jocasta after the death of Laius. Thus, the boy orphan—for it is of him whom we speak here—is led to idealizing his father, all the while internalizing the maternal ideals. Michel Butor (1961) cites De Quincey with regard to the effects on a young boy of a feminine influence which was not counterbalanced by masculine identifications:

Indeed, the men who have been brought up by women and among women do not quite resemble other men, even supposing an equality in temperament or in spiritual faculties. The attentions of nurses, maternal cajoleries, the playfulness of sisters, particularly of elder sisters, a sort of diminutive mother, transform, as they knead it, the masculine clay. The man

who from infancy has been steeped in the sweet atmosphere
of Woman, in the odour of her hands, of her breast, of her
knees, of her hair, of her soft and diaphanous clothes,

>   Dulce balneum suavibus
>   Unguentatum odoribus,

has thereby contracted a sensitivity of epidermis and a distinction of accent, a kind of hermaphroditism, without which the
harshest and most virile genius remains, in relation to artistic
perfection, an incomplete being. In other words, an early taste
for the world of women, mundus mulieribus, for all its shim-
mering, sparkling and perfumed apparatus creates superior
genius; and I am convinced that my highly intelligent lady
reader will excuse the almost sensual form of my expressions,
as she will approve and understand the purity of my thought
[pp. 51–52].

   "Woman is no doubt a light, a look, an invitation to happiness, a word sometimes; but she is above all a general
harmony" (p. 52). Isn't she before all else preponderantly a
maternal image?
   Aristotle referred to those who were abandoned when
he noted that genius is in some way linked to melancholia
and that men "melancholic on the average surpass others, either by their culture, or by their artistic capacities, or still by
their political efficacy." He called them "extraordinary men"
(perittoì), bringing out their particular emotive lability (Aristotle,
Problemata, 30, 1, 954b).
   Groddeck (1934) has related creativity to illness, A. Adler
(1917) to the feeling of inferiority (which, by abusive extension,
he made responsible for the whole pathology); it is along this
path that numerous writers go, among them Philip Roth (1974):
"I had written my second and third stories, I could not help
wondering if for me illness was not a necessary catalyst to
activate the imagination" (p. 56). Artists express the feeling
that they must fill a void, a lack, accomplish a mourning, but
that they also find a compensation in their art. Thus, the
narcissistic wound inflicted by the loss, which questions the
individual's capacity to keep what or whom he loves, is compensated for by a promise of immortality. While noting that "few

tasks are as appealing as enquiry into the laws that govern the psyche of exceptionally endowed individuals," Freud in his foreword to M. Bonaparte's work on Poe did state as well that there was no "claim to explain creative genius" (Freud, 1933a, p. xi).

It is understood that the constellation in which the child is placed influences his evolution, including the source of his creativity. We must be careful, therefore, not to include under the term *orphan state* situations that are too different one from another. Let us take, for example, Laforgue's work on Jean-Jacques Rousseau (1927). The author tries to understand, through identification with the small Jean-Jacques who lost his mother, "this childhood conflict having become his prison," the attempts of the child to win the love of his father and gain forgiveness from him for the crime with which the father seemed to reproach him. Desperately, Jean-Jacques tried to replace the woman whose death he had involuntarily caused, in this following his father's desire. This would explain, according to Laforgue, Jean-Jacques's difficulty in being a father himself, in accepting the male role, which he sought to escape by placing himself in masochistic situations where he could only fail.

The material gathered in the course of psychoanalysis leads us to believe that creation is primarily an attempt to erect an ideal image of a complete body, *bisexual*: in other words, the body of the mother is also endowed with virile attributes—it is perceived as an astonishingly beautiful Hermaphrodite.

Henry James expressed his need to transform personal experience into prose, poetry, or other artistic forms of expression. Therefore, the desires to express unfortunate experiences, to control the rage at aging, to bandage the narcissistic wound which time inflicts on us, are powerful motives for creation.

A sensibility sharpened by loss can make a child into an artist or a depressive, and sometimes both. Novalis accurately noted: "Illnesses are surely the most important factor of humanity. They are probably the most important factors and stimulants for our thoughts and actions. . . . There exists an energy through illness and weakness" (cited in Ellenberger, 1964, p. 25).

Kipling was abandoned by his parents when he was six years old. Along with his sister, he was left with a family in which the mother was rigid and sadistic and terrorized them. Shengold (1975) attributed the creative power of the author of *The Jungle Book* to this conflict which he had to deal with to avoid "the murder of his soul" in his new family. The day-dreams linked to the orphan state present variations as numer-ous as there are individuals: "Every man is an exception," said Søren Kierkegaard. In the final analysis, all situations are personal and unique, especially as seen under the magnify-ing glass of the psychoanalytic approach, and it is quite difficult to draw generalities.

According to M'Uzan (1977), literary creation is born from the need to create an inner person who would be neither the real father nor the real public, but rather a paternal image fabricated from qualities projected first on the real father and possessing "a character of total receptivity. . . . For the most violent impulses as for the most extreme manifestations of self-affirmation" (p. 19). "All that we cannot inflict on the real public, we are free to inflict on it without the anal control which is exercised upon him and risks destroying him" (p. 20). This inner father, both mediator and originator of the work, will undergo a transformation. First, he will be the object of impulses; and at a later time the inner father will become a sort of replica of its creator, permitting the restoration of the narcissistic inner self.

Others believe, and I am inclined to agree, that it is more a question of the "pregenital" mother, as in the case of Picasso who stated: "At the beginning of each picture there is someone who works with me. Towards the end I have the impression of having worked without a collaborator," (Muensterberger, 1962, p. 168).

When the desire does not reach its goal, the latter is ex-perienced as if it were lost. Each ulterior separation reopens the wound, which we try to bind as well as possible. Music, art rocks us in the enjoyment of Paradise lost and rediscovered. The myth is an attempt at reparation, as in music. Lévi-Strauss (1969) makes this connection in *The Raw and the Cooked*: "Because of the internal organization of the musical work, the act of listening to it immobilizes passing time; it catches and enfolds it as one catches and enfolds a cloth flapping in the wind. It follows that by listening to music, and while we are listening to it, we enter into a kind of immortality" (p. 16).

Helene Deutsch (1944) analyzed the impact of the early loss of her father on the life of George Sand. He died when little Aurore Dupin was only four years old. Following this, she imagined a companion, Corambe, a boy who, contrary to what usually happens, remained her hero and the source of her inspiration all her life. Helene Deutsch saw in this the representation of an idealized father. Let us note further that George Sand, by her behavior, which was masculine for the period (she wore men's clothing and smoked cigars) seemed to want to make her father live again. There were some remarkable individuals among her lovers, including Musset, Sainte-Beuve, Liszt, and Chopin; but she embalmed them in her books in order to abandon them afterwards. Even her pen name was borrowed from one of them. Wasn't it her hostility toward her father which pierced through her strange games (Kanzer, 1953) of which she was herself the victim? In *Leone Leoni* she adopts the theme of Manon Lescaut while reversing the sexes: it is the woman who is linked by a fatal love to a man who does not deserve her passion; it could very well be the love of Aurore for her father. For some people, the early loss of parents appears to lead to the development of extraordinary imaginative powers and predisposes them to the depression along with a desire to repair the "bad" and restore the "good."

Joseph Conrad's parents both died after several years of illness; the child was only seven when he lost his mother, and eleven when he lost his father. Later, in his novel *Lord Jim* the hero dedicates his life to trying to amend a youthful error (an act of cowardice), without ever succeeding. Everywhere, he encounters people who witnessed this act. This irreparable crime, never forgiven, this culpability without mercy, aren't they those of the child who believes himself to be the cause of the disappearance of his parents? Hamilton (1975) relates the troubles that Joseph Conrad incurred with regard to the death of his father. In January 1910, as he was finishing his book *Under Western Eyes*, begun at the same age his father had been at the time of his death and the theme of which is patricide, he used to continually recite the text of the Anglican burial liturgy. This acute phase lasted until May or June of the same year; during that period, he experienced clearly psychotic episodes and a dissolution of his ego. Following this crisis, according to Hamilton, we no longer find in his writing the nuances and the complexities which were characteristic of his works before that time. In a letter dated January 7, 1902, Conrad wrote: "Perhaps true literature (when you get it) is something like the disease which one feels in one's bones, sinuses and joints" (Hamilton, 1975, p. 622). We know that Joseph Conrad used to look at himself in a mirror when he experienced anguish, as if he sought to reassure himself by contemplating his own image.

"Art reunites, restores, re-creates, and conserves the lost objects; its ultimate goal is to triumph over death: Confronted with the painful sense of limitation, loss of omnipotence and omniscience, the individual seeking reparation may turn to art, religion, or science for a certain promise of immortality" (Haynal, 1985, p. 154).

Aristotle (principally in *On the Soul* and *Nichomachean Ethics*) wondered about the variety of dreams and their meanings; he wondered up to what point instincts could integrate themselves to other components of the personality, and, especially (which is the focus of our interest), up to what point frustrations can be sublimated.

If the individual is not capable of assimilating the trauma of loss, among other things, by creativity, he can become sick as a result. In the course of psychoanalysis, the working through is at the same time the suffering through, a pain provoked by the process of mourning, which is nourished by change, the loss of former ideals, and the creation of new perspectives.

The loss is not always that of a person or of certain of his or her aspects, it can be that of an ideal, a deceptive image. Naturally, its consequences will depend on the sense that the individual gives it. Those who remained creative up to the moment of their death, such as Michelangelo working on the *Pietà*, Beethoven on the Ninth Symphony, and Mahler on the Unfinished Symphony, were seeking, with indomitable courage, to overcome the premonition of their coming death.

According to Niederland (1976), the tumor which deformed Jacques-Louis David's upper lip, hindering his speech, stimulated his talent as a painter. In like manner, Goya's creativity seemed to have developed a year after the illness that left him deaf; Niederland brought out with convincing arguments that Goya's "black paintings," among others, bear the traces of this catastrophe. The same author stresses that the Douanier Rousseau had lost his left ear, that Michelangelo's face was disfigured by a scar. The painful feelings regarding such imperfections would have impelled these painters to "restore" the/their human face in all its beauty.

In his work on Leonardo da Vinci, Freud (1910) wrote:

> We must expressly insist that we have never reckoned Leonardo as a neurotic. . . . We no longer think that health and illness, normal and neurotic people are to be sharply distinguished from each other. . . . we know that neurotic symptoms are structures which are substitutes for certain achievements of repression that we have to carry out in the course of our development from a child to a civilized human being. We know too that we all produce such substitutive structures, and that it is only their number, intensity and distribution which justify us in using the practical concept of illness . . . [p. 131].

And in *Totem and Taboo*: "In only a single field of our civilization has the omnipotence of thoughts been retained, and that is in the field of art" (Freud, 1913, p. 90).

All assaults upon our integrity, all feeling of being diminished, at the time of an illness, for example, inflicts a "narcissistic wound," on us which resonates at the level of a lack and can sometimes stimulate a creative effort. Pickering (1974) insists upon the role played by physical or psychic illness in the creativity of Charles Darwin, Mary Baker Eddy, Sigmund Freud, Florence Nightingale, Marcel Proust, and Elizabeth Browning. Niederland (1976) gives a list of artists who were physically impaired: the hunchbacked such as Alexander Pope, Lichtenberg, Moses Mendelssohn; the handicapped such as Byron,

Walter Scott, Leopardi, and Toulouse-Lautrec; chronic patients, like Watteau, Chopin, John Keats, Robert Louis Steven-
son, Eugene O'Neill, Marcel Proust, Stephen Crane, George
Orwell; Kierkegaard, an invalid, recommended in order to
overcome despair that one try to reconstruct oneself; Thomas
Mann wrote in one of his first short stories, *Reserved Blood*:
"I am convinced that my talent is inseparably linked to corporal
infirmity"; H. G. Wells, who suffered from pulmonary tuberculosis since adolescence, compared his work to a "fight against
death"; for André Malraux (*Antimémoires*), the heroic act of
creation would be a defiance of death.

Numerous examples were given in Lombroso's classic work
(1864) supporting the thesis that, often, great creators have
suffered painful anomalies to their pride: debility, illness, small
stature, a speech problem, or an unpleasant physical appearance; all such deficiencies which cause problems with narcissism
would have stimulated their creativity:

> Famous for short stature as well as for genius were: Horace
> (*lepidissimum homunculum, dicebat Augustus*) . . . Alexander (*Mag-
> nus Alexander corpore parvus erat*), Aristotle, Plato, Epicurus
> . . . Laertes, Archimedes, Diogenes, Attila, Epictetus, who was
> accustomed to say: "Who am I? A little man." Among moderns
> one may name, Erasmus . . . Gibbon, Spinoza . . . Montaigne
> . . . Gray . . . Mozart, Beethoven, Goldsmith, Hogarth, Thomas
> Moore, Thomas Campbell, Wilberforce, Heine . . . Charles
> Lamb . . . Balzac, De Quincey, William Blake (who was scarcely
> five feet in height), Browning, Ibsen, George Eliot, Thiers,
> Mrs. Browning . . . Mendelssohn, Swinburne, Van Does (called
> the Drum, because he was not any taller than a drum), Peter
> Van Laer (called the Puppet) . . . Giotto . . . Pope, Leopardi,
> Talleyrand, Scott, Owen, Gibbon, Byron . . . Moses Men-
> delssohn . . . Hooke, were all either rachitic, lame, hunch-
> backed or club-footed. Lecamus has said that the greatest
> geniuses have the slenderest bodies. Caesar feared the lean
> face of Cassius. Demosthenes, Aristotle, Cicero, Giotto, St.
> Bernard, Erasmus . . . Kepler, Sterne, Walter Scott . . . D'Alem-
> bert, Fénelon, Boileau, Milton, Pascal, Napoleon, were all ex-
> tremely thin in the flower of their age. Others were weak
> and sickly in childhood; such were Demosthenes, Bacon, Des-
> cartes, Newton, Locke, Adam Smith, Boyle, Pope . . . Nelson

. . . Pascal, Wren, Alfieri, Renan. . . . Mind, a celebrated painter of cats, had a cretin-like physiognomy. So also had Socrates . . . Rembrandt, Dostoieffsky . . . Pope, Carlyle, Darwin, and, among modern Italians, Schiaparelli, who holds so high a rank in mathematics [pp. 6–8].

Men of genius frequently stammer. I will mention: Aristotle . . . Demosthenes, Alcibiades . . . Virgil . . . Erasmus . . . C. Lamb . . . and Charles Darwin, Moses Mendelssohn, Charles V. . . . Many have been left-handed. Such were: Tiberius . . . Michelangelo . . . Bertillon [p. 13].

Classical psychoanalysis found the link between creation and sublimation of sexuality. In this category, Eissler (1971) placed Goethe's sexual difficulties and problems with masturbation. The poet began to have sexual relations with women only quite late in life. The affairs were always episodic, of short duration, and highly idealistic, so that he ended up in withdrawing into his narcissism, as Thomas Mann showed in his novel *Lotte in Weimar*.

Lombroso (1864) also made a list of great men who were sterile, suggesting that lack of descendants was a springboard of their creativity. He cited great English poets: "Ben Jonson . . . Dryden . . . Addison, Pope, Swift . . . Johnson, Goldsmith, Cowper, Hobbes, Camden and many others" (p. 13).

By means of his creation, the artist overcomes his hostile daydreams and depression, feelings of incapacity, infirmity, powerlessness, and deprivation. Thus, not only does he succeed in overcoming his handicaps and inner tensions, but he makes himself beloved by the introspected mother, his double, his self ideal.

In his autobiographical writings, Swift (Davis, 1962), spoke of the feeling of insecurity from the death of his father which occurred before Swift's birth. Swift suffered from sexual problems and, according to a number of biographers, was even impotent. Does the loss of his father explain Swift's bitterness, his biting irony, or the ways in which he sabotaged his own ambitions (in writing, for example, as an Anglican pastor, *A Tale of a Tub, A Story to Make You Sleep*, a satire against Christian churches); or else, as Thackeray believed, did his troubles come from the intellectual solitude which was a consequence of the loss, which made him say to Pope: "I hate and I am contemptuous of the animal called man"? This contempt was magnificently shown in *Gulliver's Travels*, a splendid sublimation of his ferocity. Even if we are not able to determine the factors which favored his creative expression of this violence, both intellectually and artistically, the question remains: What environmental, social, and educative influences contributed to channeling his feelings in this particular fashion?

In a way, Swift made a bridge between the writer, the poet that he was, and the politician that he wanted to be. In the same way, Churchill, a neglected child though not an orphan, oscillated among his talents of painter, writer, historian, and politician. With regard to him, we can ask what psychosocial factors made a politician gifted with creativity become a leader; in other words, why did the public accept him as a leader and what were the relationships which intertwined the two? Without a doubt, the method of raising children, along with socioeconomic factors give, in each society and each generation, role models to the individuals of the group. When these factors change, the identity is questioned, the model is no longer valid, and we find ourselves in a social crisis. The charismatic leader can then reassure; around him, the group closes ranks, regressing to the search for a new identity, as the British closed in around Winston Churchill during the Second World War. They were able to identify with his strength and to extend it to Britain at a moment when it was weak and menaced. Churchill (1930) tells in his autobiography of an event of his childhood. He was playing with his younger brother and his cousin, and they were chasing him. He wished to cross a bridge over a ravine; since his pursuers blocked access, he jumped to reach a tree with the fantasy that he was going to fly, and as a result he was bedridden for three months. This attitude was interpreted psychoanalytically as resulting from a refusal to accept defeat (to be caught), with a flight into a fantasy of omnipotence, in a boy neglected by his father, presenting a great narcissistic vulnerability with megalomanic flights where he imagined that he could succeed where others had failed. This same fantasy sustained him at a time when Britain was in an almost desperate situation, and also when he himself was pushed out of political life, and launched himself into painting and into writing history, certain that he could succeed in everything, or almost everything.

To create, in science, is to discover new connections, and then, new models; in art, it is making something new or finding a new way of doing it; in politics, it is to formulate for the community a new, original concept. It is always a question of making something new.

If we refer to the model proposed above, creation aiming to "restore" a lost object, we have on the one hand the loss, the withdrawal of reality, the death, and, on the other hand, the restoration in art. We can then express these two poles of expression at the same time: realistic naturalism and ideal romanticism.

The return to reality of which we possess an image is also an art—*techni*, from which we derive the word *technique*. Science, technique, aims to transform this deceiving or frustrating reality. It is possible that the deceptions and privations of the Second World War gave an additional push to the postwar generation—children "without fathers" (Mitscherlich), orphans—seeking their own laws. We are still lacking psychohistoric studies which analyze in depth both the socioeconomic changes and their effect on the individual's life. Let us cite the pioneering work of Raymond de Saussure (1939), who seems to be a model of this genre. The author asked himself what the origin of the scientific spirit was and why it was born in Greece in antiquity. Indeed, if Greece borrowed certain material from pre-Hellenic civilizations, she was original in adopting a new attitude with regard to the real, characterized by doubt, the spirit of examination, which would lead to the scientific spirit. The geographic, ethnic, and historical explanations appear insufficient; it would still be necessary to take the inner life of the people of the community. A particular generation's autonomy of thought and of liberty with regard to the preceding one are linked to a historic change. Raymond de Saussure showed that the crushing authority of the head of the family had long maintained Hellas in an obscure and conformist position. The successive reforms of Draco, Solon, and Clisthenes displaced this authority. As religion was above all familial, the fall of the *gens* brought about the disappearance of collective thought. Each man who thought had to create a personal belief. The comparison of these individual solutions introduced doubt, then the criteria of experience which are those of science. The particular experience of Greece is not found in any previously known civilizations. This 1939 study stands alone in that era, and without any great echoes. Works of Norbert Elias (1939) and of H. Stierlin (1976a) (on Hitler, for example) underline how much the interlacing of social change and of the individual life, touching the depth of the affect, modify the manner of feeling which was molded by social structures from childhood.

Evidently, it is not enough to find new connections, they must be developed. This analytic and synthetic work takes place after the solution has been apprehended intuitively. This process was described in a very vivid manner by James D. Watson (1968) in his book on the discovery of DNA, from which it is easy to see that the creation of a scientific model also depends upon intuition. Kekule found the formula of the rings of benzene after having dreamed of a serpent biting its own tail. The mathematician Henri Poincaré (1909) discovered the theory of the fuchsian functioning after a night without sleep when he had the impression that a host of ideas collided with each other to the point of forming a stable construction. The following day, the solution presented itself to him as he was placing his foot on the first step of a bus. B. Lewin (1962) showed, with regard to Descartes, that disintegrative states such as dreams can pave the trail toward a new original synthesis. At the source of new models, we find in part intuitions, in part the synthesis of elements already known; following this comes the work of verification, analysis, and synthesis, until the hypothesis becomes *thesis*, at least for a certain time, for a scientific stage.

In our view, therefore, the process of mourning and creativity are intimately linked; early mourning impels or contributes to stimulating the work of creation. The chosen theme is probably in intimate relation with the living. We have shown it with regard to poets, and we can ask ourselves with Pollock (1977) to what degree the numerous deaths occurring in Charles Darwin's family inspired him with the feeling that he had overcome the catastrophes which brought others down and that this influenced his thesis on the "survival of the fittest."

We don't mean to say at all that loss and mourning are the only existentialist situations which stimulate creativity; it simply seems to us that we often find them in the origins of creation and of culture, even if it is clear that other human experiences, fortunate or pathological (like submanic states, for example) can play an equally important role. As a matter of fact, we are well aware that jubilant triumph only covers up a latent depression. In short, suffering in general, and particularly suffering linked to becoming an orphan, could very well be an important factor in creativity.

We cannot underestimate the influence of the environment on the *conscious*; for example, at adolescence, the encouragement or opposition of the family can direct the choice of an artistic, scientific, or political career. Thus, for Churchill, the choice of a political career followed a family tradition.

Aristotle, in his *Nichomachean Ethics,* mentioned the "possibility of being different" as one of the ways to solve a problem, when exterior circumstances remain the same. Thus, creativity can also be a choice to react to a trauma, to "get over it." Plato, in *Ion,* compares it to a sort of divine folly. In *The Republic* and *The Laws,* he insists on a particular state, in which the creator feels disconnected with regard to his senses, and which prefigures the notion of "regression in the service of the ego" (Kris, 1952, pp. 220–221, 253–254).

We find in the course of creative states that undoubling of the personality dear to Koestler (1964): a part of one's self "goes forth" in a creative leap, while the other observes, retaining a critical spirit in regard to his work. The other is sometimes lived as a *double*, the mother or its substitute, the interlocutor, the inspirer (the example of Picasso starting work with someone, then ending up alone [Muensterberger, 1962]), or still yet the twin, the imaginary companion of certain orphans, whose image latches onto the feeling of lacking, of a void to fill. Contrary to what we have at times stated, Freud (1933b) in his *New Introductory Lectures on Psycho-Analysis* recognized the importance of the decisive influence which the economic circumstances of men have upon their intellectual, ethical and artistic attitudes. He attributed to this discovery the power of Marxism, while still refusing to admit that "psychological factors can be overlooked." He takes, for example, the "impor-

tant claims made by the super-ego, which represents tradition
and the ideals of the past and will for a time resist the incentives
of a new economic situation" (pp. 178–179).

We wanted to throw a light on the personality of creators,
while being conscious of the limits of the biographical method
(Chasseguet-Smirgel, 1971). To develop a Freudian esthetic,
it would be more worthwhile to start from desire, from dreams,
that is, to utilize a specifically psychoanalytic approach. Freud
(1910) in *Leonardo da Vinci and a Memory of His Childhood* did
not try to explain genius by psychoanalysis. In "Creative Writers and Day-Dreaming" (Freud, 1908) he demonstrates how
we can understand the act of creation from the fantasy. It is
a kind of game, a kind of recuperation of pleasure, of which
the reality, the ananké (the necessity), deprives man. Freud
is nevertheless conscious of the limitation of his thesis; he writes:
"Since artistic talent and capacity are intimately connected with
sublimation we must admit that the nature of the artistic function is also inaccessible to us along psycho-analytic lines" (1910,
p. 136). In "Dostoevsky and Parricide" (1928) Freud speaks
clearly of the unanalyzable artistic talent. And yet, the links
between the dream, the vision and the poem have been con-
vincingly placed in evidence many times in psychoanalytic
literature.

When we examine under what condition the artistic or
scientific production can blossom, we are led to recognize an
"open inner space," an interior lack, where the creative forces
find their sources. The unconscious tends to reestablish the
"dual unity" by communicating with "the object"—reader, lis-
tener, or spectator—the experience of his inner world, of this
primitively arelational space. Art is then a sharing, thus re-
creating the original community of mother-child. In order
to transmit this interior experience, man creates a new language close to empathetic-archaic communication; metaphors
carry the overflow of his feelings, suggestive symbols transfuse
the emotions, aiming to find a sharing, an immediate communication, emotional and profound.

The creator places his narcissistic ideas into the work that
he is trying to accomplish; yet, these ideas are unattainable,
from which stems the dissatisfaction that he cannot fail to

experience as a result, this dissatisfaction becoming therefore the springboard for a new activity.

Diderot wrote that "absence permits all representational games, therefore all creations." Basing it on his life and work, Lewinter (1976) concludes that "a being becomes creative through death," which is confirmed by all those whose creativity was awakened when they became orphans.

Political Leaders

*The riddle of how to choose
a ruler is still unanswered,
and it is the riddle of
civilization.*
G. B. Shaw, *The Apple Cart*

We lack sufficient psychoanalytic experience to identify and interpret the factor that causes a creative personality to choose political action rather than expressing his dreams in music, the novel, or the lyric poem. The taste for social relationships, an extroverted temperament, can partly explain the reason why someone may prefer the activity of political life to the "meditation" of an artistic or scientific career. Although all these aspects are marked by the embodiments of evolution, images which have impregnated the life of the child and adolescent, we must concede that the links between the metapsychological qualities and structure of a political leader are not at all clear. The literature that reveals and "unmasks" the little man behind the great (as Stefan Zweig would say, no man is great to his butler, since the latter sees him in his bedroom slippers) satisfies the feelings and flatters the envy of mediocre people by damaging the reputation of an individual whose merits have been praised; but it does not contribute anything conclusive in the sense of leading to a better understanding of the characteristics and the events that make a leader.

It is possible that orphans more than others feel the missing something that has marked their destiny; doubtless, by creation, they seek to compensate, to restore themselves; and, for these reasons, it is possible and comprehensible that they go further along this path, that they are more creative than others in science or the arts, and also in their desire to amend which often leads them to this particular "will for power" which has struck Pierre Rentchnick.

According to Erikson (1968), the psychosocial identity depends simultaneously upon two complementary aspects of the individual: the inner synthesis of the psychic processes (of the ego) and integration with the group. In other words, historic processes would take place in relation to each generation's search for identity. Indeed, in order that a society survive, it must have the energy and the loyalty of its members, and it is in the course of the reshaping that takes place during adolescence that this identity will be confirmed as being positive. However, if this identification with society fails, the historic crisis explodes. The psychosocial identity shares in the story of the individual and that of the group. This is even more true of political leaders, who have incorporated a part of their needs and desires into their community. The society in which their leader exists is comparable to a resonating chamber which vibrates with him, to a scene where he can express his ideas and the attitudes which correspond to the desires of the group. The members of the group are linked to their leader by emotional ties, the latter personifying their self ideal since he has shown himself capable of bringing solutions to problems that they were unable to resolve.

Freud had a certain tenderness for art; great writers such as Shakespeare and Dostoyevski taught him more about the depths of the human soul than all the psychological studies of his epoch. He was less interested in politicians; if we make an abstract of his collaboration on the Wilson work (Freud and Bullitt, 1967)—and we don't know the exact extent of his role in it—there only remains his study on the legendary figure of Moses, charismatic leader of his people to which Freud felt he belonged. For him, "great men" have *father* characteristics, which confirm the identity of the child's reactions with regard to his father and of the public with regard to the leader. But this father, this great man, this hero, is often a man who revolted against another father, his own, against the preceding leader, and who finally killed him in one way or another. This is how one explains the great ambivalence felt by the general public toward leaders, political men, as well as great artists whose cult is confounded between the cult of the father and that of the hero. The hero bears a part of our self ideal, and so we see in his image an image of ourselves. This is true of religious leaders and also, every time that, on a psychological level, the religious element is put into play, untouchable, sacred in its convictions; for example, in a political situation (a savior of the world, creator of utopias), which the individual does not tolerate our modifying, because his self ideal, sometimes quite infantile, risks collapse.

> Some individual, in the exigency of his longing, may have been moved to free himself from the group and take over the father's part. He who did this was the first epic poet; and the advance was achieved in his imagination. This poet disguised the truth with lies in accordance with his longing. He invented the heroic myth. The hero was a man who by himself had slain the father—the father still appeared in the myth as a totemic monster [Freud, 1921, p. 136].

And so the political leader, like the poet, imagines a tableau where he himself is the hero with whom people will identify because he incorporates a part of their self ideal.

In *Childhood and Society*, Erikson (1950) examines Hitler's and Gorki's childhood; space is lacking to sum up this basic work, and we can only recommend that it be read. Studies on Luther (Erikson, 1962) and Gandhi (Erikson, 1970) by the same author show how great religious leaders can shape history. Luther's fundamental discovery was in placing the accent on inner conflict and the manner of obtaining salvation by means of perfecting one's inner self. Erikson compares it with the existentialist philosophy of Kierkegaard and with Freud— the comparison with Gandhi also appears significant. Luther's work is situated in the historical context of the era: the contradictions between Catholic spirituality and the economic situation of the Church in particular, the traffic in indulgences, the influence of Occamism on Catholic theology, the manner of educating children, family relations, and the complex Catholic answer to these problems. Erikson brought out how Luther developed these contradictions, took them within himself as his own conflicts, in order to finally present to the world a model for leaving them behind.

When the community has lost faith in its existence for diverse reasons, for example, the shaking up of the social equilibrium, it is the "charismatic" leader who gives it back the confidence to reestablish an ideal image of itself (as De Gaulle did for France in June 1940).

It is striking to recognize at what point the collective subconscious always attributed *exceptional qualities* to orphans, foundlings, and abandoned children. Jung and Kerenyi (1941) emphasize the fact that the god-children, Romulus and Remus, Zeus, Moses, were exposed to extraordinary dangers which they overcame thanks to the intervention of exterior, even supernatural forces. Thus, these children would have stored enough force for their subsequent exploits. The mystic imagination idealizes the solitude of the human child coming into the world deprived of the possibility of clinging to his mother; it sees in it the mark of a particular independence, of a superiority, as in Sandor Ferenczi's "wise baby" (1923).

These remarks refer to the problem of idealized orphans, mythical orphans, more often without a father, personifications of the idea that the founders (Romulus and Remus, Moses) could not have a father, as they are themselves the father; their existence refers back to no other law than their own, they are the founders of the Law. And we find here the solitude of the creator evoked by poets (e.g., the Moses of Vigny).

Anzieu (1970) showed how the individual fantasy can be shared by a group: the greater the number of individuals sharing it the more ponderous it becomes; that is, invariable in time. According to Anzieu, a given civilization exists for many centuries with the same fantasy. The latter underlies what we call traditions. Alain Besançon (Anzieu, 1970) suggests that the history of the Russian people has been following a particular form of the Oedipus complex for a millennium: the father, feeling his son to be a rival, kills him; we find this fantasy in the romanesque literature (Dostoyevski) as well as in the theology of the Orthodox Church (which gives a privileged place to the suffering Son) and in the political history (a great number of czars had their oldest son assassinated). Only great crises of civilization—such as the passage of the Roman Empire to Christianity—can change the fantasy of a civilization.

Society and Change

The path of life is marked off with changes. First of all there is the blossoming which follows the dual unity of mother and child, when the personality of the young child breaks away from this dyad and loses the security which the constant presence of the caring mother gives, satisfying all his needs. Later there is the entrance into school, adolescence (passage from childhood into adulthood), marriage, paternity or maternity, then the departure of the children, the readaptation to the life of a couple, retirement, old age. Fortunate or unfortunate, these vicissitudes span the life of human beings. Often social upheavals are added in relation to new socioeconomic structures inscribed in the historic network, the latter expressing itself by the stability or the overthrow of ideals and of proposed values by society. All this does not occur without requiring sometimes difficult efforts to adapt.

All human societies establish rites of passage (Van Gennep, 1908). In our culture, for example, we find them in the stages of religious life: Christian baptism and confirmation; circumcision and Bar Mitzvah of the Jews, and so on. All these ceremonies have as their goal to assist man at the moment of his *abandonment* of a previous identity, former attachments, all permitting him to keep some elements by incorporation. For the human being who questions the beginning and the end, certain rites are ceremonies of "rebirth" (in the Christian religion baptism involves assimilating the rebirth in Christ; ordination to the priesthood assimilates the desire to become a new man; confession abolishes the sins of the past). Thus, one of Freud's principal discoveries lies in placing the accent upon the fundamental fact of psychological continuity: the past, even submerged, can never be erased, it impregnates the future, it remains dynamically present, and even more so when it has been repressed. ("The more it changes, the more it remains the same.") Thus family ties will survive, for example, which will serve to confirm the new identity, the latter being forced to bring to the individual, thanks to the experiences that he has overcome, the tangible and socially recognized proof of his capacities, and by that, a new comfort, a compensation for what he has lost. Certain scholarly or professional examinations sometimes have an analogous function: beyond the task of eventual selection, they also aim, by a solemn and public performance, to allow children and young people to assume a new social identity.

We can try to apprehend the inner aspect of change through mourning, the inner abandoning of certain ties, of certain ideals. This renunciation is combined with a movement destined to replace what we have lost, to fill the void, "turn the page," which can either succeed after a period of suffering and depression, or fail if the change is not "digested," if it "remains in the stomach," leading to depression, extended mourning, prolonged to the point of being eternalized. A culture such as our own, in which change is constant and rapid, puts intolerable pressure on our capacity to adapt and explains the frequency of depression, which seems to be a continuing theme running through society in the late twentieth century.

It can happen that man revolts openly and seeks to reestablish the former order. At other times, there is a tendency to readopt certain elements almost without noticing, always in order to produce the illusion of stability, as was the case after the October Revolution when the repressive methods of czarist Russia were once again used.

The difficulty that we experience in adapting to the overthrow of social ideals linked to economic and technological modifications comes from their questioning of the sense of our activities. The psychological tension demanded by these adjustments has not been sufficiently taken into consideration in our reflections on the equilibrium between the individual and his surroundings.

In the domain of scientific research there coexist the necessary succession of models and the difficulty for individuals in following and *assimilating* the different operational models which are presented (let us consider the natural sciences, for example). In other disciplines, such as the human sciences, certain ideas or concepts survive with more obstinacy for emotional reasons, while their validity is questioned by facts. In the domain of ideas, after a long period of stagnation, the enlightenment takes place sometimes so brutally and rapidly that men do not always succeed in adapting to it (the evolution of the Catholic Church after the Second Concilus of the Vatican might be an example). The psychoanalyst can only plead that we keep account of the importance of affective factors in the management of changes in society or of the different domains of thought, without capturing the right to propose the formulas. Understanding that these changes follow other laws than those of the unconscious, let us recall, however, that the negation of such human factors could, in the long run, prove to be as handicapping, even as nefarious, as, for example, denial of the sexual dimension was during the Victorian era.

The fact that we are reticent in taking this dimension into consideration is probably linked to our difficulty in accepting human limitations, the most radical of which is death: "More than Life, Death holds us in subtle ties" (Baudelaire). Certain loud repercussions lead us to believe that we can, under cover of a right to good health and to life, eradicate the problem of death, and at the same time clearly indicate what explosive emotions flow beneath this theme. In order to attempt to understand the forces at play, let us cite the works of Kraus and Lilienfeld (1959), Young, Benjamin, and Wallis (1963), Parkes, Benjamin, and Fitzgerald (1969), who reveal that the mortality rate after widowhood is much higher than in the general population of the same age, showing to what degree a loss can be destructive to health. Psychosomatic medicine teaches us also that there are strong indications that even very common illnesses, such as the autumn flu, are triggered off by changes that are not well assimilated: perhaps simply the diminishing light, the return of what fall represents (work, monotony, winter); they would therefore be depressive equivalents which take the form of physical illness (see Schmale, 1958; Schmale and Engel, 1967).

Far be it for us to plead for the refusal of all change, the latter being as inevitable as it is necessary: life is change (cf. Heraclitus). Psychoanalysts are content to witness the suffering which change implies, knowing that change depends upon human vulnerability, and, consequently, imposes conscious awareness, and that it is a work of inner development which cannot be replaced by exterior decisions and by acts. The example of sexual problems indicates that the amelioration of information and of publicity cannot be a substitute for the inner evolution. The concept of something missing reflects the importance of the reorganization of the subject's inner world, and that an exterior solution does not permit easy readjustments, given its inauthenticity.

The knowledge of the intimate relationship which exists between the process of transformation and those inner relationships of mourning permits us to better understand the evolution of the individual and his dynamics. Let us take, for example, the fact that his spouse has a different significance for the young man than for the older one. This means that "the emotional investment" of the mate has changed, having lost certain aspects in order to acquire others. These transformations can either be integrated in a harmonious process of inner change—a mourning process—or, if the latter was not worked through, can end up in a crisis which the individual can sometimes overcome through his own efforts, without which he ends up with a pathology.

Even if man succeeds in obtaining decent living conditions, all his problems are not resolved: the inner conflicts, the prisoner within, presented to us in myths, Greek tragedies, the works of Shakespeare, Dante, Goethe, Dostoyevski, and so many others, pose to man as many problems as his surroundings.

The despair linked to loss is as old as humanity. We find traces of it in the first pages of written history: a papyrus from Egypt dating to 1200 B.C., *The Conversation of a Despairing One with His Ba*, is witness to a feeling of limitless solitude, of a despair with regard to a failure of justice, of tradition, of wisdom, of friendship; the writer expresses his fear of breaking up into pieces of excrement, he requests his Ba to relieve his anxiety, to prevent him from committing suicide. Later, the Book of Job also describes despair—depression, we could call it—linked to the loss of security, to a crumbling of ideals and of social stability.

Freud showed clearly, in human societies, the fragility of equilibrium between the constructive and destructive tendencies of man, in other words between Eros and Thanatos. His work was eminently semantic. He wrote about the interpretation of dreams and not about their cause. In *Introductory Lectures on Psycho-Analysis* (Freud, 1916–1917) (the chapter entitled "The Meaning of Symptoms"), he explained how neurotic symptoms have a hidden meaning, the transfer reproducing an archaic link. Likewise, social life is full of communications, often contradictory, which have a meaning. For example, on the subject of impulses, sexuality, and aggression, the individual receives double messages, so that it is difficult for him to find his identity and an authentic attitude. This lack of harmony, of authenticity, this alienation, this inner disequilibrium, explains to us why a society ends up by adopting, as political leaders, criminal individuals, and offering them a forum from which to express themselves, a resonating chamber. The improvement of the *quality* of the inner life of the members of a society perhaps brings a solution to those problems which cannot be resolved by acts, and which have caused philosophers to analyze despair (Levy, 1979). The development of a *false self* (a term created by Winnicott to designate a series of steps which culminate in the creation of an inauthentic personality) is as inefficacious on the individual level as it is at the community level. The fantasy of Paradise Lost and of the Fall represents perhaps more than a temporal sequence, the image of the coexistence in man of the sources of good and evil. The acceptance of this reality aids us more than its denial. Civilization, in the Freudian sense, is an *inner* work which permits the control of instincts in order that human beings may live together. Education contributes to the social evolution by favoring a creative understanding of itself. Paraphrasing Winnicott (who asked for children "a good enough mother"), we could hope that man be not perfect, but good enough.

The game, the activity which gives pleasure—the cultural sphere—gives the greatest satisfaction to man. This is how he is able to fill his "lack" in other ways than by rage, bitterness, vengeance, and destruction, having become self-destructive by reason of unconscious guilt. The human condition is defined by its limitations, by the lack of omnipotence (Sartre, 1947);

the acceptance of this reality structures human life. "There exists no culture in the world where it is permitted to do anything. And we have known for a long time that man does not begin with liberty, but with a *limit* and an uncrossable line" (Foucault, 1972, p. 578). Psychoanalysis approximates the deductive questioning of Socrates; it is based on a confidence in the individual's inner creative energies, it offers a framework capable of favoring the birth of the true self of the analysand. This analytic time permits a re-creation by liberating inner tensions.

For George Steiner (1961) tragic personalities appear to be broken by forces inaccessible to reason, and uncontrollable by wisdom and prudence. These are unconscious forces, linked to transgression—which are activated by tragedy, as, for example, in the story of Oedipus. For leaders, in certain situations, the tragic element resides in the transgression that they allow themselves and which confers on them a kind of seduction. The tragic vision emphasizes the inevitable nature of this demonic force and the depth of the conflict. The transgression (hybris), which, according to tradition passed on in the books attributed to Moses, precipitated the Fall from Paradise, also has a tragic aspect. In tragedies, the protagonists are powerless before the inevitability of the evolving events. They will learn only after the fact, during the suffering. Likewise, the understanding of the psychoanalyst facing the tragic events of the story does not intervene until after the deed(s), because he never possesses enough information on the individual personality and the social forces which are going to use him (Hitler). How can he prevent a menacing evolution for society? Those who would like to transform psychoanalysis, decoding the abyss of the inner world, into a provisional technology, prophylactic on the social level, would collide rapidly with its limitations.

The psychohistoric studies of world leaders have been at best only partial portraits. In fact, in the work on which Freud collaborated with Bullitt on Wilson, the tragic and weak American president of the Versailles Treaty, the authors do not succeed in giving their subject substance. The interaction of social and individual forces has been the object of a few promising studies, but this work is undoubtedly only now beginning. Clearly, one man's influence is affected by the par-

ticular social and political structures of the time, but also by
the historic moment, the socioeconomic context, and so on.
As we have said, the historic processes of change are linked
to a modification of systems of values, in an entire generation
or in a minority which has broken off from current ideals;
thus, the transmission of ideals, of values, would be an important indication of the stability of a society, or, on the contrary,
a precursor of change (A. Toynbee, 1954–1963); psychoanalysis can contribute to this hypothesis. It is even believed that
it participated as a "philosophy of suspicion" in the shaking
up of the system of values popular during the Victorian era.
It is probably true up to a certain point; for example, the
exploration of sexual beliefs has certainly played a role in the
evolution of educational principles, as well as having an effect
on attitudes toward sexuality. We have the right to ask, however, whether these changes before the Second World War,
were really so inspired by psychoanalysis, or whether to an
extent an often simplified version of psychoanalysis was used
by a quite separate movement, which had many other causes;
for example, changes in the family structure, socioeconomic
changes, the consequences of the war, and so on. Freud was
a man of his time, the Victorian era, and he could say in a
moment of bad humor that he had not "derived advantage"
from the sexual liberty he had spoken about. He remained
profoundly skeptical concerning changes in educational principles, believing that each system has its bad side. In other words,
he thought that, whatever we may do, "we do things wrong,"
and included teaching among the "impossible professions."

What is the testimony of psychoanalysis on the changes
that have occurred in the sociocultural environment since its
inception? The only thing that we can affirm in comparing
the descriptions of neuroses at the end of the last century
and the ones that we see in psychoanalysis today, is that, whereas
formerly, problems of authority and the resulting inner conflicts seemed to be foremost, in the current generation, less
exposed to parental prohibitions and injunctions, there is a
greater risk of confronting its limits (among others, the physi-
ological incapabilities of the child to have a love life). Thus,
there is no longer the escape mechanism of attributing responsibility for one's ills to one's parents: the experience of narcis-

sistic vulnerability is therefore more directly revealed, its wounds are more apparent, the naked wound appears. There is perhaps less culpability (in the Oedipean sense, which is to say linked to the Law of the Father, symbolic), less conflictual tearing up, but more abandonment, more depression, more boredom, more emptiness, apathy, drugs. Nevertheless, doesn't this new generation appear more authentic? It might seem so. At any rate, we cannot make a long-term prediction as to the consequences of such an evolution.

Utopia

The very term *Utopia* is full of ambiguity. The myth of a Paradise Lost or that of a site of total harmony, of a Paradise Regained, in heaven or on earth, has been created since Plato's Ideal State, passing through Augustine, Thomas More, the utopian socialists of the nineteenth century, up to our own time. And yet, *ou-topos* (no place) cannot be realized, the Kingdom of Heaven is not of this world.

Utopia is, in essence, antihistoric (Ruyer, 1950). It was born of an ambition to interrupt the course of history, to escape it in order to attain a stable condition of atemporal perfection, where children and parents would end up forming one generation, a world of brothers and sisters in which parents have disappeared. It appears to veer toward the human tendency to constantly rework in order to develop, adjust, and modify. It proceeds from a desire for ultimate perfection, of an idea of absolute grandeur, a throwback to the idealized image of a Paradise Lost rather than a realistic future, which, in fact, will be forever separated by a ditch from all utopian goals.

Utopias of different eras appear on the historic scene as unkept promises. As a matter of fact, they deny, as Mircea Eliade (1969a) stresses, the irreversibility of time past, which frightens man. This image of a perfect life is situated either at the origin or at the end of time, so that alpha and omega are joined. Whether or not it dons a religious cloak, this theme reappears many times in history. Mircea Eliade showed how "eschatological and paradisiacal elements in the colonization of North America by the pioneers, and the progressive trans- formation of the 'American Paradise,' [gave] rise to the myth of indefinite progress to American optimism, and to the cult of youth and novelty" (p. 90). We are not lacking in historical examples: among others, there is the "New Europe," of sinister memory, from which issue the dream of fraternity brought about by the Last Revolution.

The existence of man is precarious due to the tension between the desires and the possibility of fulfilling them, so that he always dreams of a definitive and absolute realization of desire, of a state where all psychological and social tension would be abolished. The utopia of a perfectly psychoanalyzed Man or the utopia of the Kingdom of Heaven—ecclesiastical or lay—are unrealizable illusions by their very nature and the dialectic between desire and fulfillment (between the principle of desire and the principle of reality, according to Freud's terminology). The myth of the Garden of Eden, as old as humanity, imagines a state of regression toward an original narcissism, an infantile omnipotence, comprising the automatic satisfaction of needs, without any kind of frustration.

The romantic novel, the myths of origins, are linked to utopia. The orphan includes in his daydream the presence of his lost parent: time has stopped, the lost one is idealized. The idealization of time past merges with the re-creation of an ideal former time which can never have existed. Indeed, he was never witness to the reality because the couple com- prising his parents could not be lived with each day in the evolution of time, and the orphan has not experienced their perfections and imperfections. The greater the frustrations of real life, the greater the desire to attain an ideal life. From this point of view, the ideal images can be considered, in certain phases, as the motors which drive the evolution of a group, of the progress of a society.

The one whose daydream—often an orphan—renders him sensitive to the aspirations of a certain ideal, if he succeeds in mobilizing the necessary forces (in psychoanalytic terms, the aggressive energy), to reach this goal, will become a political leader. Different factors, notably envy and jealousy, will also feed upon this aggression. Psychoanalytic experiences with certain personalities who have made a mark upon their microsociety lead us to believe that the sublimation of this envy and jealousy and this aggression propel those such as orphans who are disadvantaged to become leaders.

In *Remembrance of Things Past*, Marcel Proust writes that the real paradise is the one that is lost. Artists have been witness to the value of nostalgia: the erotization of memories, the search for the past, as Schliemann did in rediscovering the remains of the ancient city of Troy. Leoncavallo, in the prologue of his opera *Pagliacci*, describes how this work, in a painful spasm, sprang up in him all of a sudden from "a nest of memories from the depth of his soul." Nostalgia is born from the investment in the lost object, pleasant memories, people, vanished eras. Creativity, "springing forth from a soft melancholia" is the transformation of the lost past in a work of art, the latter functioning like a crutch and narcissistic support for the author. Memories, like the voices of the sirens, attract the poet. Eissler (1971) asks if the ego should not protect itself against the danger of being submerged by memories, by the archaic experiences of magic thought, the excessive imagination and feelings which could make the individual tip over into a chaotic universe, a too profound regression: psychosis. This idea is close to that of C. G. Jung on the fascination of the unconscious and its inducting power of insanity (likewise, if the barriers of the ego are weakened by drugs, it happens that adolescents and young adults swing into a psychosis which will continue beyond the period when the drugs are themselves active). After the loss of archaic unity with the mother, desire is born; in English, the word *whole*, designating totality, and *holy*, designating sacred, have the same etymology. The image of the Virgin with her child represents the sacred dual unity. We know that fear of the sacred and the fascination of archaic images derive from the same sources. Milton's *Paradise Lost*, favorite reading of Freud, evokes the Fall from Paradise (S. Friedlander); the latter places the emphasis on guilt, whose importance will become central to our civilization, even in its lay forms.

The image of a Paradise lost from its origins is situated *before the first deception*, the first separation, the first abandonment, a luminous image accompanying humanity in all the myths and legends of the "golden age." The force of this myth is no less great in historic times. Man's reflections on history always make an allusion to an image of the past that they hope to find again, bring to reality, a sort of *reference era*. Thus, for Renaissance men, it was ancient Greece, the supposed harmony of antiquity; for the men of the Reformation in northern Europe, it was primitive Christianity; for the Puritans, the simple mores of the first Christian communities; for the men of the Romantic era, it was the fairylike Middle Ages (minus the Crusades and the Inquisition); for Rousseau and for many neo-Rousseauists, the "noble savage," man before the birth of "civilization," beyond birth and evil deeds. It is easy to understand that those who have experienced a real loss, orphans, are even more inclined to believe in this eternal dimension of man, the nostalgia of beginnings, of the past, the desire to resuscitate something which was "before," the dimension of *illo tempore* (Eliade, 1969a).

The working through of mourning plays a large role in creativity. Creativity, moreover, permits the creator to consciously desire his *own immortality*, often through the work considered as immortal. In the work, as in its progeny, man seeks the satisfaction of this human desire which, for Freud (1915), is a part of each one of us. The idealization of Paradise Lost, with the negation of its loss, and its projection into the future, correspond to utopia; the immortality of a Paradise to be gained has been the springboard of great human enterprises.

Of course, a life consecrated to the realization of a utopia is not derived from one source. As an example, in the case of Mao Zedong, we may see to what point his father's tyranny, Mao's desire to save his mother, to be with her, to repair the injustice for which the father was responsible were the precipitating causes, but certainly not the unique determinants, of his activity on the historic scene. Pollock (1975) also recalls that Lenin, one of the great creators of a utopia, had lost his father at the age of fifteen, and it was after the execution of his older brother that he began his revolutionary career. Every image of the past serving as a reference for action in the present can become a utopia which will be even more dangerous in that it will be rich in a denial of reality. On the other hand, ideals which keep account of the complex reality can be a source of progress in the life of the individual and of the community.

Hope is a specifically human capacity. It assumes first of all, on the cognitive level, the construction of an axis of the continuity of time, the comparison of past experiences with those of the present and anticipation linked to the accomplishment of the future. Anticipation is the ability to project an experience into the future. It is one of the abilities of the political leader to be able to get individuals to participate in the problems which are posed in a socioeconomic moment and a given historic time. Hope implies a basic confidence (a self-image sufficiently narcissistically invested); that is, the certainty—unconscious—of being able to count upon yourself. On the contrary, in despair, with its train of rage, of destruction, of violence, you expect nothing more in the future, in the projection of one's self. It is the abandonment of all expectation. Despair, boredom, and all other forms of "eternal melancholia": a blocked horizon, violence as it was represented in Shakespeare's *Richard III*, a feeling of void, disillusion, are the multiple reflections of one who has missed the possibility of internalizing this confidence in the future. With the limits set by the sociocultural milieu and by the economic situation, the individual is the author of his destiny. His confidence in creative possibilities is linked to the assurance of being able to create a situation in which he will live in equilibrium and in harmony. This expectation of being able to count upon his creativity will permit him to live outside of utopia, to avoid rage and despair, and to fill the fundamental human dimension, for we are all orphans: that is to say, we all need something.

References

Abraham, K. (1911), Giovanni Segantini: A psycho-analytical study. *Clinical Papers and Essays on Psycho-Analysis*, Vol. 2. New York: Basic Books, 1955, pp. 210–261.

—— (1912), Amenhotep IV: Psycho-analytical contributions towards the understanding of his personality and of the monotheistic cult of aton. *Clinical Papers and Essays on Psycho-Analysis*, Vol. 2. New York: Basic Books, 1955, pp. 262–290.

Adler, A. (1917), *Study of Organ Inferiority and Its Psychical Compensation*. New York: Nervous & Mental Disease Publishing.

Aimard, G., Guyotat, J., Laurent, B., & Confavreux, C. (1976), Mort ou absence du père (Death or absence of the father). *Nouvelle Presse Médicale*, 5:1739–1742.

Ajuriaguerra, J. de (1980), *Handbook of Child Psychiatry and Psychology*. New York: Masson.

Anzieu, D. (1970), Freud et la mythologie (Freud and mythology). *Nouv. Rev. de Psychanal.*, pp. 114–145.

Aristotle, Nicomachean ethics. *The Complete Works of Aristotle: The Revised Oxford Translation*, Vol. 2, ed. J. Barnes. Princeton, NJ: Princeton University Press, pp. 729–1867.

—— On the soul. *The Complete Works of Aristotle: The Revised Oxford Translation*, Vol. 1, ed. J. Barnes. Princeton, NJ: Princeton University Press, 1984, pp. 641–692.

—— Problems, Book XXX, I. *The Complete Works of Aristotle: The Revised Oxford Translation*, Vol. 2, ed. J. Barnes. Princeton, NJ: Princeton University Press, 1984, pp. 1498–1502.

Besdine, M. (1968), The Jocasta complex, mothering and genius. *Psychoanal. Rev.*, 55:259–277, 574–600.

Bonaparte, M. (1933), *The Life and Works of Edgar Allan Poe: A Psycho-Analytic Interpretation*. New York: Humanities Press, 1971.

Breuer, J., & Freud, S. (1895), Studies in Hysteria. *Standard Edition*, 2:1–306. London: Hogarth Press, 1955.

Butor, M. (1961), *Histoire Extraordinaire: Essay on a Dream of Baudelaire's*. London: J. Cape, 1969.

Chasseguet-Smirgel, J. (1971), *Pour une Psychanalyse de L'Art et de la Créativité* (For a Psychoanalysis of Art and of Creativity). Paris: Payot.

Churchill, W. C. (1930), *My Early Life: A Roving Commission*. London: Reprint Society, 1944.

Davis, H. J., ed. (1962), Jonathan Swift. Miscellaneous autobiographical pieces, fragments and marginalia. In: *The Prose Writings of J. Swift*, Vol. 5. Oxford: Blackwell.

Deutsch, H. (1944), *The Psychology of Women: A Psychoanalytic Interpretation*. New York: Grune & Stratton.

Eissler, K. R. (1971), *Talent and Genius*. Chicago: Quadrangle Books.

Eliade, M. (1959), *Myths, Dreams and Mysteries*. New York: Harper Torchbooks, 1967.

———— (1969a), *La Nostalgie des Origines* (The Nostalgia of Origins). Paris: Gallimard, 1971.

———— (1969b), *The Quest*. Chicago, IL: University of Chicago Press.

Elias, N. (1939), *The Civilizing Process*. New York: Urizen Books, 1978.

Ellenberger, H. (1964), La Notion de maladie créatrice (The notion of creative malady). *Dialogue, Canadian Philosophical Review*, 3:25–41.

Erikson, E. (1950), *Childhood and Society*. New York: W. W. Norton.

———— (1962), *Young Man Luther*. New York: W. W. Norton.

———— (1968), Psychosocial identity. *International Encyclopedia of the Social Sciences*, 7:61–65.

———— (1970), *Gandhi's Truth*. New York: W. W. Norton.

Ferenczi, S. (1914), The nosology of male homosexuality (homoerotism). In: *Sex in Psychoanalysis*. New York: Robert Brunner, 1950, pp. 296–318.

———— (1923), The dream of the "clever baby." In: *Further Contributions to the Theory and Technique of Psycho-Analysis*. New York: Boni & Liveright, 1927, pp. 349–350.

———— (1933), Confusion of tongues between the adult and the child. *Internat. J. Psycho-Anal.*, 1949, 30:225–230.

Foucault, M. (1972), *Histoire de la Folie à l'Age Classique* (History of Madness in the Classical Age). Paris: Gallimard.

Freud, A., & Burlingham, D. (1944), *Infants Without Families*. New York: International Universities Press.

Freud, S. (1900), The Interpretation of Dreams. *Standard Edition*, 4 & 5. London: Hogarth Press, 1953.

——— (1908), Creative writers and day-dreaming. *Standard Edition*, 9:141–153. London: Hogarth Press, 1959.

——— (1910), Leonardo da Vinci and a memory of his childhood. *Standard Edition*, 11:57–137. London: Hogarth Press, 1957.

——— (1913), Totem and Taboo. *Standard Edition*, 13:vii–162. London: Hogarth Press, 1955.

——— (1915), Thoughts for the times on war and death. *Standard Edition*, 14:273–300. London: Hogarth Press, 1957.

——— (1916–1917), Introductory Lectures on Psycho-Analysis. *Standard Edition*, 15 & 16. London: Hogarth Press, 1963.

——— (1921), Group psychology and the analysis of the ego. *Standard Edition*, 18:65–143. London: Hogarth Press, 1955.

——— (1923), The ego and the id. *Standard Edition*, 19:1–59. London: Hogarth Press, 1961.

——— (1928), Dostoevsky and parricide. *Standard Edition*, 21:173–196. London: Hogarth Press, 1961.

——— (1930), The Goethe prize. *Standard Edition*, 21:205–214. London: Hogarth Press, 1961.

——— (1933a), Foreword. In: *The Life and Works of Edgar Allan Poe*, ed. M. Bonaparte. New York: Humanities Press, 1971.

——— (1933b), New Introductory Lectures on Psycho-Analysis. *Standard Edition*, 22:1–182. London: Hogarth Press, 1964.

——— Bullitt, W. C. (1967), *Thomas Woodrow Wilson*. Boston: Houghton Mifflin.

Goertzel, V., & Goertzel, M. G. (1962), *Cradles of Eminence*. Boston: Little, Brown.

Green, A. (1977), La royauté appartient à l'enfant (Royalty belongs to the child). *L'Arc*, 69:4–12.

Groddeck, G. (1934), *The World of Man: As Reflected in Art, in Words and in Disease*. London: C. W. Daniel.

Hamilton, J. W. (1969), Object love, dreaming and creativity: The poetry of John Keats. *The Psychoanalytic Study of the Child*, 24:488–531. New York: International Universities Press.

—— (1975), The significance of depersonalization in the life and writings of Joseph Conrad. *Psychoanal. Quart.*, 44:612–630.

Haynal, A. (1977), Le sens du désespoir (The sense of despair) *Rev. Française de Psychanal.*, 41:5–297.

—— (1985), *Depression and Creativity*. New York: International Universities Press.

Jung, C. G., & Kerenyi, K. (1941), *Essays on a Science of Mythology*. New York: Pantheon Books, 1949.

Kanzer, M. (1953), Writers and the early loss of parents. *J. Hillside Hosp.*, 2:148–151.

Koestler, A. (1964), *The Act of Creation*. New York: Macmillan.

Kraus, A. S., & Lilienfeld, A. M. (1959), Some epidemiological aspects of the high mortality rate in the young widowed group. *J. Chronic Dis.*, 10:207–217.

Kris, E. (1952), *Psychoanalytic Explorations in Art*. New York: International Universities Press.

Laforgue, R. (1927), Etude sur Jean-Jacques Rousseau. (Study on Jean-Jacques Rousseau). *Rev. Française de Psychanal.*, 1:378–382.

Lévi-Strauss, C. (1969), *The Raw and the Cooked*. New York: Harper & Row.

Levy, B. H. (1979), *Barbarism with a Human Face*. New York: Harper & Row.

Levy, D. (1943), *Maternal Overprotection*. New York: Columbia University Press.

Lewin, B. D. (1962), Knowledge and dreams. *Bull. Phila. Psychoanal. Assn.*, 12:97–111.

Lewinter, R. (1976), *Diderot ou les Mots de l'Absence* (Diderot or the Words of Absence). Paris: Champ Libre.

Lombroso, C. (1864), *The Man of Genius*. London: Walter Scott, 1891.

Mauron, C. (1962), *Des Métaphores Obsédantes au Mythe Personnel* (Obsessive Metaphors in Personal Myth). Paris: Corti.

Meerloo, J. A. M. (1968), Rôle psychologique du père (Psychological role of the father). *Med. & Hyg.*, 26:225–229.

Morin, E. (1973), *Le Paradigme Perdu: La Nature Humaine* (The Lost Model: Human Nature). Paris: Du Seuil.

Muensterberger, W. (1962), The creative process: Its relation to object loss and fetishism. In: *The Psychoanalytic Study of Society*, Vol. 2, ed. W. Muensterberger & S. Axelrod. New York: International Universities Press, pp. 161–185.

M'Uzan, M. de (1977), Aperçus sur le processus de la création littéraire (Overview on the process of literary creation). In: *De l'Art à la Mort* (From Art to Death). Paris: Gallimard, pp. 3–27.

Niederland, W. G. (1976), Psychoanalytic approaches to artistic creativity. *Psychoanal. Quart.*, 45:185–212.

Odier, C. (1950), *L'Homme Esclave de son Infériorité* (Man as a Slave to His Inferiority). Neuchâtel: Delachaux et Niestlé.

Parkes, C. M., Benjamin, B., & Fitzgerald, R. G. (1969), Broken heart: A statistical study of increased mortality among widowers. *Brit. Med. J.*, 1:740–743.

Pickering, G. (1974), *Creative Malady*. London: Allen & Unwin.

Plato, Ion. In: *Phaedrus, Ion, Gorgias and Symposium*. New York: Oxford University Press, 1938.

Poe, E. A. (1846), The philosophy of composition. *The Works of Edgar Allan Poe*, Vol. 6. New York: George P. Putnam's Sons, 1884.

Poincaré, H. (1909), Mathematical invention. In: *Science and Method*. New York: Dover, 1952.

Pollock, G. (1975), On mourning, immortality and utopia. *J. Amer. Psychoanal. Assn.*, 23:334–362.

——— (1977), Congrès International des Psychanalystes.

Porret, J. M. (1977), *Orphelinage et Créativité* (Orphanhood and Creativity). Genève: Thèse.

Rank, O. (1909), *The Myth of the Birth of the Hero*. New York: Brunner, 1952.

Róheim, G. (1943), *The Origin and Function of Culture*. New York: Nervous & Mental Disease Monograph, No. 69.

Roth, P. (1974), *My Life as a Man*. New York: Holt, Rinehart & Winston.

Ruyer, R. (1950), *L'Utopie et les Utopies* (Utopia and Utopias). Paris: Presses Universitaires de France.

Sartre, J. P. (1947), *Existentialism*. New York: Philosophical Library.

Saussure, R. de (1939), *Le Miracle Grec* (The Greek Miracle). Paris: Denoël.

Schmale, A. H. (1958), Relationship of separation and depression to disease. I. A report on a hospitalized medical population. *Psychosom. Med.*, 20:259–277.

——— Engel, G. L. (1967), Psychoanalytic theory of somatic disorder. *J. Amer. Psychoanal. Assn.*, 15:344–365.

Shengold, L. (1975), An attempt at soul murder: Rudyard Kipling's early life and work. *The Psychoanalytic Study of the Child*, 30:683–724. New York: International Universities Press.

Steiner, G. (1961), *The Death of Tragedy*. New York: Knopf.

Stierlin, H. (1976a), *Adolf Hitler: A Family Perspective*. New York: Psychohistory Press.

——— (1976b), Liberation and self-destruction in the creative process. In: *Psychiatry and Humanities*, ed. J. H. Smith. New Haven, CT: Yale University Press, pp. 51–72.

Toynbee, A. (1954–1963), *A Study of History*. New York: Oxford University Press.

Trilling, L. (1945), Art and neurosis. In: *The Liberal Imagination*. London: Secker & Warburg, 1951, pp. 160–180.

Van Gennep, A. (1908), *The Rites of Passage*. Chicago: Chicago University Press, 1960.

Watson, J. D. (1968), *The Double Helix*. New York: New American Library.

Young, M., Benjamin, B., & Wallis, C. (1963), The mortality of widowers. *Lancet*, 2:454–456.

APPENDIX A
Discussion With a Former Head of State: An Orphan at the Age of Four

PIERRE RENTCHNICK

Discussion With a Former
Head of State:
An Orphan at the
Age of Four

P. Rentchnick: I am looking for a common denominator among all those who wish to play a political role and wish to exercise power. Do you believe, after having wielded power in a democracy, that such a common denominator exists?

X.: Certainly, there is an internal stimulus.

P.R.: I am trying to understand if the absence of the father or the mother at a young age plays an important role by way of compensating for a state of frustration.

X.: I believe that you are right and that there must be a common denominator. I see things as follows: there exists a personal factor, and then there is a projection upon favorable ground. Hitler appears to me to be an example of this kind. You are right to seek a personal factor on the familial plane; we must think about the injustice of which we believe ourselves a victim, and then a favorable terrain that the individual interprets in his own way; he can solidify a diffused sentiment in the country. Remember that Hitler was elected in a regular manner; he did not take power by force.[1] I identify two categories: (1) those who affirm that they have wished to be heads of state since childhood; they have a visceral desire for power; (2) persons who are carried away on a political wave. For my part, I have never desired power.

I was born in a very poor family. My mother was a schoolteacher. My father died when I was four years old, but I

[1] Hitler cannot be said to have achieved power by being "elected in a regular manner." Paul von Hindenburg won the presidential election of 1932 with Hitler receiving only 36.7 percent of the votes on the second ballot. On January 30, 1933, Hitler became chancellor at the invitation of Hindenburg. Less than two months later, on March 23, 1933, Hitler was dictator of Germany—Eisenstadt.

193

hardly knew him, because my parents were separated. My father drank. My mother was a very strong woman; she is still living. She was extraordinary, she loved history and knew it very well. She was not religious, [but rather] anticlerical and liberal. My aunt, who lived with us, was also a school-teacher. I never knew the presence of a man in my house. I felt isolated. There was no discussion with a father as my friends used to tell me about. I was reading newspapers from the age of six or seven. My mother spoke to me of politics and of great historical movements; I attended secondary school from ten to fourteen; these were three or four difficult years for me. I was then placed in a commercial school. My mother and aunt wanted me to get a job; in fact, my mother was more ambitious, for I had facility in school, I had good grades, and I was easily the first in my class.

My mother wished me to study political economics. I was then twenty years old; I understood nothing in this field. I went into legal studies, which seemed to me to be closer to reality. And then I wanted to become an engineer.

At the age of twenty-two (1936), I no longer wanted to read law, for I felt: "The attorney washes the dishes of humanity": divorces, small litigations. Today's large corporate law firms did not exist. Being an engineer seemed more solid.

Then I began my apprenticeship with a humanist lawyer, who spoke Latin. He was an extraordinary guy. In 1937, I began to learn about life thanks to this man.

P.R.: This was the first time you met a man in your life, that is, at the age of twenty-three.

X.: He was a spiritual father although he did not have a paternal attitude. It was the first time I ever had discussions with a man. They were very hard times. I did not have a father when I returned home, while my friends had a father who waited for them at the railroad station. I came home, small, poor, with my suitcase, going on foot to find my mother, my aunt, these two poor women who worked to pay for my education. I envied those who had a father who spoke of his profession, of his experiences.

P.R.: Did you have a sense of frustration?

X.: I don't know. But I felt very sad. Something was missing for me in spite of my mother's intelligence.

P.R.: She must have played the dual role of father and mother and to work for you. . . .

X.: On the other hand, I had a feeling of independence (by the absence of the father). I graduated summa cum laude. I telephoned my mother announcing that I was coming home: I was happy not to worry her and my aunt both of whom were working to support me, because I felt guilty. I was leading a very thrifty life with a few friends [similarly situated] with other friends who were rich and spendthrift.

Still my mother was ambitious: she asked me to go to England and to learn English. I was stupid, I did not have a father to impose his will. I refused, as I did not want my mother to keep on working. If I had had a father, I would have left for London, for a father could make that sacrifice while my mother was poor. Today, it is a permanent regret for me not to have learned English.

P.R.: Did you daydream of an imaginary father?

X.: No, no, I daydreamed only of finding in my basement a "Guzzi" motorcycle which a father could have bought me. I still see myself going down to the cellar, hoping to find it.

P.R.: Once or twice, I was surprised to hear you say: "I have no willpower." How do you explain that?

X.: I never had any ambition, I have never asked for anything. I had a lot of luck. I succeeded in spite of my lack of ambition, because I am conciliatory, moderate, tolerant.

P.R.: Did you find a model to identify with?

X.: No model in my infancy. No schoolmaster—that was my mother. No priest, no doctor in our village. No model to emulate until my lawyer boss.

P.R.: Why did high school irritate you?

X.: It was a falsely religious atmosphere, hypocritical. I turned away from paternalistic professors. I only liked the antifascists. I liked the thinkers of the Italian Risorgimento and anti-Royalist poets, anticonservatists and anti-Papists. They were my spiritual models when I was seventeen.

P.R.: Did you have the ambition to write?

X.: My only ambition was to write articles for newspapers. I did not earn any money. I was too timid to ask for money.

P.R.: You often stress your timidity, your lack of ambition. Can you explain this?

X.: I have never wished to ask to be part of the government. But what gave me pleasure was the idea of assuming responsibility. I have no personal ambition, but I do have some for my country, in the name of the government, to render service. I then lose my shyness, I plunge in and I can be at my fiercest before the great world leaders. I remember international conferences in Paris where I violently criticized Giscard d'Estaing (then Minister of Finance). For myself, I blush with confusion, I am timid. But if I am performing the duties of the *office*, where I must ask something for my country, then I no longer have inhibitions. I am liberated.

P.R.: Don't you think that in magnifying your gratitude to your mother, you are transposing her to the level of the nation, the motherland?

X.: I don't know.

P.R.: I had a discussion with Simenon on the subject of Maigret. I was asking Simenon if he could do this or that. "Oh, no! Never—But Maigret certainly does it in your novels!—Yes, Maigret can, but not me." Did you seek power in order to liberate yourself?

X.: As soon as I have power, I exercise it totally. I was elected by the establishment. But as soon as I was in power, I did everything to be independent of this establishment. I revolted. I was from that moment the government. I am humble and have no ambitions. I would never dare to take steps to find a place for my son.

P.R.: Is that humility?

X.: I fear it might be the pride of the timid. I hesitate today to telephone former Ministers. As a lawyer, I did not like asking. I have the soul of a judge, not that of a lawyer.

P.R.: Your father was not there to disinhibit you. Is timidity a result of no paternal example?

X.: My timidity disappears when I fulfill an official function.

P.R.: Do you agree with the idea that introverts, timid persons, need an extroverted political activity?

X.: I completely agree. It is correct, it is valid. Moreover, I would like to tell you that I don't know [in personal matters] how to say no. When I act in an official function, I know how to say, I dare to say no.

P.R.: Does the official political function allow you to be something else, that is, yourself?

X.: Yes, I become someone other than myself, the one I would have liked to have been.

P.R.: You knew how to give up power at the age of sixty-two. Did it hurt you? Is power a drug? Do you miss power?

X.: I gave up power voluntarily. Power uses you up, there was a routine. I was no longer creative, so I decided to step down. But the first three months were difficult. I had a depressing feeling: I no longer had responsibilities, I had become useless, while [previously] I had been happy to be useful to my country.

P.R.: How do you explain the attitude of those who do not want to let go of power?

X.: Because it appeals to their pride, and they derive pleasure from it. While I myself, I had rendered a service to my country.

P.R.: The office did not change you since you have found again your previous timidity.

X.: It's true, but I do have responsibilities in private industry.

We find again all the themes which were discussed at length in the course of our study: the frustration after the death of the father; the injustice of which the subject feels himself a victim; the identification with the mother; the absence of contact with a paternal substitute; the feeling of independence due to the absence of the father; the daydream of the paternal gift; the need to take on an official function to serve the motherland (camouflage of the will for power placed in evidence with the phrase "As soon as I have power, I exercise it totally"); the exercise of political power as a therapeutic means which will permit him "to become the one I would have liked to have been"—Rentchnick.

APPENDIX B
Synoptic Table of Political and Religious Leaders: Parental-Loss Profiles
(These tables were compiled from data developed by Eisenstadt and Rentchnick)

Orphans Who Lost Both Parents (0–19 years)

Name		
Abdul-Hamid II	F18, M7	
4th Earl of Aberdeen		F7, M11
Alfred the Great	F9, M6	
Ernest Bevin		F before, M8
Simón Bolívar	F2, M8	
Aaron Burr		F1, M2
John Calhoun	F13, M19	
Catherine I (Russia)		F2, M3
Catherine de Médici	F0, M0	
Charles XII (Sweden)		F14, M11
Edward VI	F9, M0	
Elizabeth I (England)		F13, M2
Frederick II (Holy Roman Empire)	F2, M3	
Albert Gallatin		F4, M9
Haile Selassie	F13, M1	
William Harrison		F18, M19
Warren Hastings	F11, M0	
Henry I (England)		F18, M14
Henry IV (France)	F9, Ml8	
Henry VIII (England)		F17, M11
Adolf Hitler	F13, M18	
3rd Baron Holland		F1, M5
Herbert Hoover	F6, M8	
Ivan IV the Terrible		F3, M7
Ivan V Alekseevich	F9, M3	
Andrew Jackson		F before, M13
James III (Scotland)	F8, M11	
Benito Juárez		F3, M3
Kagawa Toyohiko	F4, M4	
Marquis de La Fayette		F1, M12
Arthur Lee	F10, M10	
Louis XV (France)		F2, M2

Louis XVI (France)	F11, M12	
Louis XVIII (France)		F10, M12
Marie de Médici	F14, M5	
Mary Queen of Scots		F0, M17
Maurice (Prince of Orange)	F16, M10	
Mohammed		F before, M6
Simon de Montfort	F10, M13	
Philip IV the Fair (France)		F17, M3
Richard II (England)	F9, M18	
Maximilien de Robespierre		F19, M6
Eleanor Roosevelt	F9, M8	
1st Earl of Shaftesbury		F9, M7
Richard Steele	F5, M5	
Sophia (Russia)		F18, M12
Albrecht von Wallenstein	F11, M9	
William III of Orange (England)		F before, M10

Orphans Who Lost
Their Fathers (0–9 years)

Aga Khan III	F7	
3rd Duke of Alba		F3
Alfonso XIII (Spain)	F before	
Jacobus Arminius		F0
Herbert Asquith	F7, M36	
Kemal Atatürk		F9, M42
Augustus (Octavian)	F4, M20	
Arthur Balfour		F7, M23
Sigismund Báthory	F9	
Thomas Benton		F8, M55
William Bradford	Fl	
Marcus Brutus		F8
2nd Duke of Buckingham	F0	
3rd Earl of Bute		F9, M23
Caligula	F7, M2l	
George Canning		Fl
Casimir IV (Poland)	F7	
Charles III the Simple (France)		F before
Charles V (France)	F6, M55	
Charles IX (France)		F9, M after, S23
Salmon Chase	F9, M24	
Chiang Kai-Shek		F8, M33
Christina (Sweden)	F5, M28	
Claudius I		Fl
Henry Clay	F4, M52	
Gaspard de Coligny		F3, M22
Confucius	Fl, M24	
Dagobert II		F6
Georges Danton	F2, M after, S34	
Eamon De Valera		F2

Demosthenes	F7	
Stephen Douglas		F0, M after, S48
William Douglas	F6	
Abba Eban		F1
Frederick Henry (Prince of Orange)	F0, M36	
James Garfield		F1, M after, S49
Hadrian	F10	
Genghis Khan	F8	
Arthur Goldberg		F8
John Hancock	F7	
Rutherford Hayes		F before, M44
Henry III (France)	F7, M37	
Henry VI (England)		F1
Henry VII (England)	F before	
Hōnen		F9
Hu Shih	F3	
James I (England)		F0, M20
James V (Scotland)	F1	
Andrew Johnson		F3, M47
Kenneth Kaunda	F8	
Jomo Kenyatta		F5
David Lloyd George	F1, M33	
Louis XII (France)		F3
Louis XIII the Just	F8, M40	
Louis XIV the Great		F4, M27
Mahmud II (Turkey)	F3	
Marcus Aurelius		F0, M35
Nero	F2, M21	
Nicholas I (Russia)		F4, M32
Olaf I Tryggvason (Norway)	F0	
Edén Pastora		F7
Spencer Perceval	F8	
Eva "Evita" Perón		F7, M after, S33
Isabel Perón	F6	
Peter the Great (Russia)		F3, M21
Philip I (France)	F8	

Philip the Magnanimous		F5
Richard III (England)	F8	
Richard (Earl of Cornwall)		F7
Cardinal de Richelieu	F4, M31	
5th Earl of Rosebery		F3, M54
William Sherman	F9, M32	
Stephen (England)		F5, M40
Tiberius	F9	
Valentinian II		F4
Valentinian III	F1	
Cyrus Vance		F5
Victoria (England)	F0, M41	
Edward White		F1
William Wilberforce	F9	

Orphans Who Lost
Their Fathers (10–19 years)

Adolf Frederick (Sweden)	F16	
Akbar		F14
Alexander III the Great	F19, M after, S32	
Mark Antony		F10
Saint Thomas Aquinas	F19, M30	
Saint Augustine		F17, M33
Francis Bacon	F18, M49	
Edward Benson		F13
Boleslaw III (Poland)	F19	
Julius Caesar		F15, M46
Charles Canning	F14, M25	
Casimir I the Restorer (Poland)		F18
Catherine II the Great (Russia)	F18, M31	
Charles II (England)		F18, M39
Charles II the Bald (Holy Roman Empire)	F17	
Charles VI (Holy Roman Empire)		F19, M35
Charles VIII (France)	F13	
Vicomte de Chateaubriand		F18, M29
1st Earl of Chatham	F18, M27	
Christian IV (Denmark)		F11
Chulalongkorn	F15	
Cleopatra VII		F18
Grover Cleveland	F16, M55	
Clovis I		F16
Thomas Cranmer	F11	
Oliver Cromwell		F18, M55
Jefferson Davis	F16, M37	
Edward III (England)		F14, M45

Edward IV (England)	F18, M after, S40	
Eleanor of Aquitaine		F15
Elizabeth (Russia)	F15	
Mohandas Gandhi		F15, M21
George III (England)	F12, M33	
1st Viscount Grey of Fallodon		F12, M43
Gustav Adolf II	F16	
Hannibal	F18	
Henry II (England)		F18, M34
Édouard Herriot	F17, M24	
Flavius Honorius		F10
Sam Houston	F14	
Idris I (Libya)		F12
James I (Scotland)	F12	
James II (England)		F15, M35
James IV (Scotland)	F15	
Thomas Jefferson		F14, M33
John III Sobieski	F17	
Nikita Khrushchev		F16, M50
Robert E. Lee	F11, M22	
Lenin		F15, M46
Leo X (Pope)	F16, M after, S46	
Louis I (Hungary)		F16
Louis II (Bavaria)	F18	
Louis III (France)		F16
Louis IV the Bavarian	F11	
Louis V the Do-Nothing (France)		F19
Louis VII the Younger (France)	F17	
Louis IX (France)		F12
Saint Ignatius of Loyola	F16	
Sean MacBride		F12
John McCormack	F13	
Matthias I (Corvinus)		F13
Matthias	F19	

Meijo Tenno (Mutsuhito)		F14
Philipp Melanchthon	F11, M32	
James Monroe		F16, M48
Napoleon I	F15, M after, S51	
Reinhold Niebuhr		F18
Origen	F17	
3rd Viscount Palmerston		F17, M20
Charles Parnell	F13, M after, S45	
Philip II (Macedonia)		F13
Philip II (Philip Augustus) (France)	F15, M40	
Philip IV (Spain)		F16
William Pitt	F18, M43	
Pompey the Great		F19
Franklin Roosevelt	F18, M59	
Theodore Roosevelt		F19, M25
José de San Martín	F18, M35	
Selim III		F12
Ludovico Sforza	F13	
Sigismund		F10, M25
Alfred Smith	F12, M50	
John Smith		F16
Joseph Stalin	F11, M57	
Theodoric		F17
Imre Thököly	F13	
Pierre Trudeau		F15, M53
Eleutherios Venizelos	F19	
George Washington		F11, M57
1st Duke of Wellington	F12, M62	
Roger Williams		F17, M31
Leonard Wood	F19	
Mohammad Zahir Shah		F19

Orphans Who Lost
Their Mothers (0–19 years)

Baudouin I	M5	
Henry Beecher		F49, M3
David Ben-Gurion	F58, M11	
1st Viscount Bolingbroke		F63, M0
Habib Bourguiba	M10	
John Bright		F39, M18
Buddha	M0	
John Bunyan		F47, M15
Charles I (England)	F24, M18	
Zhou Enlai		F44, M9
Benjamin Constant	F44, M0	
Calvin Coolidge		F53, M12
George Curzon	F57, M16	
Edward II (England)		F23, M6
Frederick William IV (Prussia)	F44, M14	
Alexander Hamilton		F44, M13
Benjamin Harrison	F44, M17	
Timothy Healy		F51, M4
Ho Chi Minh	M10	
Edward House		F22, M14
Harold Ickes	M16	
Horatio Kitchener		F44, M14
Paul Kruger	F27, M7	
Wilfrid Laurier		F44, M7
Leo XIII (Pope)	F26, M14	
Abraham Lincoln		F41, M9
2nd Earl of Liverpool	F38, M0	
Michael Mansfield		M3
Alfred Milner	F28, M15	
Thomas More		F52, M6
Gamal Nasser	F50, M8	
Horatio Nelson		F43, M9

Ignacy Paderewski	F32, M0	
Robert Peel		F42, M15
Henri Pétain	F32, M1	
Philip II (Spain)		F31, M12
John Russell	F47, M9	
Fredriech Schleiermacher		F25, M14
Henry Stimson	M8	
Earl of Strafford		F21, M18
John Tyler	F22, M7	
William I (Germany)		F43, M13

Illegitimate

Jean d'Alembert		
Cesare Borgia	F28	
Willy Brandt	M55	
Fidel Castro	F30, M39	
Frederick Douglass	M7	
Alexander Hamilton	F44, M13	
Janos Kádár		
Thomas Lawrence (of Arabia)	F30, M after, S46	
James MacDonald	M43	
Bernardo O'Higgins	F22, M61	
Napoleon III	F38, M29,	S64
Eva ("Evita") Perón	F7, M after, S33	
Shaka (Zulu)	F29, M40	
Louis Thiers	F45, M54	
Booker T. Washington		
William I the Conqueror	F8, M23	

APPENDIX C
Synoptic Table of Artists, Philosophers, Scientists, and Writers: Parental-Loss Profiles
(These tables were compiled from data developed by Eisenstadt and Rentchnick)

Orphans Who Lost
Both Parents (0–19 years)

Conrad Aiken	F11, M11	
Johann Sebastian Bach		F9, M9
Francis Beaumont	F14, M14	
William Blackstone		F before, M12
Pedro Calderón De La Barca	F15, M10	
John Calhoun		F13, M19
Thomas Campion	F9, M13	
Joseph Conrad		F11, M7
Benedetto Croce	F17, M17	
Dante		F17, M6
Eugène Delacroix	F7, M16	
Fedor Dostoyevski		F17, M15
Desiderius Erasmus	F18, M17	
John Fletcher		F16, M13
Joseph Fourier	F8, M8	
Kagawa Toyohiko		F4, M4
John Keats	F8, M14	
Gottfried Leibnitz		F6, M17
Somerset Maugham	F10, M8	
Bartolomé Murillo		F9, M9
Edgar Allan Poe	F1, M2	
Jean Racine		F3, M1
Raphael	F11, M8	
Bertrand Russell		F3, M2
Richard Steele	F5, M5	
Leo Tolstoy		F8, M1
Orson Welles	F13, M8	
Elie Wiesel		F17, M14
Dorothy Wordsworth	F12, M6	
William Wordsworth		F13, M7

Orphans Who Lost
Their Fathers (0–9 years)

John Acton	F3, M26	
James Agee		F6
Vittorio Alfieri	F1, M43	
Steve Allen		F1, M43
Arthur Balfour	F7, M23	
Erasmus Bartholin		F4
Baudelaire	F6	
Hayyim Bialik		F6
Ferdinando Bibiena	F8	
Francesco Bibiena		F6
Robert Bloomfield	F0	
William Bradford		F1
Francis Bridgwater	F9	
Thomas Browne		F8
Pieter Brueghel	F5	
George Buchanan		F7
George Gordon, Lord Byron	F3, M23	
Albert Camus		F0
Elias Canetti	F8	
Constantine Cavafy		F7
Thomas Chatterton	F0	
Samuel Taylor Coleridge		F8, M37
Marquis de Condorcet	F3	
Confucius		F1, M24
Stephen Crane	F9	
Thomas De Quincey		F7, M61
John Donne	F3, M after, S58	
Alexandre Dumas père		F3, M36
Ralph Waldo Emerson	F8, M50	
Gustav Fechner		F5
E. M. Forster	F1, M66	
François Fourier		F9, M40

François Guizot	F6, M60	
Bret Harte		F9, M38
Nathaniel Hawthorne	F3, M45	
Joseph Heller		F5
George Herbert	F3, M34	
Robert Herrick		F1, M37
Alexander von Humboldt	F9, M27	
David Hume		F2, M34
Joris-Karl Huysmans	F8, M28	
Edward Jenner		F5
Ben Jonson	F before	
Ernst Kummer		F3
Nikolay Lobachevsky	F7	
Edward Bulwer-Lytton		F4, M40
Marcus Aurelius	F0, M35	
Hermann Muller		F9
Isaac Newton	F before, M36	
Friedrich Nietzsche		F4, M52
Cesare Pavese	F6	
Charles Peale		F9
Sylvia Plath	F8	
Plato		F3
Giacomo Puccini	F5, M25	
Henry Purcell		F6
Ernest Renan	F5, M45	
Peter Rubens		F9, M31
Camille Saint-Saëns	F0, M53	
Charles Sainte-Beuve		F before, M45
George Sand	F4, M33	
William Saroyan		F3
Jean-Paul Sartre	F2	
Adam Smith		F before, M61
Tobias Smollett	F2, M45	
Aleksandr Solzhenitsyn		F before
Tom Stoppard	F4	
Sully Prudhomme		F3
Jonathan Swift	F before, M42	
William Thackeray		F5, M after, S52
Richard Wagner	F0, M34	

Joseph Wedgwood   F8
Émile Zola   F6, M40

Orphans Who Lost
Their Fathers (10–19 years)

Niels Abel	F17	
Thomas Aldrich		F12
Hans Christian Andersen	F11, M28	
Saint Thomas Aquinas		F19, M30
Matthew Arnold	F19, M50	
Saint Augustine		F17, M33
Johann Christian Bach	F14, M24	
Francis Bacon		F18, M49
Thomas Bartholin	F13	
Jean Bauhin		F18
John Berryman	F12	
Anton Bruckner		F13
Jerome Bruner	F12	
Gilbert Burnet		F17
Georg Cantor	F18	
Michelangelo Da Caravaggio		F10
René de Chateaubriand	F18, M29	
Nicolaus Copernicus		F10
Joseph Cornell	F13, M62	
Isak Dinesen		F10
Charles Eames	F10	
Michael Faraday		F19, M47
Helen Frankenthaler	F11	
Robert Frost		F11
Evariste Galois	F18	
Mohandas Gandhi		F15, M21
André Gide	F11, M25	
William Godwin		F16, M53
Oliver Goldsmith	F16, M39	
Franz Grillparzer		F18, M28
George Handel	F11, M45	
Jaroslav Hašek		F13
Lafcadio Hearn	F16, M32	

Friedrich Hebbel		F14, M25
Joseph Henry	F13	
Johann Von Herder		F19, M28
Édouard Herriot	F17, M24	
Alfred Hitchcock		F15
Eric Hoffer	F18	
Wilhelm Humboldt		F11, M29
Comtesse de la Fayette		
(Marie de la Veigne)	F15	
Lenin		F15, M46
Franz Liszt	F15, M54	
Lu Hsün		F15
Thomas Mann	F15, M47	
Philipp Melanchthon		F11, M32
Herman Melville	F12, M52	
H. L. Mencken		F19
Dmitry Mendeleyev	F13	
George Moore		F18, M43
William Morris	F13, M60	
Modest Mussorgsky		F14, M26
Reinhold Niebuhr	F18	
Flannery O'Connor		F15
Origen	F17	
John Osborne		F11
Herbert Read	F10	
Dorothy Richardson		F18
Gabriele Rossetti	F17, M39	
Anton Rubinstein		F16
Arthur Schopenhauer	F17, M50	
Robert Schumann		F16, M25
Edith Södergran	F15, M after, S31	
Robert Southey		F18, M27
Hippolyte Taine	F14, M52	
Mark Twain		F11, M54
Alfred-Victor,		
Comte de Vigny	F19, M40	
Edith Wharton		F19
James Whistler	F14, M46	

Theodore White   F16
Grant Wood   F10
Wilhelm Wundt   F11

Orphans Who Lost Their Mothers (0–19 years)

Jane Addams	F21, M2	
Joseph Addison		F31, M12
Sherwood Anderson	M19	
Carl Philipp Emanuel Bach		F36, M6
Ludwig Van Beethoven	F22, M16	
Jeremy Bentham		F44, M10
Nicolas Boileau-Despréaux	F21, M1	
Elizabeth Bowen		M12
Josef Breuer	F30, M3	
Anne Brontë		F after, M1, S29
Charlotte Brontë	F after, M5, S38	
Emily Brontë		F after, M3, S30
John Bunyan	F47, M15	
Fanny Burney		F61, M10
Thomas Chippendale	M10	
Benjamin Constant		F44, M0
William Cowper	F25, M6	
Charles Darwin		F39, M8
Daniel Defoe	F46, M8	
Edgar Degas		F39, M13
René Descartes	F44, M0	
Theodore Dreiser		F29, M19
George Eliot	F29, M16	
Henry Fielding		F34, M11
Friedrich Froebel	F20, M1	
James Froude		F40, M2
Théodore Géricault	M10	
Edward Gibbon		F33, M10
Georg Hegel	F28, M13	
A. E. Housman		M12

Laurence Housman	M5	
Victor Hugo		F25, M19
Aldous Huxley	F39, M14	
Vincent D'Indy		M0
Immanuel Kant	F21, M13	
Baron Kelvin (William Thomson)		F24, M6
Peter Kropotkin	F28, M3	
Félicité de Lamennais		F45, M5
Bernard Malamud	M14	
Stéphane Mallarmé		F21, M5
George Meredith	F48, M5	
Michelangelo		F58, M6
Molière	F47, M10	
Baron de Montesquieu		F24, M7
Thomas More	F52, M6	
Fridtjof Nansen		F23, M15
Pablo Neruda	M0	
Gérard de Nerval		M2
Giovanni Palestrina	F28, M10	
Blaise Pascal		F28, M3
Petrarch	F21, M15	
Katherine Porter		M1
Wilhelm Reich	M10	
Jean-Jacques Rousseau		F34, M0
Friedrich Schleiermacher	F25, M14	
Franz Schubert		F after, M15, S31
Giovanni Segantini	M5	
Mary Shelley		F38, M0
Richard Sheridan	F36, M14	
Ignazio Silone		M15
Benedictus de Spinoza	F21, M6	
Stendhal		F36, M7
Harriet Beecher Stowe	F51, M5	
August Strindberg		F34, M13
Emanuel Swedenborg	F47, M8	
Torquato Tasso		F25, M12
Peter Tchaikovsky	F39, M14	
Anthony Van Dyck		F23, M8

Voltaire	F27, M6	
Horace Walpole		F27, M19
James Watt	F46, M17	
Carl von Weber		M12
Karl Weierstrass	F54, M11	
Edward Weston		M5
Virginia Woolf	F22, M13	
Marguerite Yourcenar		M0

Illegitimate

Edward Albee
Leon Alberti
Jean d'Alembert
Alexander Borodin
Erasmus
Jean Genet
Jack London
Moa Martinson
James Michener
Maurice Utrillo

APPENDIX D
Who's Who

PIERRE RENTCHNICK

Who's Who

The compilation of orphanhood data is not complete, for too often the biographical documents consulted are incomplete or abridged; for example, when an illegitimate birth has been concealed, or when the biographer is not interested in that particular issue. It can be expected that the synoptic tables (see Appendices B and C) will be augmented as new research provides the necessary biographical material on political and religious leaders and those working in the arts who are not listed here.

We cannot compare Kubitscheck, ex-president of the Republic of Brazil, with Hitler, Stalin, Genghis Khan, or Ivan the Terrible. The environment, the historical period considered, the social background, the economic development will shape in a different manner the same drive for power either political or religious, according to our theory, due to the absence of the father. But it is perfectly possible to analyze the presence or absence of dynamic action, warlike or peaceful, with regard to our theory. Finally, "administrative" leaders could not be compared directly to "revolutionary" leaders.

4th Earl of Aberdeen (F7, M11)

British Prime Minister (1852–1855). His father died when Aberdeen was seven, and his mother when he was eleven. He was the oldest of seven children. In high school he was timid and never played. His adoptive father at the age of fourteen was the Prime Minister William Pitt. When he was twenty-two, Pitt died. On the very next day, Aberdeen started a diary.

Herbert Asquith (F7, M36)

British Prime Minister (1908). His father died when Asquith was seven. A grandfather took care of him, but died when Asquith was ten. Asquith had difficulty in establishing intimate friendly relationships.

Kemal Atatürk (F9, M42)

He was born in 1881. His father was a customs officer. Atatürk was orphaned at the age of nine. The family was without resources; along with his mother and his sister, he was cared for by a maternal uncle. Atatürk took care of animals. He was solitary. He returned to school, revolted, then entered military school because he knew he would wear a fine uniform and be able to meet women. Atatürk explained his ambition in the following manner: admitted to pay homage to the sultan, he refused to kiss the sleeve of the imperial caftan. Why shouldn't he install himself in this palace, since he lived in the neighborhood and this residence appealed to him? He participated in revolts, was imprisoned, then exiled.

Arthur Balfour (F7, M23)

British Prime Minister (1902–1906). His father died when Balfour was seven years old. In his autobiography, Balfour denied having any recollections of his father. His mother acted as head of the family. Chamberlain stated that Balfour had a heart of stone. He was suspected of homosexuality, but this remained unproven.

Otto von Bismarck (F30, M23)

From the age of six, Bismarck's parents handed over his education to the schoolmasters of a boarding school where the children had to obey commands signaled by beating drums. At twelve, he entered high school. At seventeen, he was violent, acted eccentrically, provoked his adversaries into dueling, drinking, and night disturbances. At the age of twenty, he learned that his parents had wasted the family fortune. He despised his mother. In more than one hundred intimate conversations, Bismarck never said a favorable word about his mother. She was hard and cold toward him. He was a stranger in the house of his parents. Since his earliest childhood he never felt at home anywhere. His education was from the start based on the principle that everything is subordinate to the perfecting of the spirit and the rapid acquisition of positive knowledge. He had a hatred of liberal ideas, in fact the very ideas espoused by his mother. His mother led a social life and left his care to others.

He had a desire to command, an ambition to be admired, to be illustrious. He had a passion similar to that of a soldier during war, of a statesman in a free country, such as Peel,

O'Connell, Mirabeau, of a man playing a role during violent political perturbations. He had an attraction, he said, "exactly as light attracts mosquitoes . . . the itching to be called Mr. President."

Simón Bolívar (F2, M8)

His father died when Bolívar was aged two; his mother died when he was eight; he was a widower at eighteen. His mother died when she was twenty-nine, while his father died at the age of sixty-one. The mother expressed little love for him, and was even harsh. She had four other children. It was his maternal grandfather who brought up Bolívar. The daughters married young, and there were no more women at home by the time Simón Bolívar was eight. A year later, the grandfather died. Bolívar's guardian was an uncle living in Spain. His nurse was black. He wrote of her as though she were his mother; he believed that her milk had nourished him, and that he knew no other father than her. Indeed, Hipolitá, a black slave, had been for him both father and mother.

Bolívar appears to have retained no conscious memory of his father, and none of the men he had been in contact with as a child had had masculine authority comparable to Hipolitá's. This woman and his mother must have been therefore the strongest links that he had with the past. Christian Spain (mother) and non-Christian Africa (governess) represented antagonistic influences. Bolívar was influenced by the romantic optimism of Rousseau and the idea of the revolution, and he identified himself with his people crushed by the Spaniards. At the age of eleven, Bolívar went to Spain to join his uncle Esteban. Later, Bolívar, at the peak of his glory, learning that Esteban had returned to Venezuela, wrote him a letter filled with impressions of his childhood and stated that his mother had come out of her tomb and stood before him to say Esteban was his second father.

At the age of eighteen, he married a Spanish woman two years his senior. His wife died eight months later. For the third time, destiny cut him off from his past. In 1803, at the age of twenty, Bolívar himself described the process which transferred his deep inner self from the domain of private affairs to that of public affairs; that is, from Spanish soil to a universal sky. In 1804, in Paris, Bolívar became attached to a woman, Madame de Villars, idealized her to the point of making her a reincarnation of his dead wife, and even gave her the same name, Theresa.

The knight needed a Dulcinea, virgin America, which was suffering atrociously under the Spanish giant. Bolívar arrived in Paris in 1804 at the time when Bonaparte became Emperor at the age of thirty-five. He attended the coronation where he was impressed by the feeling of love shown and saw the ovations given to a hero. This was all that a man could hope for, and it made him think of his country's slavery, and the glory won by the man who would bring freedom.

In Rome, on the Sacred Hill, Bolívar vowed to liberate his country and to become the Emperor of the New World. Here one can see also the identification of his personal destiny with that of his country.

Habib Bourguiba (M10)

Bourguiba's mother died when he was ten. His father was then sixty-three years of age, and it was an older brother who took care of little Bourguiba, who would go from one school to another. The fact that he was deprived of nurturing must have been important since, in 1927, at the age of twenty-four, Bourguiba married a French woman, Mathilde Lorrain, aged thirty-seven, thirteen years older than himself. When his wife was in the process of converting to Islam, in 1962, Bourguiba divorced her and married a Tunisian. It is interesting to note that Bourguiba continued regularly to visit his ex-wife and his grandchildren. Mathilde Lorrain died in 1976 at the age of eighty-six.

Willy Brandt (M55)

Former German Chancellor, Willy Brandt, was born out of wedlock, and he was always very appreciative toward his mother. He never tried to know his father. He emigrated to Norway during the Nazi era, and changed his name, thus giving himself a completely new identity, while he furnished as a completely valid reason, the need to hide from the Nazi regime. His return to Germany after 1945 and his divorce from his first wife, who was Norwegian, give the impression of a remorse toward his German motherland, and a projection of his filial affection for his mother. Brandt was traumatized by Chancellor Adenauer who, on the occasion of a bitter electoral campaign, brought out, in poor taste, Brandt's illegitimate birth.

Brandt, in spite of the self-satisfactions which the exercise of power gave him, has never wanted to evoke his painful childhood. When questioned on this crucial aspect of his biography, ex-Chancellor Brandt told the author that it was still too early to discuss it, which indicated how much the wound had remained open.

George Canning (F1)

British Prime Minister (1827). Canning's father died when the boy was one year old. At the age of eight, his uncle and grandfather separated him from his mother whose numerous liaisons were very public. He was adopted by an ambitious aunt and left her for another aunt when his uncle died. Canning, at fifteen, saw his mother's lover die in a psychiatric institution. In the meantime, his mother had remarried and had in all ten children, which included two sets of twins. At the end of his life, guilt-ridden, Canning wrote to his mother each week, until she died at the age of eighty. Canning helped his mother's last lover, but never his half-brothers.

Fidel Castro (F30, M39)

Castro's father, Angel Castro y Argez, had seven children from his marriage with a schoolteacher. His mistress, Lina Gonzalez, had five children with Angel. Fidel Castro was the third child and he was born on August 13, 1926.

At the age of seven, Castro wanted to go to a Jesuit school, but the director required legitimization of the father's marriage. Fidel resented his father's exploitation of the peasants. His father died in 1956 before Castro took power. His mother Lina opposed Fidel politically when the large land holdings were nationalized. From 1962 to 1963, she helped her younger daughter, Juana, to oppose Fidel Castro by every means.

His biographers always emphasize Fidel Castro's consistent refusal to speak of his parents.

Georges Danton
(F2, M after, S34)

Danton's father died when the boy was two. His mother remarried an elderly man, who was more of a grandfather than a father figure to Danton. Danton was homely, turbulent, intelligent, and impulsive. He lacked discipline and he was a joker, loved by his teachers and other students. He was very affectionate with his mother. With his friends, he was group leader, wielded authority, and his friends conformed easily to his decisions. He fled from school at Troyes in order to see how a king was made: he attended the coronation of Louis XVI at Rheims in 1775, at the age of sixteen. He got married in 1787, and lost his son in 1789. Like Hitler and Saint-Just, Danton affirmed that the child belongs to the nation before it belongs to his father; that the child's own interest requires that he be brought up in common; that it is not enough that a child be well brought up, he must be well brought up for everyone.

Erasmus
(F13, M13)

The famous Dutch humanist was born out of wedlock in Rotterdam on October 28, 1466. At the age of thirteen, he lost his father and mother to the plague. Erasmus's character was informed by a sense of moroseness, despair, and social isolation. He found, as Sartre did later in life, some consolation in writing, and complains of "his miserable life fit more for a wild animal than a human being."

Francisco Franco
(F49, M41)

His father was a gambler, a drinker, and a bluffer. He has completely disappeared from the official biographies of Franco. The latter considered his mother to be a saint.

Franco's father was a thorn in his son's side. The father abandoned his family and remarried to start a new family. Franco's mother, Pilar, in effect was a "widow" with a living husband.

Franco was very timid, melancholic, and overserious as a child. He wanted to become a sailor, something his father had wanted to do, but couldn't. Franco wanted to surpass his father. His brothers were more brilliant. Franco was scorned by his contemporaries for his thin voice and great timidity. He was rejected by the Naval Academy, but entered the Military Academy at the age of fifteen. It was probably there that Franco knew a certain happiness, a family, and a reason for being.

Franco loved to paint as a relaxation. One of his better works is a self-portrait in the uniform of an Admiral—the image of an old dream, although he never was a seaman; he had entered the Academy of Toledo against the will of his father.

In 1898, Franco was six years old. He heard of the shame of Spain's defeat by the United States with the loss of Cuba, Guam, and the Philippines. Franco later identified himself with the idea of defeat and revenge, as Hitler did a little later.

Franco ignored his father until his death, which occurred many years after the son's triumph, and he never wanted to know anything about him, and indeed never spoke a word to him. Franco bore grudges great and small, combining a "feminine" pettiness with the means for revenge possessed by an all-powerful man. Franco attended a mass at the death of his father. He accompanied his father's coffin to the exit of the Castle of Pardo, then he sent a company of naval infantry to the cemetery as an honor guard.

Mohandas Gandhi
(F15, M21)

Gandhi's father died when the boy was fifteen. He was married at the age of thirteen to a girl his own age. He was allowed to go to England to study law, but only after having made a triple oath to touch no meat, no alcohol, no women, and not without having been excluded from his caste for having dared to leave the sacred soil of his country. He then left for South Africa where he espoused the cause of blacks.

David Lloyd George
(F1, M33)

Lloyd George was British Prime Minister from 1916 to 1922. His father died when Lloyd George was one year old. His mother called upon her brother-in-law for help. He was a shoemaker, unmarried, and living with his eighty-year-old mother. When he was Prime Minister, Lloyd George still remembered the sale of the family farm. He would not authorize a playwright to use this episode of his life in a play. The wound had not healed. He remained very attached to his uncle, ever afterwards. His childhood was marked by sensitivity, isolation, depression, aggression, and ambition.

At forty-four, he lost his seventeen-year-old daughter as a result of complications of appendicitis. He was unable to attend the funeral and had the body exhumed in order to see her for the last time. He was a Welsh nationalist.

Adolf Hitler (F13, M18)

His father, Alois, who was illegitimate, married a second wife, his mistress and niece, Hitler's mother. Hitler's father was forty-seven years old at the time of the marriage, his mother was twenty-four. Hitler's father died when Hitler was thirteen, and his mother when he was eighteen. He explained his despair following the death of his father in *Mein Kampf*. The father was fifty when Hitler was born. The father wished Hitler to become a bureaucrat while his son wished to become a painter. Intelligent, a scrapper, a manipulator, he adored his mother who showered him with affection. At thirteen, the stories of William Tell and Lohengrin inspired Hitler. At the time, he discovered national conflict as regards the Germans in Austria.

When his mother died in 1908 (after Hitler's failure at the Painting Academy), Hitler learned that the reason was breast cancer, and he acquired a cancer phobia which was well known. He had no easy contacts, no friends. Hitler never received any packages at the front, during World War I. He adopted the doctrine that in nature might makes right. Hitler's leitmotiv was that Germany did not lose World War I, she held her position against Britain and France, had smashed Russia, but she did not take into account the power of the minuscule Jew. If only she would be delivered from the Jew, the next time she would conquer, said Hitler. He then identified himself with the avenging motherland. According to Erikson, Hitler represents the theme of the young hero who grows up in a strange land and returns to liberate and honor his captive mother, which forms the romantic counterpart of the legend of King Oedipus.

Ho Chi Minh (M10)

Ho Chi Minh had a cultured father who left his family to study in Hué, about 450 kilometers from home, and he sometimes took examinations 650 kilometers to the north. When he was thus absent, his wife died giving birth to her fourth child. Ho Chi Minh was aged ten. He was alone. His father returned to fetch his three children and took them to his parents so that he could finish his doctorate.

In 1901, when Ho Chi Minh was eleven years old, his father took an official post at Hué as secretary to the Minister of Culture. He never reestablished family ties with his children, and became something of an adventurer. At the age of fifteen, Ho became an insurgent against the French occupation, and admired a leader who threatened to revolt against the French. The leader invited Ho to pursue his education in Japan, but Ho refused. This was because, guilt-ridden, Ho's father had pressured for this invitation, which led to Ho's refusal, a rejection of the deserting father who was not loved.

Thomas Jefferson (F14, M43)

He lost his father when he was fourteen. He entered into an interesting conflict with Hamilton (an illegitimate child), Secretary of the Treasury. Hamilton and Jefferson looked on Washington as a brother, and he too was an orphan.

Andrew Johnson (F3, M47)

Johnson lost his father at the age of three. He was dependent on his mother who did laundry and sewing. He was apprenticed as a tailor and he then traveled throughout the country in search of work, followed by his mother who had remarried. He had a frustrating childhood without assistance. He sought power in words, in oratory. He did not attend school and his mother did not know how to read or write. His wife taught him how to read. He then discovered the speeches of British statesmen such as Pitt and Fox. He became president following Lincoln's death.

Kenneth Kaunda (F8)

The leader of Zambia, Kaunda was born in 1924, the eighth and last child. His father died when he was eight, which was a considerable hardship in terms of his studies. His mother had to borrow from neighbors the little money necessary to enter him in school, where he rapidly distinguished himself. He was interested in teaching, suffered under the British occupation, and identified himself with the cause of liberation; he became the first president of the Republic of Zambia.

Jomo Kenyatta (F5)

Kenyatta's father died shortly after the birth of a younger brother. We can deduce that Kenyatta was orphaned around five years of age. The mother became the wife of a younger brother-in-law, as tradition dictated, and had a new son. Kenyatta, being older, had all the responsibilities. The mother left with her child to rejoin her tribe. It appears that she may have died when Kenyatta was six years old. Kenyatta rejoined the mother's family to take care of his little brother and to take him back to his uncle-stepfather. Kenyatta worked with his uncle who did not like him, because he did not bring with him as much as a girl would have done with a dowry. Kenyatta then rejoined his grandfather and worked on a plantation, coming under the influence of English missionaries. He contracted pulmonary tuberculosis at the age of twelve.

Lenin (F15, M46)

Within sixteen months at the age of fifteen, Lenin lost his father and his older brother; the latter was hanged on the order of Czarist authorities. On the death of his father, Lenin had idealized his older brother, who became "father." Lenin later stated that his future was influenced by his older brother. In his biography of Lenin, Trotsky was impressed by these two deaths, which marked a new period of life for Lenin. The older brother failed to make the revolution; Lenin then assumed the role of revolutionary. According to Trotsky, it is upon the death of his brother that Lenin became an atheist. His sister Anna noted that the influence of the father was to constantly inhibit Lenin and his brother Alexander. In 1898, Lenin married an orphan, N. Kroupskaïa.

2nd Earl of Liverpool (F38, M0)

Liverpool was British Prime Minister from 1812 to 1827. He was responsible for the abolition of international slavery after Napoleon's defeat. He lost his mother at one month of age. His father remarried ten years later, at fifty-three years of age. Liverpool was ten years without a mother, while the father was almost always absent. Liverpool was very solitary. He was Canning's best friend, the latter having lost his father at the age of twelve months.

James Ramsay MacDonald (M43)

MacDonald was British Prime Minister in 1924 and then from 1933 to 1936. He was illegitimate, and suffered from it in his childhood. He never spoke of his birth to his children. He was completely stunned when, in 1914, a newspaper revealed his illegitimacy. "Thank God, my mother is dead!" he said.

He lived in extreme poverty as a child. His mother worked and a grandmother took care of him, recounting to him the lives of great political and religious heroes such as John Knox. The schoolmaster played the role of tutor and encouraged him to continue his studies and enter the university. On his death, he gave his gold watch to MacDonald, who wore it until his own death.

In London, MacDonald married a rich young woman, whose mother had died. He suffered the death of his son at the age of five from diphtheria, then of his grandmother (1909) whom he adored, then of his wife. He never married again, and experienced pathological mourning, which he would recall twenty-five years later. He became the first Labour Prime Minister of Britain.

Muammar Qaddafi

Qaddafi's father was sixty when he was born in 1942. He experienced total deprivation, he was illiterate, he did not like to play, stood apart. He was marked by the Italian occupation of Libya. He took Nasser as a model—serious, taciturn, reserved, introverted, sober, ascetic.

Mao Zedong (M24)

Mao had a difficult relationship with his father. At the age of ten, unable to bear it any longer, he ran away and threatened to commit suicide. Intimidated, the father gave in. "It was my first strike," Mao recounted, "and it was a total success."

In 1909, at the age of sixteen, Mao left the village. Upon leaving the paternal home, he refused to bid farewell to his father.

Jean-Paul Marat

Marat had a passionate hatred of his father, according to un-published American works. The father was a physician of Span-ish origin. He lived in Sardinia and renounced Catholicism in order to marry a Swiss Protestant (Geneva) and lived in Neuchâtel. Marat especially honored his mother. He believed that from nature came the mold of his soul, but it was from his mother that he owed the development of his character. His father never aspired to be anything else but a scientist. His mother, whose loss he deeply deplored, had nurtured him during his early years, and opened Marat's heart to philosophy, the love of justice and glory—precious sentiments. These were the only passions that fixed the destiny of his life, he believed. Through him, his mother passed on the help that she gave the needy, and the expression of interest that she had in speak-ing to them, inspired him.

Napoleon I
(F15, M after, S51)

Napoleon's father, Charles, was almost always absent from the time of his son's birth. The very year that Napoleon was born, Charles left for Pisa in order to receive a doctorate in law. The father, a dissipated man, was not serious about work. The mother was severe.

Napoleon dominated his friends in play and was the gang leader. His father never had any money. Governor Marbeuf helped him a great deal. Could he have been Laetitia's lover and Napoleon's biological father? During that time, the father was unfaithful to his wife and had numerous illegitimate chil-dren. It is a disturbing hypothesis, challenged by many; but who can explain all the kindness that Marbeuf bestowed on the Bonapartes and on Napoleon in particular throughout his life?

In 1790, when Napoleon, then twenty-one years of age, learned of the liaison of his mother with Marbeuf, he reacted. Upon returning from the campaign in Egypt, he voiced doubts on the legitimacy of his birth (his father was often absent, while Marbeuf was always present). Placed in the college of Brienne at the age of ten, he did not see his family for five years. It was then that his father died in Montpellier from cancer of the stomach when Napoleon was fifteen. There was no pathological mourning on Napoleon's part. Napoleon, an ardent Corsican patriot, did not understand his father, who accommodated himself to the French occupation. When his father died, Napoleon's "Corsicanism" was without bounds, and he identified himself with the Corsican cause. He had an isolated, studious childhood. He had to support his brothers, and economize. He "locked himself up in misery."

Napoleon III

The French emperor was born on April 21, 1808. He was the son of the Queen of Holland but not of her husband. (Hortense de Beauharnais hated her husband and bestowed her favors upon many of her friends, especially the young count Van Bylandt.) King Louis, who died in 1846, did not deny the child but would not assist at the birth or the christening. For many years, the future Napoleon III resented the King's indifference.

Gamal Abdel Nasser
(F50, M8)

Nasser was the oldest of a family of ten children from two marriages. He rarely saw his parents who had financial difficulties. At the age of six, Nasser was sent to school at an uncle's house. He wrote long letters to his mother. Two years later, in 1926, his mother died.

Nasser described the death of his mother as a cruel blow which left an indelible mark on his spirit, and he stayed away from his family for a long time. He was anguished by the idea of death. He became solitary, absent, thoughtful, and read a great deal.

In 1928, when Nasser was ten, his father remarried. Nasser did not get along with his stepmother, which drew him farther away from his father. It was then that he was sent to his grandparents.

Nasser's heroes were Nelson, Mohammed, and Gandhi. He entered the Military Academy to escape his family. He probably revolted from his father's narrow view. The father, as a postal employee, was a minor member of the Egyptian bureaucracy.

Isaac Newton
(F before, M36)

Newton was born on December 25, 1642; his father died three months before the birth. His mother remarried two years later to an older man. His mother's new husband left the two-year-old child to the care of his grandmother. During the next eleven years, until the death of his stepfather in 1653, little Isaac never saw his mother and developed intense feelings of hatred toward his stepfather. In 1662, then aged twenty, Newton wrote a few notes in which he admitted he had threatened to burn his mother and stepfather alive by setting fire to their house. Throughout his entire life Newton was affected by psychological disturbances, mainly caused by a setback in his affective maturity. He suffered manic-depressive psychosis with phases of paranoia. It was impossible for him to develop affective and friendly relationships.

Bernardo O'Higgins
(F22, M61)

His father was of Irish descent, living in Spain, and rapidly became the Spanish governor of Chile, then administrator in Peru. He fell in love with a girl less than twenty years old (an orphan). Bernardo O'Higgins was born August 20, 1778 (his father was fifty-eight). Father and son were immediately abandoned by his mother who married a knight, but became a widow in 1782.

The father ordered that the child be raised by a Portuguese friend named Pereira, who had a son nine years older than Bernardo. Bernardo's father saw little of his son. Once, when he was the king's envoy, he paid his son a visit. The father was sixty-eight years of age at the time. It was the one and only time that he saw his son. The son went to two or three schools before being sent to a Jesuit school in Peru. Four years later he returned to Spain, then was sent to London while his father became the Viceroy of Peru. We have no letters from O'Higgins's childhood, but a letter written when O'Higgins was twenty-one is interesting. He addressed his father as "Your Excellency," and reminded him that he had never received any answers to his preceding letters (like Churchill). He was filled with hatred for the Spanish ruler of whose power his father was the symbol. O'Higgins then thought of his mother's honor which had been sacrificed for his father's career in the service of the Spanish crown. He began to forget his own miseries in order to dream of the independence of his country and to identify himself with its destiny.

For O'Higgins, it was necessary to solve the dilemma of either submission to the family or answering the call of the revolutionary crusade. He did not receive any money from his father and because he was illegitimate he was unable to join the army. He expressed jealousy when his friends received letters from their parents. Even his mother did not write to him. His father, one day, became aware of his son to the extent of informing him that he was not satisfied with his attitude. He accused him of filial ingratitude (!) and told his tutor to expel him from his home. It is probable that his father had learned of his affiliations with revolutionary movements. The answer from the son, which was a real cry from the heart, was never read by the father, who died in 1801. Both the American and the French Revolutions fired O'Higgins's imagination. After having disinherited him, his father changed his feelings and left him a substantial fortune. O'Higgins liberated Chile from the Spanish occupation and became its first head of state.

Spencer Perceval (F8)

Perceval was British Prime Minister in 1809. He was the eleventh child, and his father died when he was eight. He was the child of a second marriage. Rigid, fanatical, bigoted, ascetic, austere, and unsociabnle, his biographer compared him to Robespierre, an obsessive-compulsive. He was assassinated in 1812, probably as a result of an error.

Eva ("Evita") Perón (F7, M after, S33)

Evita was an illegitimate child whose mother, an ex-concubine, was insulted constantly by the community. Later, the mother opened a café-restaurant, as part of a family boarding house. Evita wanted to become an actress, like Mary Pickford. She fell in love at twenty-four with Juan Perón, forty-nine, also illegitimate. Evita was the mother of her people incarnate, of the disinherited more than all the others. In love with her husband, but ambitious in her need for power, she sought by all means to eclipse him. She felt that the children, the women, and even the men adored her as though she were a supernatural being. She said she had been born twice. The first time, before Perón; the second time, the only true time, with Perón. She expressed an obvious need for legitimacy.

She defied tradition. She was ignored by "good society" and planned her vengeance at length.

A prisoner of her past, Evita could not forget the humiliations that she had suffered during her childhood. Above all, she resented men, whom she detested from deep within her being. She declared that she had come too late to save the hundreds of women destroyed by male narcissism. She wanted to avenge herself on the oligarchy.

In the meantime, she contributed to the ruination of the state. With her husband, she suppressed fundamental liberties, she had her enemies imprisoned knowing full well that they would be tortured. She deceived the little people whom she claimed to, and indeed may have, loved, by extracting money from them in order to build a personal fortune. She was vain, dishonest, and cruel. Finally, one must remember the funeral of her natural father when his family forbade her entry into her father's house. She herself recalled this painful memory.

Maximilien de Robespierre (F19, M6)

Robespierre's mother died when he was six years old. He was abandoned by his father shortly after. The latter, son of a lawyer, ran away because he owed many debts after the death of his wife. He reappeared from time to time. The principal disappearance dated from 1768 when Robespierre was ten. There is no doubt that Robespierre suffered indiscreet questions about this disappearance which was the subject of town gossip, and that he thus learned of his father's extravagances. In 1772, when Robespierre was fourteen, his father disappeared forever.

Robespierre wrote how he was orphaned in his early years, and early on he felt the weight of life. In school, he worked with all his might. It was the chief means of forgetting and a way to be superior to his schoolmates who had a mother, father, an inheritance, a household, and health. His work appeared to be the only way in which he could raise the family fortunes.

When he changed school, and came into contact with the children of the nobility, Robespierre became solitary, vain, and timid. Poorly dressed, he only took care of his wig. In order to visit the Bishop of Arras, he wrote how he had no good clothes and was missing a number of things without which he could not go out.

A work horse and an extraordinary student, he was the "phoenix of the Louis-le-Grand School." He was solitary and he had no friends. He was suspicious of the confidences of boys of his own age to whom he would not respond with his own confidences. At the age of eighteen, he met Rousseau and later became one of his disciples. He was designated in 1775 to make a speech before King Louis XVI. But the bad weather at the time of the visit of the sovereign prevented him from making full use of this opportunity.

His sister Charlotte remarked on the impression the death of their parents produced on Maximilien. A total change took place in him. Before, he was like all children of his age, scatter-brained, turbulent, flighty, but as soon as he saw himself in effect the head of the family as the oldest child, he became poised, reasonable, hard working; he spoke with a kind of seriousness which impressed the family; if he interceded in their games, it was to supervise. He was generous in his care and tenderness. He had the timidity of a child, even trembling when approaching the tribunal but he no longer felt anything at the moment when he started to speak.

Later, having become the great Robespierre, he presented a remarkable piece of legislation on illegitimate and abandoned children in order to give them social status.

5th Earl of Rosebery
(F3, M54)

Rosebery was British Prime Minister from 1894 to 1895. He lost his father at the age of three. His mother, an unaffectionate

woman, remarried three years later. Forty years later, Rosebery still recalled his mother's second marriage in church as
a betrayal.

The stepfather never had the time to take care of his
wife's previous family. Abandoned in a boarding school, Rosebery defended himself with his pen and paper against his
mother's indifference. He developed a great affection for his
sister. He fell in love with a dispossessed and orphaned
Rothschild. His mother's reaction was anti-Semitic; she and
his stepfather did not attend their wedding.

John Russell (F47, M9)

Russell was British Prime Minister from 1846 to 1852. He
lost his mother at the age of nine, and two years later, his
father remarried.

Short, thin, he could not tolerate alcohol. He was loved
by his mother, who would have been better able to protect
him because of his physical insufficiencies. At the age of sev-
enty, he still kept letters from his mother. He became very
aggressive after the death of his mother, cold, arrogant, and
autocratic, impatient, egocentric, and brutal. At forty, he married a widow who already had four children.

António Salazar

Salazar was born when his father was already fifty years old
and his mother forty-three. He made a veritable cult out of
his mother. When she died, he felt a great loneliness that he
compensated for in hard work: "If my mother had not died,
I would not have become Minister." He believed that she would
not have lived without him, and that he could not have worked
knowing her concern. Salazar always needed orderliness, exac-
titude. He was by nature an unsatisfied man, a man eaten

up with doubt according to his own report. All his life, Salazar gave undue importance to minor details, and to schedules.

Joseph Stalin (F11, M57)

Of the four children that Vissarion and Ekaterina Dzhugashvili had, only Joseph, the youngest survived. The parents were semiliterate peasants, descended from serfs. The father was a brutal, short-tempered drunkard.

In 1885, when Stalin was only five years old, the father went to work in Tiflis. He did not sever all ties with his family, but continued to return from time to time. For her part, his mother earned a miserable living as a laundress, seamstress, and cook in the rich houses of Gori. Joseph appeared to be a precocious boy, energetic, agile of body and spirit, who loved to play. His childhood playmates testified that winning and being feared constituted a triumph for him.

He was close to only one person: his mother. As a child and adolescent, he was a good friend provided that others submitted to his imperious will. For many years, Stalin expressed profound respect for his mother, who wished to see him become a priest. She was a woman of severe and determined character, firm and stubborn, puritanical in her ideas, inflexible in her manners, and very demanding toward herself. Joseph Stalin had an aversion for his father who was always drunk and who used to beat him. He rebelled against paternal authority and its equivalent. From childhood, the realization of his wish for vengeance became the goal of his life.

From 1888, Stalin went to a religious school. There was opposition from his father who wished him to become a shoemaker like himself. Renouncing his father, Joseph wished to identify with his mother.

In 1890, Joseph, who was then eleven, became an orphan: his father died from a knife wound received during a drunken brawl. Shortly before his death he had almost been wounded by a knife blow inflicted by his son who wanted to protect his mother.

Admired without reserve for his intelligence and his keen wit, Stalin was the best student in the school. He became enthusiastic about nationalist literature on the resistance of the Caucasian tribes against foreign rule. One of these works, *The Patricide*, made a very strong impression on Stalin. One of the heroes, Koba, was a character with whom Joseph (called Sosso up to then) identified to the point of taking his surname. The theme of vengeance runs throughout the novel. Thus, outside of the idealized image of the hero, Stalin found in *The Patricide* a message teaching him that vengeance is a cause to which it is worth dedicating one's life. Unconsciously, he was able to identify himself with the Republic of Georgia which had been occupied by the Russians since the early nineteenth century.

In 1894, Stalin entered the theological seminary of Tiflis. He was struck by the methods used which included spying on, and interfering in, the students' intimate life, and even going through their personal possessions. He specialized in history and logic.

He left school introverted, reserved, somber, spending all his leisure time in reading. He became a leader in clandestine groups, and continued to be domineering, intolerant, and rebellious.

Louis Thiers (F45, M54)

Louis Thiers was illegitimate. His father had a legitimate wife who died a month before the illegitimate son's birth. Thiers' mother was Marie-Madeleine Amic, daughter of a merchant from Marseilles and the older Thiers' mistress. In 1797, a month after the birth of Thiers, the father, who had fled, reappeared and straightened out the situation by marriage. But he was flighty, was guilty of petty thefts, and was arrested. He did not play any role in the education of the future revolutionary of 1848, who was entirely supervised by women. Thiers was an excellent student in high school and won scholarships; his aunt was the mother of the poet André Chenier. At eighteen, Thiers began his law studies at Aix-en-Provence, where he was accompanied by his mother and grandmother. The Bourbons having been restored to power by foreign means, Thiers became the enemy of the Restoration, of the *legitimacy*, drawn from the revolutionary and Napoleonic tradition. At twenty to twenty-one years of age, he indicated his ambition: "When we will be minister." Joining the Carbonarist sects, Thiers lifted his dagger swearing to exterminate the kings. While walking in the gardens of the Tuileries, Thiers said, "I will live there." Since the Tuileries burned down, Thiers resided in Versailles.

Eamon De Valera (F2)

De Valera lost his father, who was Spanish, when he was two years old. He was then abandoned by his Irish mother. Because she was very poor, his mother separated from her son in New York, where she lived, and sent him back to Ireland, where he was educated by his grandmother and his uncle. The grandmother became the substitute for both father and mother. She died when De Valera was twelve. He was a gifted student, buried in his books. His mother remarried and lived in Rochester, New York. De Valera identified with occupied Ireland, and learned the Gaelic language which would differentiate him from England. He married a woman politician five years older than himself. De Valera became the first president of a liberated Ireland.

In 1919, when he was thirty-seven, De Valera saw his mother again for the first time since he had been sent back to Ireland as a child, when he was on a political mission to the United States.

George Washington (F11, M57)

Washington lost his father at the age of eleven. He was very close to his mother who was active, capable, and resolute. His brother Lawrence played the role of father and counselor. At the age of sixteen, Washington went to Vermont to live with his brother.

Washington always yearned for honors, was always much preoccupied with his reputation. He needed the comfort of public approval. Glory meant more to him than social position.

At the age of twenty-seven, he ordered six busts in London: Alexander the Great, Julius Caesar, Charles XII of Sweden, Frederick II of Prussia, the Duke of Marlborough, and Prince Eugene.

1st Duke of Wellington (F12, M62)

Wellington was British Prime Minister in 1828. He lost his father at the age of twelve. He was very austere, had no emotional life, was apparently inhuman. His mother had an aversion for him while she showed affection for his other brothers. Wellington always found it hard to love women. When he left his family to go off to war, no one inquired about him. When he got married, he wrote to one of his friends, "I married her because I was told to do so."

APPENDIX E
The One Hundred Most
Famous Individuals in
the Study by Eisenstadt
(See Part I) by Rank Order

The One Hundred Most Famous Individuals in the Study by Eisenstadt (See Part I) by Rank Order

1. William Shakespeare
2. Plato
3. Abraham Lincoln
4. Jesus Christ
5. Napoleon I
6. George Washington
7. John Milton
8. Samuel Johnson
9. Saint Paul
10. Leonardo da Vinci
11. Homer
12. Johann Von Goethe
13. Immanuel Kant
14. Michelangelo
15. Thomas Jefferson
16. Francis Bacon
17. Martin Luther
18. Geoffrey Chaucer
19. Aristotle
20. Johann Sebastian Bach
21. Ludwig Van Beethoven
22. Dante Alighieri
23. Albrecht Dürer
24. Woodrow Wilson
25. Charles Dickens
26. René Descartes
27. Alexander III the Great
28. Dwight Eisenhower
29. Theodore Roosevelt
30. Samuel Taylor Coleridge
31. Otto Bismarck
32. Benjamin Franklin
33. Georg Hegel
34. Andrew Jackson
35. Edmund Spenser
36. Christopher Columbus
37. Euripides
38. Gottfried Leibnitz
39. Percy Bysshe Shelley
40. Socrates
41. Robert Edward Lee
42. Honoré de Balzac
43. Sir Winston Churchill
44. David Lloyd George
45. Benedictus de Spinoza
46. Queen Victoria
47. Rembrandt van Ryn
48. Duke of Wellington
49. George Gordon Byron
50. John Calvin
51. Jonathan Swift
52. Oliver Cromwell
53. Molière
54. Alexander Hamilton
55. Ben Jonson
56. Ralph Waldo Emerson
57. John Fitzgerald Kennedy
58. Robert Burns
59. Sir Walter Scott
60. Richard Wagner

61. Marcus Tullius Cicero
62. Petrarch
63. Leo Tolstoy
64. Ulysses Grant
65. Gaius Julius Caesar
66. Hannibal
67. Raphael
68. Saint Augustine
69. Diego Velazquez
70. Charlemagne
71. William Gladstone
72. Franklin Roosevelt
73. John Dryden
74. Herbert Hoover
75. Lenin
76. Wolfgang Amadeus Mozart
77. David Hume
78. William Thackeray
79. 1st Earl of Beaconsfield
80. Voltaire
81. William II (1859–1941)
82. George Frederick Handel
83. Alexander Pope
84. Jean-Jacques Rousseau
85. Jefferson Davis
86. Virgil
87. Mohammed
88. John Keats
89. John Bunyan
90. Oliver Goldsmith
91. Sigmund Freud
92. Edmund Burke
93. Thomas Macaulay
94. Johannes Brahms
95. Thomas Hobbes
96. James Madison
97. Augustus
98. John Knox
99. William Penn
100. Napoleon III

APPENDIX F

The Famous Individuals in the
Study by Eisenstadt (See Part I)
by Alphabetical Order

The Famous Individuals in the
Study by Eisenstadt (See Part I)
by Alphabetical Order

	Columns in *Britannica*	Columns in *Americana*	Combined Columns	Father Death (F)	Mother Death (M)	Age at Own Death (S)	Rank Order
Abdul-Hamid II (1842–1918)	1	2	3	18	7	75	453
Peter Abelard (1079–1142)	2	2	4	*	*	63	291
Abraham (Bible)	3	2	5	*	*	*	231
John Adams (1735–1826)	3	2	5	25	61	90	252
John Quincy Adams (1767–1848)	4	3	7	59	51	80	140
Samuel Adams (1722–1803)	1	2	3	25	*	81	500
Joseph Addison (1672–1719)	3	3	6	31	12	47	170
Aeschylus (525–456 B.C.)	6	2	8	*	*	*	118

(Combined columns were calculated on the basis of half columns as well as full columns. * means information was unavailable.)

	Columns in *Britannica*	Columns in *Americana*	Combined Columns	Father Death (F)	Mother Death (M)	Age at Own Death (S)	Rank Order
Aesop (d. 564 B.C.)	1	1	2	*	*	*	619
Louis Agassiz (1807–1873)	2	1	3	30	60	66	515
3rd Duke of Alba (1507–1582)	1	1	2	3	*	75	643
Alexander I (1777–1825)	4	2	6	23	After	47	179
Alexander III the Great (356–323 B.C.)	9	7	16	19	After	32	27
Vittorio Alfieri (1749–1803)	1	2	3	1	43	54	414
Alfred the Great (848–899)	3	1	4	9	6	51	313
Saint Ambrose (340–397)	1	1	2	*	*	57	630
Fra Angelico (d. 1455)	2	1	3	*	*	*	492
Anne Boleyn (1507–1536)	1	1	2	After	After	29	644
Marcus Antonius (82–30 B.C.)	1	1	2	10	*	52	539

	Columns in *Britannica*	Columns in *Americana*	Combined Columns	Father Death (F)	Mother Death (M)	Age at Own Death (S)	Rank Order
Saint Thomas Aquinas (1225–1274)	2	4	6	19	30	49	195
Archimedes (287–212 B.C.)	2	1	3	*	*	75	484
Aristophanes (450–388 B.C.)	4	2	6	*	*	62	202
Aristotle (384–322 B.C.)	11	8	19	*	*	62	19
Benedict Arnold (1741–1801)	1	4	5	20	18	60	241
Matthew Arnold (1822–1888)	4	4	8	19	50	65	123
Chester Alan Arthur (1830–1886)	1	2	3	45	38	56	420
Saint Athanasius (295–373)	4	1	5	*	*	78	281
Attila (d. 453)	1	1	2	*	*	*	541
1st Earl of Attlee (1883–1967)	1	1	2	25	37	84	611
Saint Augustine (354–430)	7	4	11	17	33	75	68

	Columns in *Britannica*	Columns in *Americana*	Combined Columns	Father Death (F)	Mother Death (M)	Age at Own Death (S)	Rank Order
Augustus (63 B.C.–14 A.D.)	6	3	9	4	20	76	97
Jane Austen (1775–1817)	3	1	4	29	After	41	327
Johann Sebastian Bach (1685–1750)	13	6	19	9	9	65	20
Francis Bacon (1561–1626)	12	8	20	18	49	65	16
Roger Bacon (1220–1292)	2	1	3	*	*	72	461
Arthur James Balfour (1848–1930)	2	1	3	7	23	81	454
1st Baron of Baltimore (1580–1632)	1	1	2	*	*	53	650
Honoré de Balzac (1799–1850)	7	7	14	30	After	51	42
George Bancroft (1800–1891)	1	1	2	38	38	90	580
1st Earl of Beaconsfield (1804–1881)	7	3	10	43	42	76	79
Pierre de Beaumarchais (1732–1799)	2	1	3	43	26	67	503

	Columns in *Britannica*	Columns in *Americana*	Combined Columns	Father Death (F)	Mother Death (M)	Age at Own Death (S)	Rank Order
Francis Beaumont (1584–1616)	2	2	4	14	14	32	296
Thomas Becket (1118–1170)	3	2	5	*	21	52	247
Bede (673–735)	1	3	4	*	*	62	363
Henry Ward Beecher (1813–1887)	1	3	4	49	3	73	399
Ludwig Van Beethoven (1770–1827)	11	6	17	22	16	56	21
Giovanni Bellini (1430–1516)	2	1	3	40	*	86	493
Jeremy Bentham (1748–1832)	2	1	3	44	10	84	443
Thomas Hart Benton (1782–1858)	2	1	3	8	55	76	469
Henri Bergson (1859–1941)	1	4	5	38	*	81	246
George Berkeley (1685–1753)	2	3	5	*	*	67	251
Hector Berlioz (1803–1869)	3	2	5	44	34	65	237

	Columns in *Britannica*	Columns in *Americana*	Combined Columns	Father Death (F)	Mother Death (M)	Age at Own Death (S)	Rank Order
Ernest Bevin (1881–1951)	2	1	3	Before	8	70	478
Otto Bismarck (1815–1898)	14	2	16	30	23	83	31
Bjornstjerne Bjornson (1832–1910)	1	1	2	39	65	77	675
Sir William Blackstone (1723–1780)	3	1	4	Before	12	56	388
James Gillespie Blaine (1830–1893)	2	2	4	20	41	63	356
Robert Blake (1599–1657)	1	1	2	26	39	58	560
William Blake (1757–1827)	5	1	6	26	34	69	184
Giovanni Boccaccio (1313–1375)	5	2	7	36	*	62	147
Anicius Boethius (480–524)	2	1	3	*	*	44	489
1st Viscount Bolingbroke (1678–1751)	3	1	4	63	0	73	321
Simón Bolívar (1783–1830)	6	1	7	2	8	47	165

	Columns in *Britannica*	Columns in *Americana*	Combined Columns	Father Death (F)	Mother Death (M)	Age at Own Death (S)	Rank Order
Boniface VIII (1235–1303)	2	1	3	*	*	68	430
Sir Robert Borden (1854–1937)	1	2	3	46	60	82	475
Jacques Bossuet (1627–1704)	2	1	3	39	33	76	439
James Boswell (1740–1795)	5	1	6	41	25	54	210
Sandro Botticelli (1445–1510)	2	2	4	37	*	65	359
Tycho Brahe (1546–1601)	1	1	2	24	*	54	647
Johannes Brahms (1833–1897)	4	5	9	38	31	63	94
John Bright (1811–1889)	4	1	5	39	18	77	280
Anne Brontë (1820–1849)	2	1	3	After	1	29	518
Charlotte Brontë (1816–1855)	2	1	3	After	5	38	516
Emily Brontë (1818–1848)	2	1	3	After	3	30	517

	Columns in *Britannica*	Columns in *Americana*	Combined Columns	Father Death (F)	Mother Death (M)	Age at Own Death (S)	Rank Order
Henry Brougham (1778–1868)	3	1	4	31	61	89	328
John Brown (1800–1859)	1	2	3	56	8	59	514
Sir Thomas Browne (1605–1682)	1	2	3	8	*	77	411
Elizabeth Barrett Browning (1806–1861)	2	1	3	51	22	55	449
Robert Browning (1812–1889)	5	2	7	54	36	77	160
Filippo Brunelleschi (1377–1446)	1	1	2	*	*	69	547
Giordano Bruno (1548–1600)	1	1	2	41	*	52	552
Viscount Bryce (1838–1922)	1	1	2	39	65	83	678
George Buchanan (1506–1582)	1	3	4	7	*	76	317
James Buchanan (1791–1868)	1	4	5	30	42	77	242
Bernhard Bülow (1849–1929)	2	2	4	30	44	80	374

	Columns in *Britannica*	Columns in *Americana*	Combined Columns	Father Death (F)	Mother Death (M)	Age at Own Death (S)	Rank Order
John Bunyan (1628–1688)	8	2	10	47	15	59	89
Edmund Burke (1729–1797)	5	4	9	32	41	68	92
Gilbert Burnet (1643–1715)	1	1	2	17	*	71	566
Robert Burns (1759–1796)	6	5	11	25	After	37	58
Aaron Burr (1756–1836)	1	2	3	1	2	80	444
Samuel Butler (1612–1680)	1	1	2	*	*	68	563
Samuel Butler (1835–1902)	2	2	4	51	37	66	357
Richard Byrd (1888–1957)	1	1	2	37	*	68	696
George Gordon, Lord Byron (1788–1824)	6	7	13	3	23	36	49
Gaius Julius Caesar (100–44 B.C.)	8	3	11	15	46	56	65
Pedro Calderón De La Barca (1600–1681)	3	2	5	15	10	81	260

	Columns in *Britannica*	Columns in *Americana*	Combined Columns	Father Death (F)	Mother Death (M)	Age at Own Death (S)	Rank Order
John Calhoun (1782–1850)	2	1	3	13	19	68	416
John Calvin (1509–1564)	6	6	12	21	*	54	50
Luis Vaz de Camões (1524–1580)	3	2	5	28	After	56	234
Michelangelo Da Caravaggio 1573–1610)	1	1	2	10	*	36	555
Thomas Carlyle (1795–1881)	3	5	8	36	58	85	126
Lazare Carnot (1753–1823)	1	1	2	44	35	70	572
Lewis Cass (1782–1866)	1	1	2	47	53	83	664
Catherine II the Great (1729–1796)	2	2	4	18	31	67	369
Marcus Cato Censor (234–149 B.C.)	1	2	3	*	*	85	485
Gaius Valerius Catullus (84–54 B.C.)	3	1	4	*	*	30	360
Conte di Cavour (1810–1861)	5	1	6	39	35	50	189

	Columns in *Britannica*	Columns in *Americana*	Combined Columns	Father Death (F)	Mother Death (M)	Age at Own Death (S)	Rank Order
Benvenuto Cellini (1500–1571)	1	2	3	28	*	70	433
Miguel de Cervantes Saavedra (1547–1616)	6	2	8	37	46	68	136
Paul Cézanne (1839–1906)	2	3	5	47	58	67	226
Marc Chagall (1887–1985)	1	1	2	33	*	97	612
Joseph Chamberlain (1836–1914)	5	2	7	37	39	78	161
Samuel de Champlain (1567–1635)	1	1	2	*	*	68	554
Charlemagne (743–814)	7	4	11	26	41	71	70
Charles I (1600–1649)	6	2	8	24	18	48	132
Charles II (1630–1685)	4	2	6	18	39	54	178
Charles V (1500–1558)	8	1	9	6	55	58	101
Charles VI (1685–1740)	1	1	2	19	35	55	652

	Columns in Britannica	Columns in Americana	Combined Columns	Father Death (F)	Mother Death (M)	Age at Own Death (S)	Rank Order
Charles XII (1682–1718)	3	1	4	15	11	36	322
Salmon Portland Chase (1808–1873)	1	3	4	9	24	65	330
Vicomte de Chateaubriand (1768–1848)	3	1	4	18	29	79	326
1st Earl of Chatham (1708–1778)	5	3	8	18	27	69	124
Geoffrey Chaucer (1340–1400)	9	10	19	26	*	60	18
Chiang Kai-Shek (1887–1975)	1	1	2	8	33	87	613
Thomas Chippendale (1718–1779)	1	1	2	*	10	61	653
Frédéric Chopin (1810–1849)	2	3	5	34	After	39	265
Christina (1626–1689)	1	1	2	5	28	62	565
Sir Winston Churchill (1874–1965)	8	6	14	20	46	90	43
Marcus Tullius Cicero (106–43 B.C.)	7	4	11	39	*	64	61

	Columns in *Britannica*	Columns in *Americana*	Combined Columns	Father Death (F)	Mother Death (M)	Age at Own Death (S)	Rank Order
George Clark (1752–1818)	1	2	3	46	46	65	505
Paul Claudel (1868–1955)	1	1	2	44	60	86	605
Henry Clay (1777–1852)	4	5	9	4	52	75	106
Georges Clemenceau (1841–1929)	3	3	6	55	*	88	193
Grover Cleveland (1837–1908)	4	5	9	16	45	71	104
William Cobbett (1763–1835)	3	2	5	30	*	72	236
Richard Cobden (1804–1865)	2	1	3	29	21	60	448
Sir Edward Coke (1552–1634)	1	1	2	9	17	82	553
Jean Colbert (1619–1683)	2	1	3	*	39	64	438
Samuel Taylor Coleridge (1772–1834)	10	6	16	8	37	61	30
Gaspard de Coligny (1519–1572)	1	1	2	3	22	53	645

	Columns in *Britannica*	Columns in *Americana*	Combined Columns	Father Death (F)	Mother Death (M)	Age at Own Death (S)	Rank Order
Christopher Columbus (1451–1506)	9	6	15	*	*	54	36
Auguste Comte (1798–1857)	4	3	7	After	39	59	144
Marquis de Condorcet (1743–1794)	2	1	3	3	*	50	504
Confucius (551–479 B.C.)	2	4	6	1	24	72	173
William Congreve (1670–1729)	3	1	4	38	38	59	387
Joseph Conrad (1857–1924)	1	2	3	11	7	66	476
Benjamin Constant (1767–1830)	1	1	2	44	0	63	660
Constantine I (280–337)	4	2	6	26	50	57	174
James Cook (1728–1779)	2	1	3	After	40	50	502
James Fenimore Cooper (1789–1851)	2	2	4	20	28	62	351
Pierre Corneille (1606–1684)	2	2	4	32	52	78	346

	Columns in *Britannica*	Columns in *Americana*	Combined Columns	Father Death (F)	Mother Death (M)	Age at Own Death (S)	Rank Order
Jean Corot (1796–1875)	2	3	5	51	54	78	277
Hernán Cortés (1485–1547)	1	2	3	*	*	62	408
William Cowper (1731–1800)	2	3	5	25	6	68	222
Thomas Cranmer (1489–1556)	3	2	5	11	*	66	273
Benedetto Croce (1866–1952)	1	1	2	17	17	86	602
Oliver Cromwell (1599–1658)	8	4	12	18	55	59	52
George Curzon (1859–1925)	1	1	2	57	16	66	600
Saint Cyprian (200–258)	1	1	2	*	*	58	628
Cyrus II the Great (d. 530 B.C.)	1	1	2	*	*	*	620
Gabriele D'Annunzio (1863–1938)	1	2	3	30	53	75	424
Dante Alighieri (1265–1321)	10	7	17	17	6	56	22

	Columns in *Britannica*	Columns in *Americana*	Combined Columns	Father Death (F)	Mother Death (M)	Age at Own Death (S)	Rank Order
Georges Danton (1759–1794)	3	1	4	2	After	34	391
Darius I (d. 486 B.C.)	1	1	2	*	*	*	536
Charles Darwin (1809–1882)	3	3	6	39	8	73	200
Honoré Daumier (1808–1879)	1	1	2	*	*	71	669
David (Bible)	3	2	5	*	*	*	232
Jefferson Davis (1808–1889)	4	6	10	16	37	81	85
Claude Debussy (1862–1918)	1	1	2	48	52	55	690
Daniel Defoe (1660–1731)	3	4	7	46	8	71	139
Edgar Degas (1834–1917)	2	1	3	39	13	83	523
Charles De Gaulle (1890–1970)	1	1	2	*	49	80	697
Eugène Delacroix (1798–1863)	2	1	3	7	16	65	513

	Columns in *Britannica*	Columns in *Americana*	Combined Columns	Father Death (F)	Mother Death (M)	Age at Own Death (S)	Rank Order
Democritus (d. 370 B.C.)	2	1	3	*	*	*	482
Demosthenes (384–322 B.C.)	5	2	7	7	*	62	151
Thomas De Quincey (1785–1859)	2	3	5	7	61	74	224
René Descartes (1596–1650)	14	2	16	44	1	53	26
John Dewey (1859–1952)	2	1	3	31	40	92	421
Charles Dickens (1812–1870)	11	6	17	39	51	58	25
Denis Diderot (1713–1784)	4	1	5	45	35	70	275
Charles Dilke (1843–1911)	1	1	2	25	10	67	682
Diocletian (245–313)	3	1	4	*	*	68	379
Johann von Dollinger (1799–1890)	1	1	2	*	*	90	667
Donatello (1386–1466)	3	1	4	*	44	80	337

	Columns in *Britannica*	Columns in *Americana*	Combined Columns	Father Death (F)	Mother Death (M)	Age at Own Death (S)	Rank Order
John Donne (1572–1631)	3	2	5	3	58	58	220
Fedor Dostoyevski (1821–1881)	4	2	6	17	15	59	180
Stephen Douglas (1813–1861)	1	1	2	0	After	48	584
Sir Francis Drake (1543–1596)	1	2	3	*	*	53	434
Theodore Dreiser (1871–1945)	1	1	2	29	19	74	693
Alfred Dreyfus (1859–1935)	2	1	3	*	*	75	528
John Dryden (1631–1700)	5	5	10	22	44	68	73
Alexandre Dumas (1802–1870)	3	2	5	3	36	68	278
John Duns Scotus (1265–1308)	3	2	5	*	*	43	257
Albrecht Dürer (1471–1528)	4	13	17	31	43	56	23
Eleonora Duse (1859–1924)	1	1	2	34	14	65	689

	Columns in *Britannica*	Columns in *Americana*	Combined Columns	Father Death (F)	Mother Death (M)	Age at Own Death (S)	Rank Order
Mary Baker Eddy (1821–1910)	1	3	4	44	28	89	341
Edward I (1239–1307)	3	1	4	33	51	68	316
Edward II (1284–1327)	2	1	3	23	6	43	491
Edward III (1312–1377)	3	1	4	14	45	64	380
Edward IV (1442–1483)	2	1	3	18	After	40	432
Edward VII (1841–1910)	2	1	3	20	59	68	452
Edward VIII (1894–1972)	2	1	3	41	58	77	459
Jonathan Edwards (1703–1758)	3	6	9	54	After	54	111
Albert Einstein (1879–1955)	3	4	7	23	41	76	142
Dwight Eisenhower (1890–1969)	7	9	16	51	55	78	28
Elijah (Bible)	1	1	2	*	*	*	618

	Columns in *Britannica*	Columns in *Americana*	Combined Columns	Father Death (F)	Mother Death (M)	Age at Own Death (S)	Rank Order
George Eliot (1819–1880)	3	2	5	29	16	61	267
Thomas Stearns Eliot (1888–1965)	1	1	2	30	40	76	616
Elizabeth I (1533–1603)	5	4	9	13	2	69	105
Ralph Waldo Emerson (1803–1882)	5	7	12	8	50	78	56
Epicurus (341–270 B.C.)	3	2	5	*	*	71	233
Desiderius Erasmus (1466–1536)	5	2	7	13	13	70	163
2nd Earl of Essex (1567–1601)	1	1	2	8	After	33	649
Euripides (485–407 B.C.)	13	2	15	*	*	79	37
Ezekiel (Bible)	2	3	5	*	*	*	256
Michael Faraday (1791–1867)	2	1	3	19	47	75	418
David Farragut (1801–1870)	1	1	2	15	7	69	581

	Columns in *Britannica*	Columns in *Americana*	Combined Columns	Father Death (F)	Mother Death (M)	Age at Own Death (S)	Rank Order
Johann Fichte (1762–1814)	5	3	8	*	*	51	125
Henry Fielding (1707–1754)	3	5	8	34	11	47	115
Millard Fillmore (1800–1874)	2	1	3	63	31	74	470
Firdausi (935–1020)	1	4	5	*	*	85	272
John Fletcher (1579–1625)	2	2	4	16	13	45	295
Ferdinand Foch (1851–1929)	4	1	5	28	32	77	287
François Fourier (1772–1837)	1	1	2	9	40	65	575
Charles Fox (1749–1806)	5	1	6	25	25	57	215
George Fox (1624–1691)	1	1	2	*	50	66	564
Francis Joseph I (1830–1916)	2	3	5	48	41	86	268
Benjamin Franklin (1706–1790)	9	6	15	38	46	84	32

	Columns in Britannica	Columns in Americana	Combined Columns	Father Death (F)	Mother Death (M)	Age at Own Death (S)	Rank Order
Frederick II (1194–1250)	4	1	5	2	3	56	238
Frederick II the Great (1712–1786)	5	3	8	28	45	74	116
John Fremont (1813–1890)	2	2	4	5	34	77	305
Sigmund Freud (1856–1939)	2	8	10	40	74	83	91
Sir Martin Frobisher (1539–1594)	1	1	2	3	*	55	551
Friedrich Froebel (1782–1852)	1	2	3	20	1	70	510
James Froude (1818–1894)	1	1	2	40	2	76	587
Margaret Fuller (1810–1850)	1	1	2	25	After	40	670
Thomas Gainsborough (1727–1788)	2	1	3	21	42	61	501
Galileo Galilei (1564–1642)	4	3	7	27	56	77	154
Albert Gallatin (1761–1849)	1	2	3	4	9	88	466

	Columns in *Britannica*	Columns in *Americana*	Combined Columns	Father Death (F)	Mother Death (M)	Age at Own Death (S)	Rank Order
Vasco da Gama (1460–1524)	1	1	2	35	*	64	640
Mohandas Gandhi (1869–1948)	6	2	8	15	21	78	138
James Garfield (1831–1881)	2	1	3	1	After	49	472
Giuseppe Garibaldi (1807–1882)	1	1	2	36	44	74	668
David Garrick (1717–1779)	2	1	3	20	23	61	441
William Lloyd Garrison (1805–1879)	3	1	4	*	17	73	329
Genghis Khan (d. 1227)	3	1	4	*	*	*	336
George III (1738–1820)	6	1	7	12	33	81	153
George V (1865–1936)	3	1	4	44	60	70	406
Edward Gibbon (1737–1794)	4	4	8	33	10	56	120
Giotto (d. 1337)	4	1	5	*	*	*	282

	Columns in *Britannica*	Columns in *Americana*	Combined Columns	Father Death (F)	Mother Death (M)	Age at Own Death (S)	Rank Order
William Gladstone (1809–1898)	7	4	11	41	25	88	71
Christoph Gluck (1714–1787)	5	1	6	33	36	73	183
Boris Godunov (1552–1605)	1	1	2	*	*	54	648
William Godwin (1756–1836)	2	1	3	16	53	80	415
Johann von Goethe (1749–1832)	13	9	22	32	59	82	12
Oliver Goldsmith (1730–1774)	7	3	10	16	39	43	90
Charles Gordon (1833–1885)	5	1	6	32	40	52	190
Francisco de Goya (1746–1828)	3	1	4	35	*	82	324
Ulysses Grant (1822–1885)	4	7	11	51	61	63	64
Thomas Gray (1716–1771)	2	2	4	24	36	54	299
El Greco (1541–1614)	4	1	5	*	*	73	239

	Columns in *Britannica*	Columns in *Americana*	Combined Columns	Father Death (F)	Mother Death (M)	Age at Own Death (S)	Rank Order
Horace Greeley (1811–1872)	2	2	4	56	44	61	304
Nathanael Greene (1742–1786)	1	1	2	28	10	43	656
Robert Greene (1558–1592)	2	2	4	*	*	34	345
Gregory I (540–604)	2	1	3	30	*	64	460
Gregory VII (1025–1085)	3	1	4	*	*	60	314
Saint Gregory of Tours (538–594)	1	1	2	*	*	56	542
Sir Edward Grey (1862–1933)	1	2	3	12	43	71	422
Franz Grillparzer (1791–1872)	2	1	3	18	28	81	419
Hugo Grotius (1583–1645)	2	2	4	57	60	62	365
François Guizot (1787–1874)	2	1	3	6	60	87	447
Hadrian (76–138)	3	1	4	9	*	62	378

	Columns in *Britannica*	Columns in *Americana*	Combined Columns	Father Death (F)	Mother Death (M)	Age at Own Death (S)	Rank Order
Ernst Haeckel (1834–1919)	1	1	2	37	55	85	593
Alexander Hamilton (1755–1804)	7	5	12	44	13	49	54
Hammurabi	1	1	2	*	*	*	534
George Frederick Handel (1685–1759)	9	1	10	11	45	74	82
Hannibal (247–183 B.C.)	9	2	11	18	*	64	66
Warren Harding (1865–1923)	3	2	5	After	44	57	230
Thomas Hardy (1840–1928)	3	1	4	52	63	87	333
Benjamin Harrison (1833–1901)	2	1	3	44	17	67	473
William Henry Harrison (1773–1841)	1	2	3	18	19	68	507
Bret Harte (1836–1902)	1	1	2	9	38	65	677
William Harvey (1578–1657)	4	1	5	45	27	79	245

	Columns in *Britannica*	Columns in *Americana*	Combined Columns	Father Death (F)	Mother Death (M)	Age at Own Death (S)	Rank Order
Warren Hastings (1732–1818)	5	2	7	11	0	85	164
Nathaniel Hawthorne (1804–1864)	3	5	8	3	45	59	113
Franz Joseph Haydn (1732–1809)	3	1	4	31	21	77	323
Rutherford Hayes (1822–1893)	1	3	4	Before	44	70	401
William Hazlitt (1778–1830)	2	1	3	42	After	52	445
Timothy Healy (1855–1931)	1	1	2	51	4	75	597
Lafcadio Hearn (1850–1904)	2	1	3	16	32	54	526
William Randolph Hearst (1863–1951)	1	1	2	27	55	88	691
Friedrich Hebbel (1813–1863)	1	1	2	14	25	50	585
Georg Hegel (1770–1831)	10	5	15	28	13	61	33
Heinrich Heine (1797–1856)	4	2	6	31	After	58	199

	Columns in Britannica	Columns in Americana	Combined Columns	Father Death (F)	Mother Death (M)	Age at Own Death (S)	Rank Order
Henry VIII (1491–1547)	3	1	4	17	11	55	338
Joseph Henry (1797–1878)	2	1	3	13	*	80	512
Patrick Henry (1736–1799)	1	3	4	36	48	63	390
Johann Herbart (1776–1841)	3	1	4	33	26	65	393
George Herbert (1593–1633)	1	1	2	3	34	39	558
Johann von Herder (1744–1803)	4	2	6	19	28	59	204
Herod the Great (73–4 B.C.)	1	1	2	30	*	69	623
Herodotus (5th cent. B.C.)	5	1	6	*	*	*	211
Robert Herrick (1591–1674)	1	1	2	1	37	83	557
Edouard Herriot (1872–1957)	1	1	2	17	24	84	606
Paul von Hindenburg (1847–1934)	5	1	6	54	45	86	187

	Columns in *Britannica*	Columns in *Americana*	Combined Columns	Father Death (F)	Mother Death (M)	Age at Own Death (S)	Rank Order
Adolf Hitler (1889–1945)	6	3	9	13	18	56	110
Thomas Hobbes (1588–1679)	6	3	9	*	*	91	95
William Hogarth (1697–1764)	2	5	7	20	37	67	156
Hans Holbein the Younger (1497–1543)	3	2	5	27	*	46	219
Oliver Wendell Holmes (1809–1894)	3	1	4	27	53	85	340
Homer	21	1	22	*	*	*	11
Winslow Homer (1836–1910)	1	3	4	62	48	74	342
Herbert Hoover (1874–1964)	5	5	10	6	8	90	74
Horace (65–8 B.C.)	6	2	8	*	*	57	130
Edward House (1858–1938)	1	2	3	22	14	79	477
William Howells (1837–1920)	2	1	3	57	33	83	451

	Columns in *Britannica*	Columns in *Americana*	Combined Columns	Father Death (F)	Mother Death (M)	Age at Own Death (S)	Rank Order
Charles Evans Hughes (1862–1948)	2	1	3	47	52	86	423
Victor Hugo (1802–1885)	6	1	7	25	19	83	166
Alexander von Humboldt (1769–1859)	2	3	5	9	27	89	223
David Hume (1711–1776)	7	3	10	2	34	65	77
James Leigh Hunt (1784–1859)	1	3	4	25	28	74	394
Thomas Huxley (1825–1895)	2	2	4	30	27	70	372
Henrik Ibsen (1828–1906)	4	2	6	49	41	78	176
Ignatius (d. 110?)	1	1	2	*	*	*	540
Sir Henry Irving (1838–1905)	1	1	2	38	*	67	679
Washington Irving (1783–1859)	2	2	4	24	34	76	350
Isocrates (436–338 B.C.)	2	1	3	*	*	98	483

	Columns in *Britannica*	Columns in *Americana*	Combined Columns	Father Death (F)	Mother Death (M)	Age at Own Death (S)	Rank Order
Andrew Jackson (1767–1845)	8	7	15	Before	13	78	34
Thomas (Stonewall) Jackson (1824–1863)	1	5	6	3	6	39	186
James I (1566–1625)	3	1	4	0	20	58	384
James II (1633–1701)	2	1	3	15	35	67	498
Henry James (1843–1916)	3	1	4	39	38	72	403
William James (1842–1910)	4	1	5	40	40	68	286
John Jay (1745–1829)	1	2	3	36	31	83	413
Thomas Jefferson (1743–1826)	11	10	21	14	33	83	15
Jeremiah (Bible)	2	5	7	*	*	70	150
Jesus Christ (Bible)	30	9	39	*	*	*	4
Saint John the Apostle (Bible)	1	2	3	*	*	*	487

	Columns in *Britannica*	Columns in *Americana*	Combined Columns	Father Death (F)	Mother Death (M)	Age at Own Death (S)	Rank Order
Andrew Johnson (1808–1875)	2	3	5	3	47	66	264
Samuel Johnson (1709–1784)	17	8	25	22	49	75	8
John Paul Jones (1747–1792)	2	4	6	20	*	45	197
Ben Jonson (1572–1637)	8	4	12	Before	*	64	55
Juvenal (60–after 128)	2	1	3	*	*	*	429
Kalidasa (fl 400)	1	1	2	*	*	*	631
Immanuel Kant (1724–1804)	13	8	21	21	13	79	13
John Keats (1795–1821)	3	7	10	8	14	25	88
1st Baron Kelvin (1824–1907)	1	1	2	24	6	83	673
John Fitzgerald Kennedy (1917–1963)	4	8	12	After	After	46	57
Nikita Khrushchev (1894–1971)	1	2	3	16	50	77	481

	Columns in *Britannica*	Columns in *Americana*	Combined Columns	Father Death (F)	Mother Death (M)	Age at Own Death (S)	Rank Order
Rudyard Kipling (1865–1936)	2	2	4	45	45	70	376
1st Earl Kitchener (1850–1916)	3	2	5	44	14	65	228
John Knox (1515–1572)	6	3	9	*	*	57	98
Peter Kropotkin (1842–1921)	1	1	2	28	3	78	681
Stephanus Kruger (1825–1904)	1	1	2	27	7	78	591
Marquis de La Fayette (1757–1834)	2	2	4	1	12	76	301
Jean de La Fontaine (1621–1695)	2	2	4	36	*	73	347
Alphonse de Lamartine (1790–1869)	1	1	2	49	39	78	665
Charles Lamb (1775–1834)	3	2	5	24	21	59	262
Hugues Lamennais (1782–1854)	1	1	2	45	5	71	576
Joseph Lancaster (1778–1838)	1	1	2	*	*	59	662

	Columns in *Britannica*	Columns in *Americana*	Combined Columns	Father Death (F)	Mother Death (M)	Age at Own Death (S)	Rank Order
Walter Landor (1775–1864)	2	1	3	30	54	89	508
Duc de La Rochefoucauld (1613–1680)	2	1	3	36	59	66	437
Sieur de La Salle (1643–1687)	1	1	2	21	*	43	567
Ferdinand Lassalle (1825–1864)	1	1	2	37	After	39	674
Orlando Lasso (1530–1594)	2	1	3	*	*	62	409
Hugh Latimer (1485–1555)	1	1	2	35	*	70	641
Sir Wilfrid Laurier (1841–1919)	2	2	4	44	7	77	358
Thomas Edward Lawrence (1888–1935)	1	1	2	30	After	46	615
Le Corbusier (1887–1965)	1	1	2	*	72	77	614
Robert Edward Lee (1807–1870)	4	10	14	11	22	63	41
Gottfried Leibnitz (1646–1716)	8	6	14	6	17	70	38

	Columns in *Britannica*	Columns in *Americana*	Combined Columns	Father Death (F)	Mother Death (M)	Age at Own Death (S)	Rank Order
Lenin (1870–1924)	6	4	10	15	46	53	75
Saint Leo I (d. 461)	1	1	2	*	*	*	632
Leo X (1475–1521)	3	1	4	16	After	46	382
Leo XIII (1810–1903)	2	3	5	26	14	93	254
Leonardo da Vinci (1452–1519)	11	12	23	52	*	67	10
Gotthold Lessing (1729–1781)	3	1	4	41	48	52	339
Li Hung-Chang (1823–1901)	1	1	2	32	59	78	672
Abraham Lincoln (1809–1865)	16	23	39	41	9	56	3
Charles Lindbergh (1902–1974)	1	1	2	22	52	72	699
Carolus Linnaeus (1707–1778)	1	1	2	41	26	70	568
Franz Liszt (1811–1886)	3	1	4	15	54	74	371

	Columns in *Britannica*	Columns in *Americana*	Combined Columns	Father Death (F)	Mother Death (M)	Age at Own Death (S)	Rank Order
David Livingstone (1813–1873)	3	1	4	43	52	60	400
Livy (59 B.C.–17 A.D.)	5	1	6	*	*	76	212
David Lloyd George (1863–1945)	9	5	14	1	33	82	44
John Locke (1632–1704)	7	1	8	28	22	72	119
Henry Wadsworth Longfellow (1807–1882)	1	4	5	42	44	75	243
Louis XIV (1638–1715)	1	2	3	4	27	77	499
Louis XVI (1754–1793)	1	1	2	11	12	38	659
James Lowell (1819–1891)	2	2	4	41	31	72	355
Saint Ignatius of Loyola (1491–1556)	3	2	5	16	*	65	259
Erich Ludendorff (1865–1937)	4	1	5	39	48	72	288
Saint Luke (Bible)	1	1	2	*	*	*	625

	Columns in *Britannica*	Columns in *Americana*	Combined Columns	Father Death (F)	Mother Death (M)	Age at Own Death (S)	Rank Order
Martin Luther (1483–1546)	14	6	20	46	47	62	17
Edward Bulwer-Lytton (1803–1873)	1	3	4	4	40	69	397
Douglas MacArthur (1880–1964)	1	1	2	32	55	84	610
Thomas Macaulay (1800–1859)	4	5	9	37	30	59	93
George McClellan (1826–1885)	2	2	4	20	After	58	307
James MacDonald (1866–1937)	2	1	3	*	43	71	458
Sir John MacDonald (1815–1891)	1	1	2	26	47	76	586
Niccolo Machiavelli (1469–1527)	5	3	8	40	27	58	114
William McKinley (1843–1901)	3	2	5	49	54	58	227
James Madison (1751–1836)	3	6	9	49	77	85	96
Ferdinand Magellan (1480–1521)	2	2	4	*	*	41	292

	Columns in *Britannica*	Columns in *Americana*	Combined Columns	Father Death (F)	Mother Death (M)	Age at Own Death (S)	Rank Order
Mahmud II (1785–1839)	1	1	2	3	*	53	577
Maimonides (1135–1204)	1	1	2	31	*	69	635
Sir John Mandeville (fl 1356)	2	1	3	*	*	*	431
Edouard Manet (1832–1883)	1	1	2	30	After	51	592
Henry Manning (1808–1892)	3	1	4	27	39	83	398
Andrea Mantegna (1431–1506)	3	1	4	*	*	75	381
Guglielmo Marconi (1874–1937)	2	2	4	29	46	63	312
Marcus Aurelius Antoninus (121–180)	2	2	4	0	35	58	343
Saint Mark (Bible)	1	1	2	*	*	*	626
1st Duke of Marlborough (1650–1722)	3	1	4	37	48	72	386
Christopher Marlowe (1564–1593)	3	1	4	After	After	29	318

	Columns in *Britannica*	Columns in *Americana*	Combined Columns	Father Death (F)	Mother Death (M)	Age at Own Death (S)	Rank Order
John Marshall (1755–1835)	5	2	7	46	54	79	149
Martial (40–104)	2	1	3	*	*	64	488
Karl Marx (1818–1883)	1	1	2	20	45	64	588
Saint Mary (Bible)	3	6	9	*	*	*	107
Mary Queen of Scots (1542–1587)	6	2	8	0	17	44	135
Tomás Masaryk (1850–1937)	2	1	3	57	37	87	527
Philip Massinger (1583–1640)	1	2	3	23	*	56	464
Cotton Mather (1663–1728)	1	1	2	60	51	65	651
Henri Matisse (1869–1954)	1	1	2	*	*	84	692
Guy de Maupassant (1850–1893)	3	1	4	After	After	42	375
Jules Mazarin (1602–1661)	1	1	2	52	*	58	561

	Columns in *Britannica*	Columns in *Americana*	Combined Columns	Father Death (F)	Mother Death (M)	Age at Own Death (S)	Rank Order
Giuseppe Mazzini (1805–1872)	2	2	4	43	47	66	353
Lorenzo de' Médici (1449–1492)	1	1	2	20	33	43	639
Meijo Tenno (1852–1912)	1	1	2	14	*	59	686
Philip Melanchthon (1497–1560)	2	2	4	11	32	63	294
Herman Melville (1819–1891)	4	1	5	12	52	72	285
Gregor Mendel (1822–1884)	2	1	3	35	40	61	519
Felix Mendelssohn (1809–1847)	3	3	6	26	33	38	171
George Meredith (1828–1909)	4	2	6	48	5	81	208
Michelangelo (1475–1564)	11	10	21	58	6	88	14
John Stuart Mill (1806–1873)	6	3	9	30	48	67	112
Jean Millet (1814–1875)	1	3	4	21	38	60	331

	Columns in *Britannica*	Columns in *Americana*	Combined Columns	Father Death (F)	Mother Death (M)	Age at Own Death (S)	Rank Order
Alfred Milner (1854–1925)	2	1	3	28	15	71	455
John Milton (1608–1674)	16	12	28	38	28	65	7
Comte de Mirabeau (1749–1791)	4	2	6	40	After	42	205
Francisco Miranda (1750–1816)	1	1	2	41	*	66	658
William Mitchell (1879–1936)	1	1	2	24	43	56	609
Mohammed (570–632)	6	4	10	Before	6	62	87
Mohammed Ali (1769–1849)	1	1	2	*	*	80	574
Molière (1622–1673)	9	3	12	47	10	51	53
Claude Monet (1840–1926)	1	1	2	*	*	86	680
James Monroe (1758–1831)	1	3	4	16	48	73	325
Michel de Montaigne (1533–1592)	3	1	4	35	After	59	383

	Columns in *Britannica*	Columns in *Americana*	Combined Columns	Father Death (F)	Mother Death (M)	Age at Own Death (S)	Rank Order
Baron Montesquieu (1689–1755)	3	2	5	24	7	66	261
Simon de Montfort (1206–1265)	1	1	2	10	13	57	545
George Moore (1852–1933)	1	1	2	18	43	80	687
Thomas Moore (1779–1852)	2	1	3	46	52	72	509
Hannah More (1745–1833)	1	1	2	37	*	88	657
Sir Thomas More (1478–1535)	5	1	6	53	*	57	209
William Morris (1834–1896)	2	2	4	13	60	62	309
Moses (Bible)	1	2	3	*	*	*	428
Wolfgang Amadeus Mozart (1756–1791)	6	4	10	31	22	35	76
Joachim Murat (1767–1815)	1	2	3	32	39	48	468
Bartolomé Murillo (1617–1682)	3	1	4	9	9	64	319

	Columns in *Britannica*	Columns in *Americana*	Combined Columns	Father Death (F)	Mother Death (M)	Age at Own Death (S)	Rank Order
Benito Mussolini (1883–1945)	5	1	6	27	21	61	188
Mustafa Kemal, Atatürk (1881–1938)	2	1	3	9	42	57	479
Fridtjof Nansen (1861–1930)	2	1	3	23	15	68	530
Napoleon I (1769–1821)	25	12	37	15	After	51	5
Napoleon III (1808–1873)	6	3	9	38	29	64	100
Jacques Necker (1732–1804)	1	1	2	30	22	71	655
Horatio Nelson (1758–1805)	6	3	9	43	9	47	109
John Henry Newman (1801–1890)	3	4	7	23	35	89	145
Sir Isaac Newton (1642–1727)	6	3	9	Before	36	84	108
Michel Ney (1769–1815)	1	1	2	After	22	46	661
Nicholas I (1796–1855)	3	1	4	4	32	58	396

	Columns in *Britannica*	Columns in *Americana*	Combined Columns	Father Death (F)	Mother Death (M)	Age at Own Death (S)	Rank Order
Nicholas II (1868–1918)	2	1	3	26	After	50	426
Reinhold Niebuhr (1892–1971)	1	1	2	18	*	78	698
Friedrich Nietzsche (1844–1900)	5	2	7	4	52	55	162
Viscount Northcliffe (1865–1922)	2	1	3	24	After	57	457
Johan van Oldenbarnevelt (1547–1619)	2	1	3	40	*	71	495
Eugene O'Neill (1888–1953)	1	2	3	31	33	65	480
1st Earl of Orford (1676–1745)	2	2	4	24	35	68	348
Origen (185–254)	5	1	6	17	*	69	213
James Otis (1725–1783)	1	1	2	53	*	58	654
Ovid (43 B.C.–18 A.D.)	5	2	7	*	*	61	158
1st Earl of Oxford & Asquith (1852–1928)	6	1	7	7	36	75	167

	Columns in *Britannica*	Columns in *Americana*	Combined Columns	Father Death (F)	Mother Death (M)	Age at Own Death (S)	Rank Order
Ignacy Paderewski (1860–1941)	1	1	2	32	0	80	601
Walter Page (1855–1918)	1	1	2	44	42	63	598
Thomas Paine (1737–1809)	1	2	3	49	54	72	465
Giovanni da Palestrina (1526–1594)	3	2	5	28	10	68	248
3rd Viscount Palmerston (1784–1865)	5	1	6	17	20	81	216
Francis Parkman (1823–1893)	1	1	2	29	47	70	589
Charles Parnell (1846–1891)	5	1	6	13	After	45	191
Blaise Pascal (1623–1662)	3	2	5	28	3	39	221
Louis Pasteur (1822–1895)	2	2	4	42	25	72	306
Saint Patrick (5th cent. A.D.)	2	2	4	*	*	*	289
Saint Paul (Bible)	17	7	24	*	*	*	9

	Columns in *Britannica*	Columns in *Americana*	Combined Columns	Father Death (F)	Mother Death (M)	Age at Own Death (S)	Rank Order
Sir Robert Peel (1788–1850)	5	1	6	42	15	62	185
William Penn (1644–1718)	3	6	9	25	37	73	99
Samuel Pepys (1633–1703)	2	2	4	47	34	70	297
Pericles (490–429 B.C.)	3	2	5	*	*	61	271
John Pershing (1860–1948)	1	3	4	45	42	87	405
Henri Pétain (1856–1951)	1	1	2	32	1	95	599
Saint Peter (Bible)	4	2	6	*	*	*	203
Peter I the Great (1672–1725)	4	1	5	3	21	52	284
Petrarch (1304–1374)	7	4	11	21	15	70	62
Phidias (498–432 B.C.)	1	1	2	*	*	66	621
Philip II (382–336 B.C.)	1	1	2	13	*	46	538

	Columns in *Britannica*	Columns in *Americana*	Combined Columns	Father Death (F)	Mother Death (M)	Age at Own Death (S)	Rank Order
Philip II (1165–1223)	3	1	4	15	40	57	315
Philip II (1527–1598)	1	1	2	31	12	71	646
Philip IV (1268–1314)	1	1	2	17	3	46	637
Philo Judaeus (30 B.C.–40 A.D.)	3	1	4	*	*	70	334
Pablo Picasso (1881–1973)	2	1	3	31	58	91	533
Franklin Pierce (1804–1869)	2	3	5	34	34	64	279
Pindar (522–443 B.C.)	6	2	8	*	*	80	134
Luigi Pirandello (1867–1936)	1	1	2	*	*	69	604
William Pitt (1759–1806)	8	1	9	18	43	46	102
Pius IX (1792–1878)	5	2	7	41	49	85	152
Pius XII (1876–1958)	1	1	2	41	44	82	608

	Columns in *Britannica*	Columns in *Americana*	Combined Columns	Father Death (F)	Mother Death (M)	Age at Own Death (S)	Rank Order
Plato (428–348 B.C.)	32	11	43	*	*	80	2
Plautus (254–184 B.C.)	3	1	4	*	*	70	377
Pliny the Elder (23–79)	2	2	4	*	*	56	361
Plutarch (46–120)	2	2	4	*	*	74	362
Edgar Allan Poe (1809–1849)	2	3	5	1	2	40	225
Raymond Poincaré (1860–1934)	2	1	3	51	52	74	529
James Knox Polk (1795–1849)	2	2	4	32	After	53	303
Marco Polo (1254–1324)	3	3	6	*	*	70	196
Alexander Pope (1688–1744)	5	5	10	29	45	56	83
Porphyry (233–304)	1	1	2	*	*	71	629
Nicolas Poussin (1593–1665)	1	1	2	*	*	72	559

	Columns in *Britannica*	Columns in *Americana*	Combined Columns	Father Death (F)	Mother Death (M)	Age at Own Death (S)	Rank Order
Praxiteles (fl 345 B.C.)	1	1	2	*	*	*	622
William Prescott (1796–1859)	2	2	4	48	56	62	352
Proclus (410–485)	1	1	2	*	*	75	633
Pierre Proudhon (1809–1865)	1	1	2	36	38	55	583
Ptolemy (100–170)	3	1	4	*	*	70	335
Pythagoras	4	2	6	*	*	*	194
François Rabelais (d. 1553)	4	2	6	*	*	*	175
Jean Racine (1639–1699)	2	2	4	3	1	59	298
Sir Walter Raleigh (1552–1618)	2	2	4	29	42	66	364
Leopold von Ranke (1795–1886)	1	1	2	*	*	90	666
Raphael (1483–1520)	6	5	11	11	8	37	67

	Columns in *Britannica*	Columns in *Americana*	Combined Columns	Father Death (F)	Mother Death (M)	Age at Own Death (S)	Rank Order
Rembrandt van Ryn (1606–1669)	6	7	13	23	34	63	47
Ernest Renan (1823–1892)	2	1	3	5	45	69	520
Guido Reni (1575–1642)	1	1	2	27	*	66	556
Auguste Renoir (1841–1919)	1	1	2	*	74	78	594
Cecil Rhodes (1853–1902)	3	2	5	25	20	48	269
Richard I (1157–1199)	2	1	3	31	After	41	490
Richard II (1367–1400)	1	1	2	9	18	33	546
Samuel Richardson (1689–1761)	2	2	4	41	47	72	367
Cardinal Richelieu (1585–1642)	2	3	5	4	31	57	250
Rainer Maria Rilke (1875–1926)	2	1	3	30	After	51	532
1st Earl Frederick Roberts (1832–1914)	2	1	3	41	49	82	522

	Columns in *Britannica*	Columns in *Americana*	Combined Columns	Father Death (F)	Mother Death (M)	Age at Own Death (S)	Rank Order
Maximilien de Robespierre (1758–1794)	4	3	7	19	6	36	155
Franklin Roosevelt (1882–1945)	3	8	11	18	59	63	72
Theodore Roosevelt (1858–1919)	10	6	16	19	25	60	29
5th Earl of Rosebery (1847–1929)	1	1	2	3	54	82	596
Dante Gabriel Rossetti (1828–1882)	2	2	4	25	After	53	308
Gioacchino Rossini (1792–1868)	1	3	4	47	35	76	395
Jean-Jacques Rousseau (1712–1778)	5	5	10	34	0	66	84
Peter Rubens (1577–1640)	4	2	6	9	31	62	177
John Ruskin (1819–1900)	5	3	8	45	52	80	128
Bertrand Russell (1872–1970)	3	2	5	3	2	97	255
John Russell (1792–1878)	2	1	3	47	9	85	511

	Columns in *Britannica*	Columns in *Americana*	Combined Columns	Father Death (F)	Mother Death (M)	Age at Own Death (S)	Rank Order
Ernest Rutherford (1871–1937)	1	1	2	57	63	66	694
Charles Sainte-Beuve (1804–1869)	1	1	2	Before	45	64	582
Augustus Saint-Gaudens (1848–1907)	1	1	2	*	25	59	685
Camille Saint-Saëns (1835–1921)	1	1	2	0	53	86	676
Comte de Saint-Simon (1760–1825)	1	1	2	22	*	64	573
George Sand (1804–1876)	4	2	6	4	33	71	207
José De San Martín (1778–1850)	1	1	2	18	35	72	663
John Sargent (1856–1925)	3	1	4	33	50	69	404
Andrea Del Sarto (1486–1530)	1	1	2	*	38	44	549
Girolamo Savonarola (1452–1498)	5	2	7	32	42	45	159
Friederich von Schelling (1775–1854)	3	1	4	37	*	79	392

	Columns in Britannica	Columns in Americana	Combined Columns	Father Death (F)	Mother Death (M)	Age at Own Death (S)	Rank Order
Johann von Schiller (1759–1805)	3	4	7	36	42	45	143
Friedrich Schleiermacher (1768–1834)	2	1	3	25	14	65	506
Arthur Schopenhauer (1788–1860)	3	3	6	17	50	72	198
Franz Schubert (1797–1828)	5	3	8	After	15	31	127
Robert Schumann (1810–1856)	3	3	6	16	25	46	192
Albert Schweitzer (1875–1965)	1	1	2	50	41	90	607
Sir Walter Scott (1771–1832)	6	5	11	27	48	61	59
Lucius Seneca (4 B.C.–65 A.D.)	1	1	2	43	43	69	624
William Seward (1801–1872)	2	1	3	48	43	71	471
1st Earl of Shaftesbury (1621–1683)	3	1	4	9	7	61	385
William Shakespeare (1564–1616)	41	20	61	37	44	52	1

	Columns in *Britannica*	Columns in *Americana*	Combined Columns	Father Death (F)	Mother Death (M)	Age at Own Death (S)	Rank Order
George Bernard Shaw (1856–1950)	4	2	6	29	56	94	181
Percy Bysshe Shelley (1792–1822)	8	6	14	After	After	29	39
Philip Sheridan (1831–1888)	1	2	3	44	57	57	521
Richard Sheridan (1751–1816)	2	2	4	36	14	64	300
William Sherman (1820–1891)	1	3	4	9	32	71	332
Algernon Sidney (1622–1683)	2	1	3	55	28	61	497
Sir Philip Sidney (1554–1586)	2	1	3	31	31	31	435
Sigismund (1368–1437)	1	1	2	10	25	69	638
Luca Signorelli (1441–1523)	1	1	2	*	*	82	548
Adam Smith (1723–1790)	5	1	6	Before	61	67	214
Alfred E. Smith (1873–1944)	1	3	4	12	50	70	407

	Columns in *Britannica*	Columns in *Americana*	Combined Columns	Father Death (F)	Mother Death (M)	Age at Own Death (S)	Rank Order
John Smith (1579–1631)	4	1	5	16	*	51	240
Tobias Smollett (1721–1771)	1	3	4	2	45	50	368
Jan Smuts (1870–1950)	2	1	3	44	30	80	427
Socrates (470–399 B.C.)	10	4	14	*	*	71	40
Sophocles (496–406 B.C.)	6	2	8	*	*	90	129
Robert Southey (1774–1843)	2	2	4	18	27	68	349
Herbert Spencer (1820–1903)	3	4	7	46	47	83	146
Edmund Spenser (1552–1599)	6	9	15	*	*	47	35
Benedictus de Spinoza (1632–1677)	10	4	14	21	6	44	45
Madame de Staël (1766–1817)	2	1	3	38	28	51	467
Joseph Stalin (1879–1953)	4	3	7	11	57	73	157

	Columns in *Britannica*	Columns in *Americana*	Combined Columns	Father Death (F)	Mother Death (M)	Age at Own Death (S)	Rank Order
Sir Henry Stanley (1841–1904)	3	1	4	0	45	63	402
Stendhal (1783–1842)	2	1	3	36	7	59	417
Stephen (1097–1154)	1	1	2	5	40	57	634
Robert Louis Stevenson (1850–1894)	3	2	5	36	After	44	229
Joseph Story (1779–1845)	2	1	3	25	After	66	446
1st Earl of Strafford (1593–1641)	2	1	3	21	18	48	496
August Strindberg (1849–1912)	2	1	3	34	13	63	474
Sir Arthur Sullivan (1842–1900)	1	1	2	24	40	58	595
Charles Sumner (1811–1874)	1	6	7	28	55	63	168
Sun Yat-Sen (1866–1925)	1	1	2	21	*	59	603
Emanuel Swedenborg (1688–1772)	2	3	5	47	8	84	235

	Columns in *Britannica*	Columns in *Americana*	Combined Columns	Father Death (F)	Mother Death (M)	Age at Own Death (S)	Rank Order
Jonathan Swift (1667–1745)	5	7	12	Before	42	77	51
Algernon Swinburne (1837–1909)	2	2	4	39	59	72	310
Cornelius Tacitus (55–120)	3	2	5	*	*	65	218
William Howard Taft (1857–1930)	3	3	6	33	50	72	172
Hippolyte Taine (1828–1893)	2	1	3	14	52	64	450
Charles de Talleyrand-Périgord (1754–1838)	5	3	8	34	55	84	133
Roger Taney (1777–1864)	3	1	4	43	37	87	370
Torquato Tasso (1544–1595)	2	3	5	25	12	51	249
Zachary Taylor (1784–1850)	2	3	5	44	45	65	276
Peter Tchaikovsky (1840–1893)	2	2	4	39	14	53	311
Alfred Tennyson (1809–1892)	4	4	8	21	55	83	122

	Columns in *Britannica*	Columns in *Americana*	Combined Columns	Father Death (F)	Mother Death (M)	Age at Own Death (S)	Rank Order
Dame Ellen Terry (1847–1928)	1	1	2	48	45	81	684
Tertullian	2	1	3	*	*	*	486
William Thackeray (1811–1863)	3	7	10	5	After	52	78
Thales (d. 548 B.C.)	1	1	2	*	*	*	535
Louis Thiers (1797–1877)	1	1	2	45	54	80	578
Henry Thoreau (1817–1862)	4	1	5	41	After	44	244
Tintoretto (1518–1594)	3	3	6	*	*	75	169
Alfred von Tirpitz (1849–1930)	2	1	3	*	*	81	525
Titian (1490–1576)	4	7	11	*	*	86	63
Leo Tolstoy (1828–1910)	5	3	8	8	1	82	117
Anthony Trollope (1815–1882)	2	2	4	20	48	67	354

	Columns in *Britannica*	Columns in *Americana*	Combined Columns	Father Death (F)	Mother Death (M)	Age at Own Death (S)	Rank Order
Leon Trotsky (1879–1940)	1	1	2	42	31	60	695
Harry S. Truman (1884–1972)	4	4	8	30	63	88	121
Baron de l'Aulne Turgot (1727–1781)	2	1	3	23	37	53	442
Joseph Turner (1775–1851)	4	2	6	54	29	76	206
Mark Twain (1835–1910)	6	2	8	11	54	74	137
John Tyler (1790–1862)	2	2	4	22	7	71	302
William Tyndale (1492–1536)	1	1	2	*	*	42	550
Martin Van Buren (1782–1862)	2	3	5	34	35	79	263
Sir Anthony Van Dyck (1599–1641)	4	1	5	23	8	42	283
Diego Velazquez (1599–1660)	4	7	11	*	*	61	69
Eleutherios Venizelos (1864–1936)	2	1	3	19	*	71	456

	Columns in *Britannica*	Columns in *Americana*	Combined Columns	Father Death (F)	Mother Death (M)	Age at Own Death (S)	Rank Order
Giuseppe Verdi (1813–1901)	2	3	5	53	37	87	266
Paolo Veronese (1528–1588)	2	1	3	*	*	60	494
Vespasian (9–79)	1	1	2	*	*	69	627
Amerigo Vespucci (1454–1512)	2	1	3	28	*	58	463
Gil Vicente (1465–1536)	2	2	4	*	*	71	344
Giambattista Vico (1668–1744)	1	2	3	40	27	75	440
Victoria (1819–1901)	9	4	13	0	41	81	46
François Villon (b. 1431)	1	2	3	*	*	*	462
Virgil (70–19 B.C.)	6	4	10	27	*	51	86
Voltaire (1694–1778)	8	2	10	27	6	83	80
Richard Wagner (1813–1883)	6	5	11	0	34	69	60

	Columns in *Britannica*	Columns in *Americana*	Combined Columns	Father Death (F)	Mother Death (M)	Age at Own Death (S)	Rank Order
Morrison Waite (1816–1888)	1	1	2	53	51	71	671
Alfred Wallace (1823–1913)	1	1	2	20	*	90	590
Albrecht von Wallenstein (1583–1634)	2	1	3	11	9	50	436
Horatio Walpole (1717–1797)	1	1	2	27	19	79	569
Walther von der Vogelweide (1170–1230)	1	1	2	*	*	60	544
George Washington (1732–1799)	16	20	36	11	57	67	6
James Watt (1736–1819)	1	1	2	46	17	83	571
Antoine Watteau (1684–1721)	1	2	3	After	After	36	412
Daniel Webster (1782–1852)	3	4	7	24	34	70	141
John Webster (fl 1602–1624)	1	1	2	*	*	*	562
1st Duke of Wellington (1769–1852)	7	6	13	12	62	83	48

	Columns in *Britannica*	Columns in *Americana*	Combined Columns	Father Death (F)	Mother Death (M)	Age at Own Death (S)	Rank Order
H. G. Wells (1866–1946)	1	2	3	44	39	79	425
John Wesley (1703–1791)	5	2	7	31	39	87	148
James Whistler (1834–1903)	2	2	4	14	46	69	373
Edward White (1845–1921)	1	1	2	1	*	75	683
Walt Whitman (1819–1892)	3	3	6	36	54	72	201
John Greenleaf Whittier (1807–1892)	3	2	5	22	50	84	253
Christoph Wieland (1733–1813)	1	1	2	39	55	79	570
Oscar Wilde (1854–1900)	1	1	2	21	41	46	688
John Wilkes (1727–1797)	3	1	4	33	53	70	389
William I the Conqueror (1027–1087)	2	2	4	8	23	60	290
William I (1533–1584)	3	2	5	26	47	51	274

	Columns in *Britannica*	Columns in *Americana*	Combined Columns	Father Death (F)	Mother Death (M)	Age at Own Death (S)	Rank Order
William I (1797–1888)	1	1	2	43	13	91	579
William II (1056–1100)	1	1	2	31	27	44	543
William II (1859–1941)	8	2	10	29	42	82	81
William III (1650–1702)	3	1	4	Before	10	51	320
Roger Williams (1603–1683)	1	2	3	17	31	80	410
Woodrow Wilson (1856–1924)	8	9	17	46	31	67	24
Ludwig Wittgenstein (1889–1951)	1	1	2	23	*	62	617
Wolfram von Eschenbach (fl 1170–1220)	1	1	2	*	*	*	636
Thomas Wolsey (1473–1530)	3	2	5	23	*	57	258
William Wordsworth (1770–1850)	5	4	9	13	7	80	103
Sir Christopher Wren (1632–1723)	1	3	4	23	*	90	366

	Columns in *Britannica*	Columns in *Americana*	Combined Columns	Father Death (F)	Mother Death (M)	Age at Own Death (S)	Rank Order
Frank Lloyd Wright (1869–1959)	1	2	3	*	56	89	531
Sir Thomas Wyatt (1503–1542)	1	1	2	33	*	39	642
John Wycliffe (1320–1384)	6	2	8	*	*	64	131
Xenophon (430–after 355 B.C.)	3	2	5	*	*	*	217
William Butler Yeats (1865–1939)	3	2	5	56	34	73	270
Zeno of Elea (490–430 B.C.)	1	1	2	*	*	60	537
Emile Zola (1840–1902)	1	2	3	6	40	62	524
Zoroaster (630–553 B.C.)	5	1	6	*	*	*	182
Huldreich Zwingli (1484–1531)	2	2	4	29	31	47	293

NAME INDEX

SUBJECT INDEX